Praise for *Ultimate Guide to Instagram for Business*

If you want to figure out how your business can win with Instagram grab
a copy of *Ultimate Guide to Instagram for Business*.

—MICHAEL A. STELZNER, CEO AND FOUNDER OF SOCIAL MEDIA EXAMINER, AUTHOR OF *LAUNCH AND WRITING WHITE PAPERS*,
HOST OF "SOCIAL MEDIA MARKETING" PODCAST

If you have been curious about using Instagram for your business, this is the
definitive guide you've been looking for. Instagram doesn't come with a user manual,
so most businesses are left resorting to trial and error, which can be a massive waste of
time and frustrating to boot. Do yourself a favor, and pick up a copy of this guidebook
which will give you the why and the how to turn Instagram into a powerful spigot
spouting out more clients, sales, and revenues.

This book doesn't stop at teaching you how to share pretty pictures on your phone
using Instagram. Instead, Kim dives deep into the step-by-step of how to grow your
following (even if you're starting from nothing), how to nurture that following, what
to avoid, and how to turn that community into a valuable source of business. And
best of all, Kim uses an easy-to-follow format sprinkled with valuable case studies and
interviews with today's top Instagram experts. I highly recommend this book.

—JOHN CORCORAN, FORMER CLINTON WHITE HOUSE AIDE AND WRITER, FOUNDER OF SMART BUSINESS REVOLUTION
AND CO-FOUNDER OF RISE25, LLC

In a sea of social media charlatans, Kim is the only person I trust to get
dollar-measurable results.

—DAN S. KENNEDY, DIRECT RESPONSE MARKETING LEGEND AND AUTHOR OF THE *NO B.S. BOOK SERIES*

This powerful book shows you how to create and nourish an Instagram following
then turn it into dollars in the bank! Kim's advice is very practical and timely and
helps businesses become more influential.

—MATTHEW LOOP, SOCIAL MEDIA REVENUE STRATEGIST, SPEAKER, AND AUTHOR OF *SOCIAL MEDIA MADE ME RICH*

This book is incredible! I'm not a big social media guy, but now I see that we were completely misunderstanding Instagram (and all social media for that matter). After reading the *Ultimate Guide to Instagram for Business,* I'm now clear on how to use the platform to find customers and build relationships that make money by using direct marketing to something I honestly didn't think we'd ever use. Thank you so much for a huge boost in understanding, your attention to detail and caring about creating real results. Killer read. Well worth it!

—MICAH MITCHELL, FOUNDER OF MEMBERIUM

Driving traffic, generating leads, and acquiring customers is the lifeblood of any business. For that reason, there's never been a better time to fully leverage the power of Instagram. The *Ultimate Guide to Instagram* pulls back the curtain to reveal every practical aspect of capitalizing on the platform whilst covering all the nuances along the way. Kim takes you through everything you need to know and how to use Instagram effectively for your business.

—OLIVER BILLSON, DYNAMIC RESPONSE MARKETING EXPERT

Using stats, stories, and strategic ideas, Kim brings together a complete guide to Instagram that any business can follow. If you want Instagram demystified, and to form a solid social marketing plan, this book is for you.

—JILL SCHIEFELBEIN, AUTHOR OF *DYNAMIC COMMUNICATION: 27 STRATEGIES TO GROW, LEAD, AND MANAGE YOUR BUSINESS*

Businesses should continually be focused on the bottom line and how to bring more leads into the pipeline. This book is the perfect tool to help businesses scale their marketing and bring more sales in the door with a fresh, ROI-based approach to Instagram.

—RYAN FARRELL, DIRECTOR OF MARKETING AT LINKEDSELLING

Ultimate Guide to Instagram for Business is an eye-opening, practical approach to leveraging Instagram to build client relationships that ultimately lead to an increase in your bottom line.

—TYLER ANDERSON, SOCIAL MEDIA MARKETING ENTREPRENEUR, SPEAKER, HOST OF THE "SOCIAL MEDIA SOCIAL HOUR" PODCAST, AND FOUNDER AND CEO OF CASUAL FRIDAYS

Ultimate Guide to Instagram For Business is a completely approachable and beginner-friendly how-to, from sign-up to creating your own Instagram stories. Kim Walsh Phillips writes, as always, with both warmth and authority, and her guides are the next best thing to having an expert sitting behind you, walking you through the whole process with humor and confidence.

—LESLIE GRAY STREETER, POP CULTURE COLUMNIST FOR *THE PALM BEACH POST*

From the opening quote to the food references that made me hungry, Kim Walsh Phillips connects with you from the moment you start reading her book. She can draw empathy and empowerment within the confines of the same sentence, making you feel like you are a part of her life and rooting for her all the while realizing that she is rooting for you. Change is never easy, but I believe taking the journey with Kim will help readers tackle the unpredictable world of social media in a way that will not only make them hungry for jam but starving for the next steps for success.

—JASON PLOTKIN, PHOTOGRAPHER FOR USA TODAY NETWORK

Kim Walsh Phillips is the real deal. She dispels the fluff most "gurus" put out there and gives practical advice on how to use Instagram to get more leads and sales. Read this book if you want Kim to practically take your hand lead you through a step-by-step how-to to get real results.

—DAVE DEE, FOUNDER OF DAVEDEE.COM

I can tell you there is no one on the planet who better exemplifies the words ultimate, entrepreneur, or social media more than Kim Walsh Phillips. Kim has created an accurate, relevant, and timely guide that lays the foundation for all entrepreneurs to create and monetize their Instagram accounts if they move as quickly and decisively as Kim did in creating this guide. So, open your Instagram account, pull out a pen, write in the book, do what Kim guides you to do, and watch the leads and the profits roll in.

—WES SCHAFFER, FOUNDER OF THE SALES WHISPERER

Entrepreneur
MAGAZINE'S

ULTIMATE GUIDE TO

INSTAGRAM
FOR BUSINESS

- Reach more than 600 million of today's visual shoppers
- Develop a picture-perfect promotion strategy
- Increase your sales, brand recognition, and digital presence

Entrepreneur
PRESS®

KIM WALSH PHILLIPS

Entrepreneur Press, Publisher
Cover Design: Andrew Welyczko
Production and Composition: Eliot House Productions

This publication is designed to provide accurate and authoritative information in regard to the
subject matter covered. It is sold with the understanding that the publisher is not engaged in
rendering legal, accounting or other professional services. If legal advice or other expert assistance is
required, the services of a competent professional person should be sought.

Library of Congress Cataloging-in-Publication Data
    Names: Walsh Phillips, Kim, author.
    Title: Ultimate guide to Instagram for business/by Kim Walsh Phillips.
    Description: Irvine, California : Entrepreneur Media, Inc., [2017] | Series: Ultimate series
    Identifiers: LCCN 2016054460 (print) | LCCN 2017006455 (ebook) | ISBN 978-1-59918-602-3
        (alk. paper) | ISBN 1-59918-602-0 (alk. paper) | ISBN 978-1-61308-357-4
    Subjects: LCSH: Photography—Digital techniques. | Instagram (Firm) | Computer file sharing. |
        Image files.
    Classification: LCC TR267.5.I57 W35 2017 (print) | LCC TR267.5.I57 (ebook) | DDC 770.285/
        53—dc23
    LC record available at https://lccn.loc.gov/2016054460

Printed in the United States of America

Contents

Acknowledgments

This book is dedicated first and foremost to God. Without Him, nothing is possible. With Him, this book was actually completed on time and without my family disowning me. Second is my snuggle tribe—my very tall, smart, and better-at-numbers than me husband, Ian, who is the most supportive and understanding human on Earth, and my two glitter-and-all-things-pink-obsessed girls, Bella and Katie. You are my "why," and I don't know how it is possible, but I love you more every day. Thank you for agreeing to eat Panera and Atillo's in order for me to get this book done. (Never mind that you like their food better than my cooking. And you were right, Bella—writing this book was easier than a chicken trying to do a cartwheel.)

To Mom and Dad, Gloria and Jack Walsh, because you are definitely the most awesome parents and MeMaw and PopPop that ever graced this Earth. I hope to someday be at least half the parent you've been for me.

Thank you to my Elite Digital Group staff who each contributed to the book and picked up slack when I dove into my writing cave (aka beachfront hotel, lest you think I was roughing it). You are an amazing group of talented and inspiring professionals I am blessed to know. Thank you especially to Kelly LeMay, who has been with me longer than my marriage, and who knows where all the bodies are buried; Samantha Melhorn, our in-house Instagram aficionado; Tanner Stolte, responsible for the first client campaign with a measurable sale on Instagram and the nicest tech geek you will ever meet; Ryan Olszewski, a graphic design super hero; Tracey-Lee Whetstine, the best assistant in the world (seriously, if there were assistant Olympics, I would sponsor Tracey and cry tears of joy as she took home the gold. She would probably find a way to answer our office calls while competing, she is that good.); Mike Stodola, marketing superstar and my forever marketing sensei who I am honored to have on my team; and Dana Nolan and Claire Wallace for rocking the casbah.

Thank you to my tribe of advisors, colleagues, confidants, and posse—basically those who make the journey fun and support me when it isn't: Dave Dee (Where's your book, Dave—get to it!); Andrew Warner (your podcast and cheerleading are awe-inspiring), Jon Toy, Kris Mae, Kate Kohler, Brittney Walton, Leslie Streeter (Girl, I'm on book three now—get yours done! You are a much better writer than me, and it's time!); my "Everyday I'm Hustling" Mastermind Group: Oli Billson, Shaun Buck, Micah Mitchell, and Wes Schaeffer (you are the sprinkles on my cupcake each week); my church community of amazing peeps, including Lauren Fisher, Amy Lober, Pastor Jason Tucker, Karin Tucker, Lindsey Larken, DeeAnn Memon, Larisa Weaver, and Karen Gyimesi (you are the best thing about New Jersey, and I thank God every day that I know you and am a part of Tower Hill Church community—I mean, a group of people I can laugh, play, and drink wine with—miracles do happen); my editorial powerhouse, Demi Stevens, of Year of the Book Publishing, my personal editor and writing coach, you are my writing fairy godmother, and I want to make sure the clock *never* hits midnight; the Entrepreneur Press team of Vanessa Campos and Jennifer Dorsey, my editor Michelle Martinez, the promotions team Rocky Vy and Ralph Li (coolest names, ever!), y'all are social media and marketing super troopers; and to Green Bean Roasting Company, the drive-through Starbucks on the Pennsylvania Turnpike (genius!), and my Keurig Machine, for your caffeine contributions to fuel all my words. You are delicious (mmm . . . coffee . . .).

And to YOU, fearless reader, not only for picking up this book but for also wanting to find out how to make your social media more effective for your business. Keep on keeping on. You are going to change the world.

Why Instagram for Business? How to Make It Work for Yours

One of my favorite quotes is:

The opposite of courage is not cowardice, it is conformity. Even a dead fish can go with the flow.

—JIM HIGHTOWER

I tend to fall on the opposite side of most. When they yin, I yang. When they zig, I zag.

Perhaps you can relate?

The reality is, the majority is often wrong. Most business owners are spending time and money on marketing activities that aren't getting them a return on investment. According to a recent study by *Social Media Examiner*, out of 5,000 marketers surveyed, only 42 percent of businesses can measure their marketing's effectiveness. Of that group, only about half are seeing increased revenue because of it. Yet 76 percent of the 5,000 surveyed said they plan to *increase* their social media activities this year. So even though most don't know if it is working, they are sure they want to do more of it.

This is why we need to do the opposite of the majority if we want to get an ROI from Instagram. And getting an ROI is my jam. And I am guessing it's your jam, too. (Mmm . . . jam. Quick confession: Whenever I mention food in this book, which isn't too often, but often enough, I start to picture the food item. It gets me hungry, and then I literally debate for like 90 seconds whether I am going to get up and get the mentioned food item. I may have finished this book in 2015 if I could have stopped mentioning food. And perhaps gotten back into my pre-pregnancy jeans quicker. The struggle is real, people.)

Most entrepreneurs aren't getting the results they want, but they keep on keeping on with what they are doing so they don't risk having to change. You see, change is scary. Change is hard. But staying the same as everyone else is easy. It requires no risk and no effort.

Yet I don't wear high heels every day because they are comfortable. I have never been one to take the easy way out. I'm guessing you aren't either, which is why you are reading a book on Instagram in order to improve your Instagram ROI for your business.

Before jumping on another social media network, it is paramount to ask: *Why* should I use this for my business? Before you keep going through these pages of ROI yumminess, ask yourself if you should. Be discerning each day with each minute and how you spend it, as you will never get this time back.

So, should you keep going with this book and Instagram marketing in general? First let's look at the facts:

1. *Businesses are using the platform.* (https://blog.hootsuite.com/instagram-statistics-for-business/)
   - There are now more than 200,000 businesses using Instagram for promoting products and services.
   - In 2015, 32.3 percent of U.S. companies with 100 employees or more used Instagram for marketing activities.
   - Engagement with brands on Instagram is 10 times higher than Facebook, 54 times higher than Pinterest, and 84 times higher than Twitter.

2. *Businesses are spending money on Instagram.* Instagram's global mobile ad revenues are expected to close in on nearly $3 billion by 2017. That figure would account for over 10 percent of its parent company Facebook's revenues.

3. *Consumers* are purchasing *through Instagram*. (My favorite fact!) Nearly a third of online shoppers (31 percent) say they are using social media channels to browse for new items to buy (www.marketingweek.com/2016/03/23/social-commerce-how-willing-are-consumers-to-buy-through-social-media/). Facebook is the most popular network for shopping (26 percent), followed by Instagram (8 percent) and Pinterest (6 percent).

4. *Consumers trust brands more because they saw them on Instagram.* (This one is good, too.) A majority of millennials surveyed—70 percent—valued non-celebrity endorsements, particularly from influencers that they consider peers (http://www.marketplace.org/2016/03/31/business/consumers-trust-social-media-stars-more-celebrities-or-ads).

This book was created to give you the tools you need to leverage all the buying power Instagram brings to the table and serve it to you on a silver platter. And I didn't stop there, as most social media books do. Inside these pages, you will also find strategies for moving your Instagram audience seamlessly from follower to high-value customer for life. This was a prerequisite for my agreement to write this book in the first place.

You see, I am not just a social media educator or theorist. I am a small business owner who wants to monetize our Instagram page. I read, researched, and studied everything I could find about Instagram marketing and monetization. This book is a compilation of what worked, what failed miserably, and the best of the best strategies that have allowed me to grow my account quickly and effectively just with not followers but with buyers.

I have included interviews with the top minds in business, Instagram marketing, and traffic monetization. You'll see example after example that you can swipe and deploy for your own marketing efforts.

Keep reading and we'll laugh together, cry together, imagine jam together.

More important, read this book so you are armed with the strategies you need to realize real ROI through account growth and traffic monetization from Instagram.

Let's get down to biscuits—err—I mean business.

IT WAS A LETTER THAT CHANGED EVERYTHING

And why I said yes to writing this book. For you.

Maybe you can relate to this.

In the beginning, I thought it should be easier. I saw people around me enjoying success, taking time off, having the ability to donate large sums to charity—I felt lost.

I was working all of the time and was completely broke. And there are a lot more fun ways to be broke than working *all of the time*. My answer to covering cash flow or trying to make ends meet was to work harder. What could I do more of? What one thing could I push a little bit further that would finally make things easier?

I was at home with my infant daughter, barely two weeks old and (finally!) sleeping and not crying. The easiest-going kid now, she was a colicky baby then and cried unless she was sleeping or nursing. So here she was sleeping soundly, looking like a cherub, peacefully enjoying rest, and I started to cry.

I had just read a letter from my bank telling me they weren't going to cover my overdrafts any longer. This was how I had made sure we had enough money for payroll. I couldn't qualify for a line of credit so I used my overdraft to make ends meet. Before I had my daughter, when our overdraft got too high, I would go out and attend more networking events, follow up with more prospects, and do everything I could to hustle another project. I would end up taking anything offered to us, never being paid what we were worth, always just to get enough money in the moment. Always in crisis. Always in fear.

Well, this time I couldn't follow my "kill yourself until you make it happen" business model. My daughter was barely born and needed me. But my employees needed me, too. And they had trusted me when they came to work for me. Alas, that coupled with the crazy-town hormones one has after giving birth produced ugly, gut-wrenching tears.

I am a woman of faith and I did what I could in that moment—I prayed. I prayed that God would show me a way out. That I could take care of my daughter and take care of my staff. I prayed that I wouldn't have to work as much so I could be more present for my sweet child. I prayed that things could just get a little easier. I was so tired of being tired and living in constant fear of everything falling apart.

It was at this time that my good friend, Jon Toy, provided me the answer to my prayers. He gave me a book that *changed everything*. It was called *No B.S. Direct Marketing: The Ultimate No Holds Barred Kick Butt Take No Prisoners Direct Marketing for Non-Direct Marketing Businesses* (Entrepreneur Press) by Dan Kennedy. This book showed me not only can marketing equal results, but it can equal results quickly. Marketing could be my salesperson. Marketing could go out and hustle my next job while I stayed home and took care of my daughter.

The problem was that Dan Kennedy—the guy who wrote the book that changed everything—*hated* social media.

But that wasn't going to stop me. I was on a mission to bring change to my path so I could reach a different destination.

I started implementing right away (more on the "what" later in this book). And for the love of my then-sad-now-fabulous shoe collection, something incredible happened. It was a Saturday morning, and I remember it as clear as if it was yesterday. I received a message on LinkedIn as shown in Figure I–1 on page xvii.

I couldn't believe it. Someone I didn't know had contacted me directly. I hadn't met him at a networking event, sat in on a committee meeting with him, or chased him down after a networking group. I didn't have to compete in an RFP in order to land the job. For the first time ever, my marketing had brought me a client. My marketing had gone out and hustled for me.

My marketing was WORKING!

I am proud to say that I did land that client. It was for a few hours of consulting, at about 100 times higher than what I'd been paid for projects before. My social media marketing had successfully repositioned me as the expert. This attracted a higher-quality client and meant that I didn't have to compete on projects any longer because those that came to me were ready to hire my firm specifically and not shop around. It meant that my perfect prospect came to me, asking to work with me, and expecting to pay top dollar for the privilege.

> Hi Kim,
>
> I don't believe we've ever met, however I am familiar with you and your company via the social mediasphere.
>
> I'm looking for a marketing firm, with a robust understanding of social media, to advise/provide feedback on a periodic basis as it relates to our marketing strategy and marketing and social media initiatives/campaigns.
>
> If this is something you'd like to explore further, please call me at ▓▓▓▓▓▓▓ or drop me an email.
>
> Steve
>
> 7:01 AM

FIGURE I–1. The Letter That Changed Everything.

I had spent years struggling in a tiny apartment with no cable (this was before Netflix, back when that meant you had only one channel, and it was fuzzy), unable to afford health insurance, and without a vacation for over ten years to a complete, 180-degree turnaround.

In one year of using direct-response marketing with social media, we grew our email list from 1,555 to over 21,000 people. In one year we increased our income 327 percent.

I've now been able to work with some of the top companies in the world like Harley-Davidson Motor Co., Sandler Training, Hilton Hotels, Chem-Dry, and more. I've also worked with top marketers who have my firm handle their in-bound marketing, such as GKIC Insider's Circle, Dan Kennedy, Rich Schefren, Speaking Empire, Ted Thomas, Scott Carson, Ron LeGrand, Newsletter Pro, Sixth Division, and more.

And one astonishing thing happened. Small businesses, entrepreneurs, and freelancers started to ask how they could learn to do this type of marketing for their own businesses so they could also attract their perfect prospect who would then pay them what they were worth. They wanted to grow their audiences and make a difference in the world, too, all while bringing themselves and their families the financial peace and prosperity they longed for (and deserved). In response to growing interest, my team and I formed Marketing Insiders Elite (www.marketinginsiderselite.com), an association that now has hundreds of members focused on creating raving fans and converting them into buyers for life.

The most rewarding part is the difference it is making in others' lives. I get messages from members all the time that what they are discovering through Marketing Insiders Elite is allowing them to attract a higher-quality prospect who expects to pay more. I hear how they've been able to grow their tribes successfully and how what they are doing is helping others.

Since I've pivoted from broke to booming I've still cried many times, but they've been tears of joy as I've been at an event and someone I didn't know has come up to me to tell me the difference this has made in their lives. Moms who were able to quit their full-time jobs are now able to work from home and be there more for their kids. Professionals who were able to build bigger tribes can finally get paid what they are worth. Dreamers are finally putting their ideas into action now that they know how.

Deep down we all want to know that what we are doing has meaning. We want to know that what we do matters.

Knowing that what I am doing is actually impacting lives is the greatest gift of all. That and finally having the peace and prosperity I craved for such a long time. Before, I would automatically wake up every night at 3 A.M. (because that is the time my bank would turn over the night's numbers) and see how negative my bank account was. It was then that I would know which check bounced and what crisis I would have to fix next. I truly didn't have a single peaceful night's sleep for more than ten years.

Flash to the present where I can finally take vacations with my family and disconnect without fear that it is all going to fall apart. We are a Disney family and even though we live in the Northeast, we have annual passes because we are able to visit there often now. It should come as a surprise to no one. After one has ten years of stress, she craves a little "Happiest Place on Earth" time.

I now spend virtually no time in fruitless networking or chasing down leads. In fact, I don't belong to a single networking group and haven't done an RFP in years. I can spend my time doing things that matter to me versus things I have to do. I can volunteer for my church and Operation Homefront—an organization serving military families while their loved ones are deployed—because they matter to me rather than because I hope I can get my next client from them.

When I was struggling, I remember seeing others' success and wishing I could have their "breakthrough," and that one day someone would discover me and what I was doing, and magically everything would turn around. It was like I was hoping for a "Breakthrough Fairy" to come along and make it all better.

It took that moment in the kitchen with my daughter finally sleeping, me finally breaking down, to realize that it wasn't a fairy who was going to solve this. It was me. I had to do something different if things were going to be different. I had to be the one to make that change. And it wasn't going to be one big moment that would change everything. It would be the little steps I would take each day that would make the big differences later on. Little things, just like you picking up this book and deciding to read it so that you can improve your results.

Are you ready for a change in your path? Are you ready to attract more raving followers and turn them into buyers for life?

Follow along in this book and then make sure to check out www.UGIGbook.com for more resources, such as a 30-day content template, sales strategies, resources, and more!

But most important, put what you discover into action.

This book will take you through the steps to discover who your perfect prospect is, how to communicate effectively to them, and then how to turn followers into buyers for life. Instagram can be a money-making machine for businesses of all types. But it's not just about engagement—it's about the right kind of engagement. Along the way, you will read case studies of other entrepreneurs and business that have successfully used Instagram to produce results.

I will share examples from my own business and those of my clients and colleagues who are effectively using Instagram to grow their business. You'll meet Nathan Chan of *Foundr* magazine, who grew his Instagram following in just a few short weeks to thousands of followers; DigitalMarketer who uses Instagram ads to drive subscribers to their popular podcast Perpetual Traffic; Josh Harcus of Hüify who uses the platform to promote company culture and recruit new hires; Timothy Sykes, who has leveraged Instagram into a multi-million dollar education enterprise; and many more. With a variety of both common mistakes and success stories of entrepreneurs who use Instagram for their businesses, you can create your own engaging Instagram brand that will help you attract and retain your ideal clients. From sales funnels, to follower contests, to product launches, you'll learn killer techniques to turn nearly any Instagram audience into a network of loyal customers.

One thing I caution you against is reading their examples and thinking, "My business is different. This won't work for me." Instead think, "*How* can I apply this to my business?" That is how you can make lasting change in your current situation and create the future you once only hoped was possible.

Are you ready?

Today is the first day of the rest of your journey. Think of any failures from the past as plot twists getting you ready for this next chapter. Your story is being written every day, and you have control over the next chapter.

And it's going to be a good one. Are you in? Post on Instagram and use the hashtags #IAmIn #InstagramforBusiness, and I will give you a shoutout. Plus, you can win one of hundreds of prizes.

Let's get started.

#INSTAGRAMFORBUSINESS POSTABLES

Note: Throughout the book, you will find a synopsis of key points and resources you can use. Share the postables on Instagram and your other social media networks. Be sure to use the hashtag #InstagramforBusiness. We will be monitoring this hashtag and will jump in to reply, continue the conversation, and give out prizes. Go ahead and post one from the list below now.

- Deep down we all want to know that what we are doing has meaning. We want to know that what we do matters. #InstagramforBusiness
- Today is the first day of the rest of your journey. Think of any failures from the past as plot twists getting you ready for this next chapter. #InstagramforBusiness
- Your story is being written every day. You have control over the next chapter. And it's going to be a good one. #InstagramforBusiness
- When successful business owners hear a good idea, they do not think, "My business is different. This won't work for me." Instead they think, "HOW can I apply this to my business?" #InstagramforBusiness
- I'm in! #InstagramforBusiness

Visit www.UGIGbook.com for behind the scenes private photos of the stories I share throughout this book and to get your Instagram 21-Day Explosion Plan today.

Chapter 1

Questions, Questions: Understanding the Why of Instagram

The history of Instagram reminds me of the quote:

If you want to make God laugh, tell him about your plans.

While the birth of Instagram was just a few years ago, in 2010, the idea for the photo app happened years before, and it happened because of a different project.

WHERE DID INSTAGRAM COME FROM ANYWAY?

Kevin Systrom and Mike Krieger are the official founders of Instagram. Systrom grew up in an upper-middle-class family in Massachusetts. According to rumors, he used to believe that getting rich quick through startups was something that happened to the other guy. (There was nothing quick about his story.)

Systrom left the East Coast to attend Stanford. After graduating, he wound up working for tech giants like Twitter and Google. Eventually, he started working in the marketing department of NextStop, which is a New York City subway directions app. At this time, Systrom decided to embark upon a new project featuring an app called Burbn. He intended for Burbn to become an HTML5-based merger of the online game *Mafia Wars* and

Foursquare's check-in service. During production, Burbn turned into Instagram (http://gramlike.com/the-history-of-instagram).

Thank goodness they changed the name.

After many iterations, the app was released in the fall of 2010. It went from a few users, which mainly included friends of Systrom and Krieger along with several early testers, to the number-one free photo app in only a few hours. By December of 2010, more than one million users had downloaded the program to their Apple devices.

Over the next two years, Instagram continued to grow, and the founders started to add features like hashtags, high-resolution photo support, one-click rotate, and new filters. In August of 2011, the 150 millionth photograph was uploaded to the app. A month later, Instagram had more than 10 million users, and at this time, the company was able to secure $7 million in Series A funding (http://thenextweb.com/magazine/2013/06/21/instagram-a-brief-history/#gref). This deal valued Instagram at around $25 million. (They are valued at $50 billion now—score!)

The Facebook Adoption

Since Instagram was initially set up as an iOS app, the program was available only through Apple's platform until April of 2012. At that time, the company finally released a version for Android devices. After taking that step, Facebook jumped in and bought the company for $1 billion in cash and stock. The final purchase amount was less, though, because the social site's value took a hit on the stock market.

The deal received approval in August of 2012, but by December, the new owners ran into trouble with the app. The problem began when a change was made to the company's terms of service, giving Instagram the right to sell users' pictures to third parties without compensating them or providing a notification. Understandably, people weren't too happy about this, and the consumer backlash began. People even vowed that they would never use Instagram again. Due to the program's current success, I suspect that a number of those people have now recanted.

You may recall, the backlash was enough to cause the company to retract the sections of its terms of service regarding the sharing of photos with third parties. Unfortunately to some degree, the company's reputation took a hit. This is just another example of the delicate balance between public, private, and social media networking.

Growing with Facebook

After Facebook purchased Instagram, the company introduced popular features like photo tagging and a "Photos of You" option. It also extended photo tagging to include brands. This move gained the attention of companies that were looking to expand their social media presence and jump into organic advertising.

To become even more social, the company made it easier for users to share posts and videos through links and embed codes. This function lets you show content on Instagram in its original state. You can do this by just copying and pasting an embed link with a website or an article. This was a clever move by the company because it lets users share their content in other places while potentially reeling in new traffic.

The Facebook purchase also brought us natural-looking ads within Instagram. The social media giant claimed it wanted to use natural ads because Instagram users weren't used to seeing advertisements on the app. Facebook started slow with just a handful of high-quality photos presented by a few brands. This marketing approach proved to be successful since about 5 percent of the app's users liked the ads. By incorporating marketing, Instagram gave businesses a new advertising platform to help them reach new consumers. The "warm" look of an effective Instagram ad from this time period continues to work today on not only Instagram but on Facebook as well.

By the end of 2013, Instagram added a private chat feature. With it, the app's users can send private videos and photos to each other. Prior to the chat feature, the only way for people to communicate through Instagram was publicly through comments and likes. Today, users can send private content to as many as 15 people at a time on the company's network. They're able to write captions for the images they are sharing, and after releasing a picture, they can have a conversation. With Facebook at the helm, the recent updates were strategic moves designed to increase the engagement levels of Instagram users and expand the site's traffic.

The Future of Instagram for Commerce

Social and mobile commerce are embracing Instagram in a big way. Not only is organic advertising a welcome form of marketing on the app, it also highly engages users, placing Instagram in the unique position of supporting social and mobile commerce.

Since mobile marketing is still "new" to many businesses (despite the fact that 87 percent of people have a mobile device, only 12 percent of businesses have any type of mobile marketing program), most companies are still trying to determine the best way to use it in their marketing strategies, and for retailers, Instagram has made it easier.

Instagram was one of the first networks to supply call-to-action tools for advertisers. They did this in the form of "Install Now" or "Shop Now" links. When it comes to commerce, Instagram offers intimacy and immediacy for both consumers and companies. These options are engaging more users.

Millennials are especially influenced by these kinds of call-to-action tools because they are seeing their friends and other influencers install or buy those items (while my age group, aka over 40, is more influenced by the ability to find our reading glasses—but I digress). This, more than branded content, gives companies more credibility with millennials. These tools are transitioning Instagram from a marketing platform into a conduit for ecommerce, which decreases the number of clicks a consumer needs to purchase an item. It also makes mobile sales tracking easier for companies.

Ah, the refreshing melody of "making it easier to purchase." Beautiful.

Businesses that have been waiting to enter the mobile advertising market are starting out on Instagram because the infrastructure is already there for them. For Instagram to remain a favorite advertising spot for commerce, the company will require them to embrace business trends and needs consistently without annoying its customer base. No one wants another spama-palooza like MySpace again. I do miss the constant requests for buying coins from Russia I got in my in-box, though—not!

Instagram's Future with Everyday Users

Recently, Kevin Systrom said, "We believe you can see the world happening in real time through Instagram, and I think that's true whether it's Taylor Swift's *1989* tour, which trends on Instagram all the time, or an important moment like a protest overseas, or a march like 'Je suis Charlie' in Paris. We want to make all of those, no matter how serious, no matter how playful, discoverable, and accessible on Instagram." He went on to say, "At the end of the day, there's no better way to consume what's happening in the world other than through images and video. I think Instagram is at the natural nexus of both of those."

As you know, our world is one that changes quickly, so while Instagram may be a service we continue to embrace for years, it's also one that could be gone in an instant. Only time will truly show us the future of Instagram (http://time.com/4059656/this-is-what-the-future-of-instagram-looks-like/). My hope is that with this book, Instagram will help your business achieve ROI in the here and now.

Let's start first with the "what" of Instagram and then in the chapters to follow, the "how," in order to achieve maximum ROI for your time, money, and energy spent in the app.

IT'S A POST, NOT A MARRIAGE.

Let me start by sharing a story. My husband, Ian, and I have been married for several years. Like most, it was a while after we started dating before we told each other how we felt, and a while after that before we got engaged.

Later on, we would admit to each other that we fell in love on our second date (truthfully these feelings may have been aided by the Italian guitarist serenading us, or the wine that preceded it). But neither of us told the other then because that would have been weird and a bit creepy at the time. Before we got serious, way back when, there was a series of events that needed to take place to build trust and commitment between us.

The same is true for your business.

At the time of this publication, Instagram allows only one clickable link in your account, and that falls into your bio. This means that your individual posts won't have links in them, forcing you to create content that connects. Focusing on that content and your messaging—and how it connects back to growing your business—can be confusing, and sadly most businesses get it wrong. Most fall in one of two categories:

1. *The Spammy McSpammerson.* Unfortunately, many businesses begin their relationships with prospects by asking to get married on the first date. *Yuck!* Or even worse, they show up like a used car salesman looking to hawk goods from hello. They make all their posts about their products, programs, or services and never about what their prospect really cares about—themselves.

2. *Too Chicken to Make a Move.* Some companies do the complete opposite and never connect their content with anything that will convert the follower into a buyer. They post and post and post forever and do nothing to turn the follower into a customer. This is like dating the love of your life forever and wanting to marry your beloved, but never asking your sweetie to marry you. Not only will this result in the two of you not getting married, but most likely when someone who has more serious intentions comes along, your twosome will also become a onesome.

When you never create a clear path on how to do business with you, and why someone *should* do business with you, they won't. And they will move on to something else that meets their needs. Or even worse, they will do nothing at all.

What Your Prospects Really Want

The truth is, you have a purpose. You have a mission. You have a pain to solve and it is your duty to find those who need you so you can heal their pain. Done well, the process can be seamless and can create lifelong client relationships instead of one-time, love 'em and leave 'em interactions. It doesn't have to be complicated. Start with value, build trust, and then ask for the sale.

Using Instagram as the start of your funnel is an effective way to create authority, credibility, and celebrity, while magnetically attracting your perfect prospects. But first, you have to start with making your content all about your prospect and what they care about.

So what do they care about?

The reality is, no one cares about your products, programs, or services. What they care about is how your products, programs, and services will make their lives better. Focusing on what they care about—as in how you are going to make their life better in some way—is vital to creating a tribe of loyal followers who become your customers for life.

Take time to consider what they are thinking when their thoughts wander during the day that causes them anxiety. What do they repeatedly hope will become different? What keeps them up at night?

Before you move forward with your Instagram marketing (or any type of marketing for that matter) answer this question:

How would your target market finish this sentence: "If I could just . . ."

For example, clients of the following might say:

- _Recruiter's clients._ "If I could just find a career that suits me so I can enjoy what I do."
- _Personal trainer's clients._ "If I could just get my abs back so I could finally feel comfortable on the beach."
- _Financial advisor's clients._ "If I could just take my wife on vacation without worrying about finances."
- _Realtor's clients._ "If I could just sell my house for enough money so we can move closer to our grandkids."

My amazing tribe thinks:

If I could just fill my sales pipeline and get more clients, I could reach and help more people and my business would bring my family and me the financial peace and prosperity we long for. (Yes, my tribe is the bee's knees.)

This translates into posts like the ones shown in Figure 1–1 on page 7.

I focus my @KWalshPhillips posts on the motivation and mindset necessary for taking your business to the next level, along with some quick how-to tips. These posts tie into how my tribe wants to build an audience of qualified leads, turn those leads into clients, and then become financially prosperous in the process.

Truthfully though, it can be difficult to get into your prospect's mind. We are so used to focusing on our own products, programs, and services that we tend to spend too much of our marketing power focused on ourselves instead of our audience.

An effective way to get into the mindset of your prospect is to write yourself a letter as though you are them. In the letter, go deep into the problem and what effect it is having on your emotional well-being—go beyond facts to feelings. And in the letter make sure to answer the "If I could just" longing. This will put you into your

FIGURE 1–1. These Posts Focus on Motivation.

customer's mindset (instead of your own) and help you to focus your promotion all on them.

Set a timer for ten minutes, and write yourself this letter from your prospect. (You should set a timer, because you and I both know that if you don't make yourself sit there and get this done, it won't happen. When you are done, feel free to treat yourself, and if you're buying, I'll take a non-fat cappuccino with cinnamon. Thanks.)

How would your prospect finish this sentence: "If I could just_____"?

Spending time outside Instagram before you launch can be hard for the impatient get-it-done-now kind of person (ask me how I know), but it's imperative for quickly succeeding on this platform. Getting inside your prospect's mindset before beginning to create content will give you a head start in having an effective Instagram campaign.

Once you have determined this, you can set forth on the rest of your marketing and sales funnel.

WHAT IS A SALES FUNNEL?

If you hear someone mention a sales funnel, they are not talking about some type of super-human ride at the beach where tourists climb up and pay money to ride down into the ocean on a slide that gets perpetually smaller (although that would be fun). A sales funnel is the general buying process that companies guide their customers through during a purchase-based transaction.

When companies embrace the sales funnel technique, they usually divide the process into several steps. These stages range from when a customer first becomes aware of a product or service, to repurchasing it after discovering its helpful properties. The term "sales funnel" is a good description of the process because the top of the funnel consists of potential customers. These prospective clients are just learning about a product or service and are expressing some degree of interest in it. The bottom of the funnel features the clients who have already invested in a company's product or service. The sales industry uses the funnel comparison because potential prospects drop off along the way. The ones who stay funnel down through the buying process.

What the Funnel Should Look Like

Developing a sales funnel is the most important step in your Instagram marketing. It is also where most businesses make terrible mistakes. (Don't be one of them!)

When a private client or one of my coaching members first comes to us, typically there is no congruency between what they are posting for their business and what they ultimately want their prospect to do.

Think of it this way:

Imagine you are invited to your friend's daughter's birthday party. You received the invitation, and you can't help but smile at the princesses, glitter, and feathers that fill the cover. You can tell this is going to be one adorable gathering.

Because you have manners, you show up to the party with a present for the little girl. When your friend greets you upon arrival, you hand her a present for the birthday princess.

Your friend then looks at you very confused and asks: "Are you sure this is for Jenny?"

You: "Yes. Isn't it pretty wrapping paper?"

Your confused friend: "It is indeed. It's just that it says, 'Happy Retirement.'"

You: "I know. I wanted to use it because the images are so beautiful."

Your confused friend: "Um. Okay. Thanks."

And then, with much hesitation, she takes the present. Later, at the end of the party, the little girl Jenny opens up the gift you brought.

Jenny: "Mommy, I don't know what this is."

You: "It's a shoe polish kit! The best in the world. You'll be able to polish your shoes until the end of time. It's been around since 1985 and with its great formula it is the #1 choice for shoes. There are endless uses and due to the fact that it is a concentrate, a little amount—just the size of a dime—goes a long way."

Jenny: "Mommy, do I need shoe polish?"

Your confused friend: "You don't. Please give me the present."

You: "Wow. This party is a problem. You should have loved my gift. It is an amazing shoe polish kit."

And with that, you are never invited to a gathering at your friend's house again. (*Dang!* That is too bad. Their crab dip was out of this world. You are going to miss it, I am sure. But you can come over to my house. I make great crab dip as well and would love a shoe shine kit.)

Too often, businesses do this very same thing. They show up to the wrong party with branding and/or an offer that is a terrible match for their target market. They use images because "they are pretty" or offer opt-in opportunities that don't match the audience. Then they blame the medium for their lack of ROI, when actually, it is the marketing campaign itself that is to blame.

How do you prevent this from happening? Focus on who your target market really is. Focus on what they want, not what they need. Attract them with images that will resonate with them. Make each step of the process make sense. The process works like this:

First, someone comes across an Instagram post, such as the one below, from a friend who liked or shared it, or through a hashtag search (see Figure 1–2 on page 10).

Your messaging resonates with the new follower, and this person wants to learn more. Your new audience member goes to the link in your bio (see Figure 1–3, page 10) and clicks on it. Your link sends them to a lead magnet that gives this person an incentive to give you their contact information so you can continue the conversation outside of Instagram. This should *always* be the goal, because then you can nurture the

FIGURE 1–2. One of My Instagram Posts that Someone Shared.

FIGURE 1–3. My Bio That Sends Customers to a Lead Magnet.

relationship over time without the distraction of other shiny objects in the networking platform.

The lead magnet (see Figure 1–4, page 11) addresses the pain point of your perfect prospect and has a similar look and feel as your Instagram posts. This way, the prospect who is clicking through feels like they are in the right place. Then they enter their contact information to receive a reward in return (see Figure 1–5, page 11).

If it can make sense for your business, this is an excellent time to convert the lead into a customer. Once they have opted in, give them a chance to buy something. In this example, the new subscriber is given an offer for 35 ad designs for $1 (see Figure

FIGURE 1–4. An Example of a Lead Magnet.

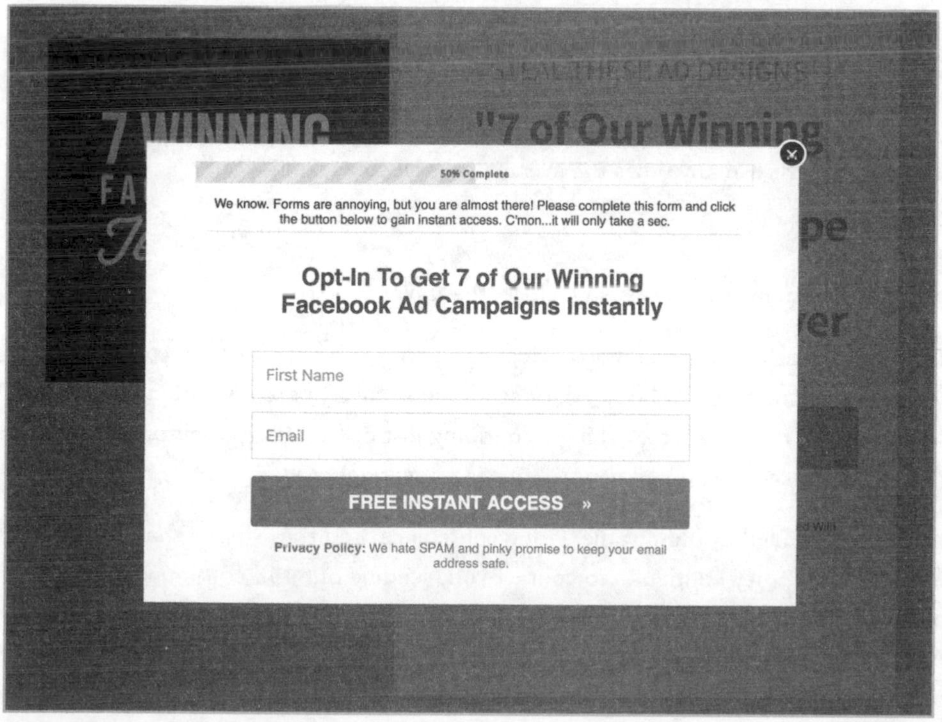

FIGURE 1–5. A Lead Magnet Gets Customers to Enter in Their Contact Information.

1–6 on page 13). This is congruent with the lead magnet they just requested, and the wording is focused on solving the pain point. Always make sure yours is as well.

The prospect is given the option to take a test drive of Marketing Insiders Elite membership, a direct-response marketing association of their peers. Again, the wording focuses on the pain point of the customer (see Figure 1–7, page 13).

The marketing and sales path continues even if someone doesn't take membership. This is so important to get the highest ROI, because many will not be ready to pull the trigger the first time they go through your sales funnel. In this example, in the confirmation email, there's an invitation to attend a free training at www.FBSalesLaunch. com. See Figure 1–8 on page 14.

In our sales funnel example, when the report is delivered, an opportunity to attend a valuable training on Facebook is presented. While the contact is of course top-notch, there is also an opportunity to enroll in a paid course at the end, hence giving this newbie another chance to become a customer. See Figure 1–9 on page 14.

THE FORTUNE IS IN THE FOLLOW UP

Dr. Herbert True of Notre Dame studied selling behaviors and prospect behaviors to find where people became interested. He found that on average, it took five times of being asked for a person to say yes.

Do you know how many times the average salesperson asked?

Once.

Imagine how many sales are being left on the table!

The same holds true for marketing. Most companies send out one direct-mail piece, run one Instagram or Facebook ad, or send one email and are disappointed with the results. Frankly, if they get anything from doing just one touch to their prospects, they should be thrilled because in general, one is not enough.

I recently attended a sold-out marketing conference, and they shared that until you registered, they continued to contact you, sending out 138 communication pieces. 138! Talk about persistent. Did I mention they sold out the conference? Always develop a path to purchase for those not ready to buy right now. (See more in my conversation with Oli Billson in Chapter 6 for more on that topic.)

FIGURE 1–6. Once a Customer Has Opted In, Give Them a Chance to Buy Something.

FIGURE 1–7. Make Sure the Wording Focuses on the Pain Point of the Customer.

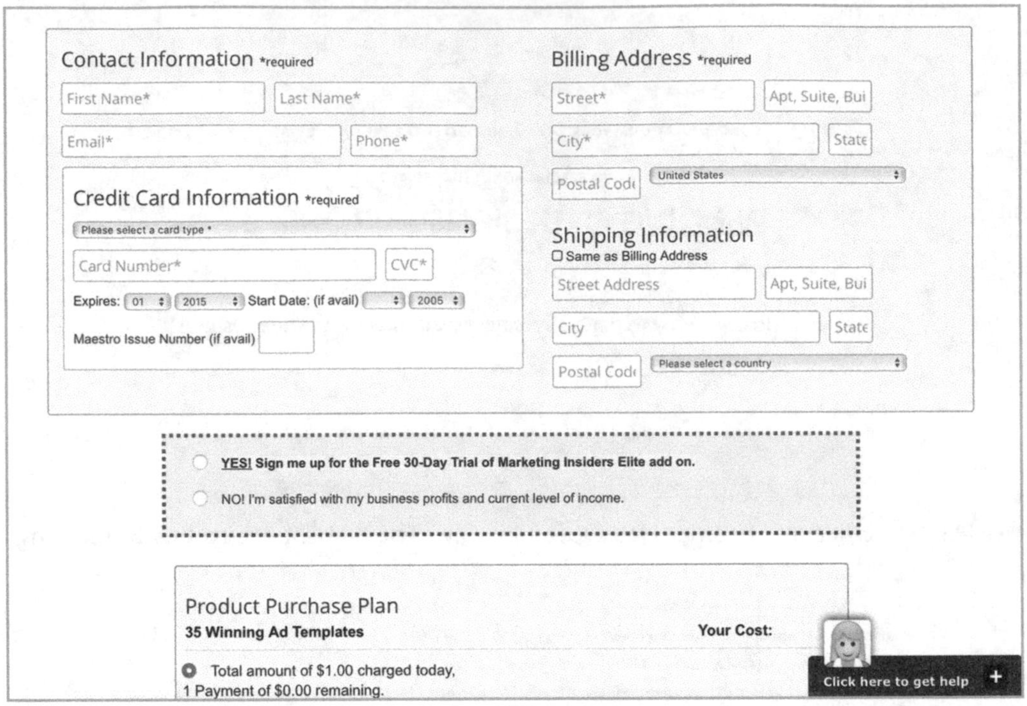

FIGURE 1–8. Give Customers the Option of Taking a Test Drive of the Product.

Hi Kim,

Below you will find a link to download your 7 Winning Facebook Campaigns. I encourage you to use these campaigns to attract the most fantastic leads and sales into your business. (Why the most-fantastic? Because you don't have time for lame leads or problemsome customers...you are too busy doing way more important things.)

Please let me know what campaign you launch and how it goes on my Facebook page. (And if you haven't liked the page to start following my stream of tips and strategies each day, do a girl a solid and like the page now please. And thank you. You are the best.)

Also, if you want even more Facebook Sales Strategies, join me for a free training by clicking here ☻. I hope to see you there!

Your fan,
Kim Walsh-Phillips

📎 7WinningFacebookCampaigns.pdf ☻

FIGURE 1–9. This Confirmation Email Offers the Prospect an Opportunity to Take a Free Webinar.

The path from post to sale makes sense and is all geared toward the same perfect prospect.

So how do you ensure yours is as well? You start by keeping it simple.

CREATING YOUR MARKETING AND SALES PATH

Begin with the end in mind.

While it may seem counterintuitive, begin with the last step you want your prospect to take. What is it that you want your prospect to do? Should they contact you to schedule a client consultation? Purchase a product? Subscribe to your blog? Listen to your podcast?

Determine the last thing you want your prospect to do because it will allow you to walk your full campaign in reverse so that every image, blog post, lead magnet, and email all lead seamlessly to the sale. After you've determined that last step, work backward to create a lead magnet that would be valuable only to your perfect prospect who would want to take the last step you want them to take. Then create blog posts about that same topic. Finally, create quote image posts that pull content directly from the blog posts. This way, every marketing message you put out there is all leading to the same conclusion—doing business with you.

In one of my prospect paths, my goal for my fans is that they join our Summit Academy, a 90-day program to attract more high-quality clients to pay you what you are worth and have more of a life while doing it. That is the final goal, and not one that I *ever* talk about in my Instagram posts, but if the product is focused on solving my prospects' pain points—and I keep my Instagram posts focused on those four topics—then when I am in promotion mode, this funnel will also make sense.

So, why Instagram? Well, Instagram is a tangible, visual representation of your business and your brand. That captivating quality of your brand and content will allow you to continually market to your prospective and current followers. By doing so, you will achieve low-effort, high-impact marketing that directly calls your audience to action and moves followers along your sales funnel with every post. Throughout this book, I will share how to effectively develop each stage of that marketing funnel. I will walk you through brand development, content creation, and communication techniques to ensure each step is congruent and effective for your target market.

Ready to get started? In the next chapter, I will demonstrate how to set up your Instagram account for maximum success.

#INSTAGRAMFORBUSINESS POSTABLES

- It's a post. Not a marriage. #InstagramforBusiness
- The truth is, you have a purpose. You have a mission. You have a pain to solve ,and it is your duty to find those who need you so you can heal their pain. #InstagramforBusiness
- Focus on who your target market really is. #InstagramforBusiness
- Always develop a path to purchase for those not ready to buy right now. #InstagramforBusiness

Resource spotlight: Visit www.UGIGbook.com to download the "Path to Purchase" worksheet.

Chapter 2

First Things First: Creating a Solid Foundation

had no idea that what I was doing before was wrong and most don't. I thought it *should* work, but it just didn't. And when it did, I didn't know why. I had no idea what part of my marketing was working and what wasn't, so I just did more of it, and more often, with that hope that it would work.

As I shared in this book's introduction, I struggled for an extremely long time to make my business successful. I labored harder than I thought possible, at times doing a million "things," hoping *something* would produce revenue.

When I did get a major sale, I usually had no idea why, other than what the prospect told me about where they came from. This tends to be the way most businesses track clients and sales, and it is riddled with assumptions and false data. When you start tracking your leads and sales sources, however, you will often find the prospect is wrong about where they think they came from. Accurate measurement requires more sophisticated ways of measuring ROI.

THE LAWS OF DIRECT-RESPONSE MARKETING

When I first read Dan Kennedy's book, *No B.S. Guide to Brand-Building by Direct Response: The Ultimate No Holds Barred Plan to Creating and Profiting from a Powerful Brand Without Buying It*, I was blown away.

For the first time ever, I saw how marketing could equal results—how each action could be tracked. When I found something that worked, I could scale it. And quickly I would. When I found something that didn't work, it would be eliminated quicker than an anchorman after a vulgar tweet.

Over the years, I have tweaked Dan Kennedy's strategies and those of other mentors I have learned from, and added a few of my own as I find what works and what doesn't, and what is my taste for doing things. Digital marketing gives us tracking options that go far and above what was ever possible before. It would be downright silly not to take advantage of these. And while Dan tends to be a gruff guy, as do many direct-response marketers, I tend to be a bit glam and have adjusted accordingly. (Hint, your marketing *does not* need to be ugly—more on that in a sec.)

Many direct-response marketers think social media is complete fluff, and for most companies, it is. That is because most marketers do not apply *any* direct marketing tactics to their strategic approach (if they are even strategic at all).

My firm places millions of dollars in ad spend in social media advertisements and is using direct-response marketing principles to achieve financially rewarding results for our clients—and frankly, for us, too (which makes us giddy).

For the sake of this book, I will share how to apply these principles to Instagram, but they work for all types of marketing. And they should be used accordingly.

It is my hope that you will find these principles as profitable as I have.

Direct-Response Marketing Rule 1: There Will Be TRACKING and MEASUREMENT

Ever hear that John Wannamaker quote, "I know 50 percent of my marketing is working. I just don't know which 50 percent?" This philosophy is bogus. Everything in marketing is measurable. Everything.

And if it is not, you should find another strategy quickly or fire the person running your marketing. How will you ever know the ROI on your social media marketing unless you track it?

When it comes to Instagram marketing, do the following:

1. *Use a unique URL and landing page in your bio.* This way you know that every lead that comes in came from this source. Use tinyurl.com, bitly.com, or buy a new domain name to create this link.
2. *Use a unique email address in your bio description.* Create an email address just for Instagram so that when leads come in with this "To" line, you know where they came from.

Direct-Response Marketing Rule 2: There Will ALWAYS Be an OFFER or OFFERS

In Instagram, you never want to come across as a sales predator pouncing on his next kill, but you do need to ensure that you are giving your prospects a consistent opportunity to connect and do business with you. If you don't, you will not realize a return of your marketing dollars and staff resources spent online.

Your marketing funnel will launch with the click of your bio link from your Instagram profile's visitor. Make sure you draw attention to this link in your post description and bio so that visitors are given an opportunity to buy at some time. Remember, you are providing a solution to a need, and you are doing your prospects a service by giving them a chance to buy.

There are many types of offers you can run in an Instagram marketing and sales funnel.

Lead Generation

An incentive for your recipient to provide contact information. This is done through offering something of inherent value that is so good your recipient would pay for it, except they won't because you will be giving it away for free. This can include any incentive such as:

- A report/white paper/guide
- Chapter of your book
- Ebook
- Video
- Gift certificate
- Sample
- Webinar
- Checklist
- Script
- Templates
- Swipe file
- Video training series
- Ticket to a live event
- Discount code/certificate
- Sample

Sale

It *is* possible to sell directly to cold traffic on social media. We do it every day, but there are a few key things to remember. There should be something special about your offer, such as:

- It is being sold there first.
- It is being sold for less money.
- It starts with a free trial.
- It comes with bonuses.
- It is time sensitive.
- It is an outrageous offer—as in it is so good it is impossible to say no.

In contrast, if you sell the exact same thing on social media as you do everywhere else, for the exact same price, then you are most likely not going to realize great results. Social media is a cocktail party, not a shopping mall, and the only way to get people to pay attention to something being sold is to make sure it is a really good deal. Do that and *everyone* will pay attention and want in first.

At any one time, only a small percentage of people have intent to buy. According to Google, 18 percent of local searches leads to sales in contrast to only 7 percent of non-local searches (https://searchenginewatch.com/sew/study/2343577/google-local-searches-lead-50-of-mobile-users-to-visit-stores-study). For the rest of your target market, you need to create intent, so an incentive is needed.

Some examples of offers our clients are running effectively on social media:

- Women's Institute for Gynecology & Minimally Invasive Surgery, LLC, runs a campaign starting with a guide on how hormones affect your body and mind and then encourages the prospect to schedule an appointment.
- The American Society for Tax Problem Solvers offers accountants five letter templates they can use with their clients to communicate with the IRS.
- Financial planner John Smallwood offers a guide on ways to cut expenses so you can have more money for retirement.
- Phelan Dental offers a free training for other dentists and sells a training course at the end—bringing in over six figures each month, on autopilot. (This does not suck.)
- Modoma Health and Wellness offers an introductory massage for $39.

All very different offers for different types of businesses. But all are offering something of value as a first step in the collection of contact information.

Direct-Response Marketing Rule 3: There Will ALWAYS Be a REASON to RESPOND NOW

"I really could be busier. It's just that I don't have enough to do. If you could give me a few more things to fill my day, I would appreciate it," said no one, ever.

Let's face it. No one is walking around hoping you will give them more to do. Every prospect you encounter is busy and distracted, and unless you give them a reason to act now, they won't. It is why so many gyms now offer boot camps. "Sign up now for the 21-Day Challenge: Abs from Flab to Fab!"

Adding in a reason to respond now gives that thing you can keep putting off "until next Monday" a deadline so you need to act now. Time-sensitive triggers include limited quantities, limited time, or are event, day, or time specific.

Direct-Response Marketing Rule 4: There Will ALWAYS Be CLEAR INSTRUCTIONS on How to RESPOND

Want your followers to comment on your post? Tell them. Want "hearts," request the double tap. Simply telling your audience what you'd like them to do (call to action) can increase your engagement. A study by Search Engine Land (www.searchengineland.com) showed that simply giving clear instructions that lay out, step by step, exactly what you want your target market to do, will increase your conversions (actions taken by your target market) up to five times.

Direct-Response Marketing Rule 5: Brand Is Important but It Is Just the FIRST Step of a Marketing and Sales Funnel

In contrast to some old-school direct-response marketers, I believe your marketing need not and should not be ugly. If you make branding just the first step in a strategically executed marketing and sales funnel, brand can be leveraged to develop trust and authority positioning.

Bop Design (www.BopDesign.com) states, "80 percent of consumers are more likely to evaluate solutions from the brands they follow on social channels. Social media channels are a one to many solution for getting the word out about your products and services. By creating a strong brand presence on social media, you can reach a broader audience."

After all, you are looking for lifetime customers here. Not one-time transactions. Branding is a strong way to start to build that trust. (See Chapter 3 for more on building your Instagram brand.)

Direct-Response Marketing Rule 6: RESULTS RULE. Period

There is an endless supply of conjecture by marketers, PR professionals, and "branding experts." Be very cautious whenever you hear a universal truth about any type of marketing. My Elite Digital Group team places thousands of ads each week for clients across industries, geography, and products, and what we have found is that *nothing* can be deemed a universal truth, not even within the same industry. The only thing that should be used to determine your spend and marketing direction are the results of your own marketing. This is why *everything* needs to be tracked and checked *every day*.

Our reporting to clients tells them exactly what they spent on ads and our fee and how many qualified leads or customers they received that day. Keeping a hawk's eye on spending and results allows us to quickly scale up or down a campaign without guessing if it is working.

As you develop your marketing and sales funnels, you will most likely find your own set of "laws." I encourage you to start with the ones I outlined in this chapter and then tweak and add as you find a system that works for you. Above all else, let results, not conjecture, be your guiding force.

HOW TO SET UP YOUR ACCOUNT FOR MAXIMUM SUCCESS

Unfortunately for those of us (me included!) who prefer working on our desktops versus mobile apps, Instagram really is a mobile-only app. (For all of us over 40, let's say a collective, "Dagnabit." For all of those under, pretend that didn't just happen. Please.)

While you can edit your profile and see your timeline on a desktop, pretty much everything else needs to be done on a mobile device. I have found a few workarounds, though, and we will get to those in a sec.

Finding Success with Instagram Begins with Setting Up Your Account Correctly

After you have downloaded the application from your app store you can get started. When you open the application, the registration screen will appear. Here you have the option of Signing In with your email or through Facebook (see Figure 2–1, page 23).

Signing Up with Your Email

Step 1. Select the option to sign up with your email address. You will need to have a valid email address to continue (see Figure 2–2, page 23).

Step 2. You will be taken to a page titled New Account. Put in your valid email address (there will be a verification email sent later on). Create a username. If the one you want is taken, you will be notified and given alternative username suggestions. Then you will create a password for your account. On this page you are given the option to add your phone number. This can make it easier for Instagram to verify your profile (see Figure 2–3 on page 23).

Step 3. Next you will be taken to the Edit Profile page. Here you will be asked to put in the name that you want to appear when someone views your profile, your username,

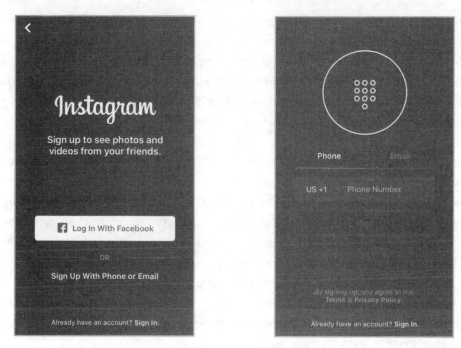

FIGURE 2–1. You Have the Option of Signing Up for Instagram Either Through Facebook or with Your Email.

FIGURE 2–2. Enter Your Email Address.

FIGURE 2–3. Pick a Username That You Want to Appear When Someone Views Your Profile.

website, and a brief bio. Definitely play around with your description in a Microsoft Word® document before pasting it into your profile.

Write your bio to really be about "them"—your target market.

Share with readers why they should connect with you by stating your unique selling proposition (USP). Tell viewers quickly why they would want to do business with you versus anyone else in the world and how it benefits *them*. Then follow it up with a link to a landing page offering value. If you have a lead magnet—like a free report, chapter download, or video—that is a great place to start. If not, then send them to your blog or other value-rich page on your site.

You can also add a profile picture on this page. You have the option of uploading an existing picture from your mobile device, taking a new picture right then, or choosing not to have a profile picture at all. Remember, this is your chance to let your followers get to know you a little bit, so make your personality show. (Don't let too much "show," if you know what I mean. And I am pretty sure you do.)

My recommendation here from a branding perspective is to *only* use a professional headshot, and no matter what, do not use a selfie. If you want to be treated like a market expert, show up that way.

Step 4. Check your email to verify your account. Once you complete that confirmation step, you are ready to search for friends, family, and celebrities to follow. You can also upload pictures because you are now an Instagram user.

Signing Up with Your Facebook Account

Since the big Facebook owns Instagram, they allow you to sign up for the platform using your Facebook account. Here's how to do that:

Step 1. Select the option to "Log In with Facebook" and enter your username and password just like you would if you were signing into your Facebook account (see Figure 2–4, page 25).

Step 2. Verify that you would like to continue to create your Instagram account using your Facebook account (see Figure 2–5, page 25).

Step 3. The next screen will show your Facebook profile picture along with your profile name on Facebook. Here you can choose to change your profile picture or your display name (or you can keep both as they appear, see Figure 2–6, page 25).

Step 4. Next you will be asked to create a username. There will be a suggested username provided based on your Facebook profile name. You can choose to use the suggested

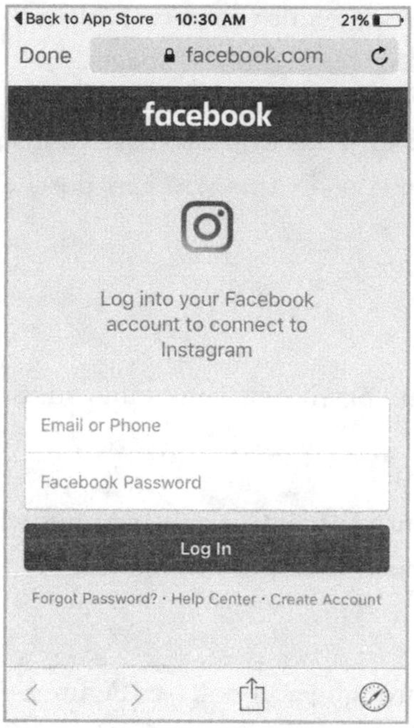

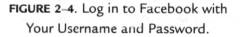

FIGURE 2–4. Log in to Facebook with Your Username and Password.

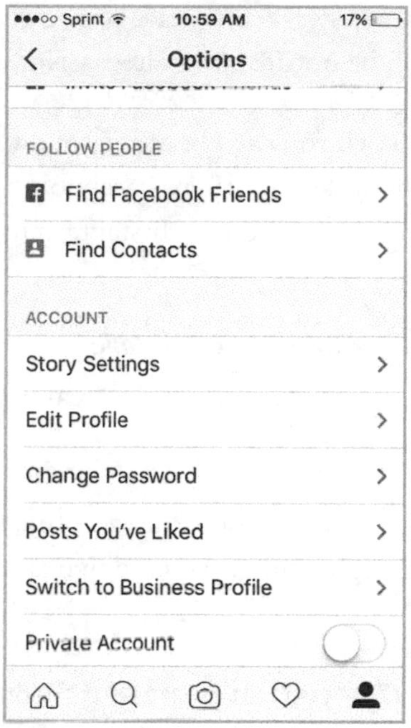

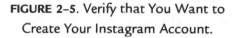

FIGURE 2–5. Verify that You Want to Create Your Instagram Account.

FIGURE 2–6. You Can Choose to Keep Your Profile Picture and Username from Your Facebook Account or You Can Create a New One.

username or you can create your own. Again, if the username you enter is already taken, you will be notified and alternatives will be provided (see Figure 2–7, page 27).

Step 5. Then you can choose to follow your Facebook friends who also have an Instagram account linked to their Facebook account. Once you do this you can post pictures because you are now an Instagram user.

Creating Your Business Profile

Now that you've successfully created your Instagram profile you can build your business profile.

Step 1. Open your personal account and go to your profile. Click the settings wheel in the top-right corner. Scroll down and select "Switch to Business Profile" (see Figure 2–8, page 27).

Step 2. Now you can create your Business Profile through Facebook (see Figure 2–9, page 27). You can flip through the features and see that you can use your phone number, email, or location to connect to potential customers and see how well your posts are performing.

Step 3. Once you select to continue to use your Facebook profile, just enter your business account information. Profile details from your Facebook profile will automatically be displayed. You can choose to use this information or enter your own based on your personal preferences.

Step 4. After entering all your information you will be taken back to your Instagram page, which will now be a business profile!

At any time, you can view your profile from a visitor's point of view so that you can see what your profile looks like to everyone else. (Don't you wish you could do this in real life? I mean, how would the world see this black dress I am going to wear to Friday's dinner?) By clicking the Contact button on your profile page you will see the engagement options that your followers and visitors will see when they view your business profile. Depending on your personal preferences, you can decide whether or not you want to edit the information your visitors will see.

Obviously the first thing a client will search for when trying to find your business is the name; however, the difference that will both set you apart from other users and gain landings is choosing a name and profile picture that make your brand linger in your viewers' minds. Your assigned username should be the name of your business for

FIGURE 2–7. If You Want to Create a New Username and Add a New Profile Picture, This Is Where You Will Enter the Information.

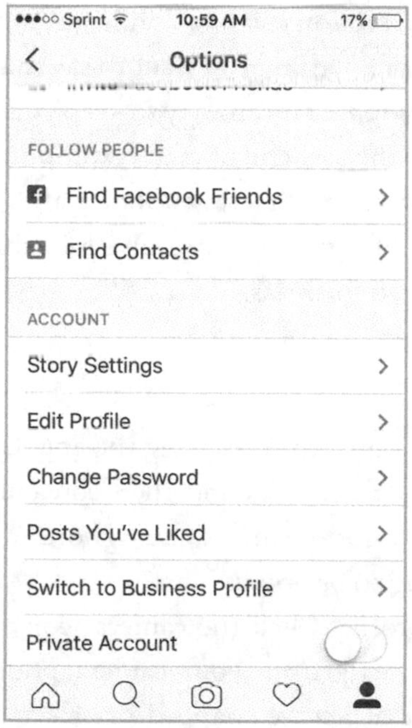

FIGURE 2–8. Click Switch to Business Profile to Create Your Business Profile.

FIGURE 2–9. Connect Your Instagram Business Account with Your Facebook Business Profile.

people to easily find you online. The only problem with using your business name is that your establishment may have a name that already exists somewhere else in the world. In that event, it will be your profile picture and description that uniquely identifies your business in search results.

If you are the face of your company, use your professional headshot as the account profile picture. If your company does not have a figurehead, use your company logo as your profile picture. (More on that later.)

If your business doesn't have a logo, get one. Not only is it essential for a business to have a logo, this is the first thing users will see when typing your name into the search bar within Instagram. You can have a professional logo created quickly for just $5 on www.Fiverr.com. This logo should be the same image you use across all your social media platforms to make your personal branding consistent. Navigation between your various social media platforms will be more intuitive for your clients if all the pages have identical imagery.

You may be thinking, "Seriously, what kind of logo can I get for $5?!" I have ordered a bunch from Fiverr and have been really happy with them. And getting something done is way better than nothing at all—no excuses! (Hear me yelling that at you in the deepest Jillian Michaels voice possible, and while you are down there, *gimme 20!*)

The last step in setting up your profile is adding a description that gives a brief summary of what your business is all about. The Bio section can be a condensed version of your mission statement, a message for your fans, or anything you want to say that will convey the soul of your enterprise. Just like your personal branding, try to keep your info blurb similar across all your social media profiles. At the very end of your text input there should be a URL hyperlinked to your professional website. Directing online traffic to an actual website from your social media profile will add legitimacy to your establishment and ultimately result in conversions that will gain you business.

How to Use Instagram

Now that you've finished setting up your profile, it's time to start using the app. Unlike that Steps app you downloaded last year, used for three days and then conveniently moved to the fourth page of your screen search, do not download and ignore. We are about to get our Instagram ROI on and this is going to be good!

Let's start by adding some pictures to your profile. Click the camera icon at the bottom of the screen to either take a picture directly from your camera phone or import a photo from your library. Once you have a picture snapped or selected, it's time to edit the photo using the filter presets within the app or tweaking the individual characteristics of the image. Click *Next* when you've finished editing the photo (see Figure 2–10, page 29).

FIGURE 2–10. First, Find an Image You Want to Upload to Instagram.

You are then presented with all of the tagging and linking options that make Instagram great for businesses. Let's break down what each section does and how to best utilize it.

The first box allows you to write a caption for your photo (see Figure 2–11, page 30). In this space, you want to insert text that communicates the intent behind posting the picture, along with some categorized keywords (otherwise known as "hashtags"—see Figure 2–12, page 30). A hashtag, denoted by a "#" symbol preceding a single word or unbroken string of words, is how Instagram creates searchable content categorizes.

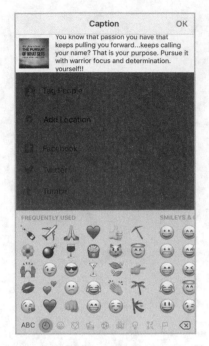

FIGURE 2–11. Then Add a Caption to Your Photo.

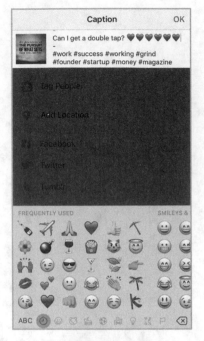

FIGURE 2–12. Be Sure to Include Hashtags That Will Get Your Prospects' Attention.

Hashtags are used by businesses to gain followers by attracting the attention of public users. It is important that you include a large number of hashtags to cover a broad range of user traffic and keep them relevant to your industry to avoid spamming. For example, if I were the owner of a coffee shop I wouldn't include #Roofing in my caption because that has nothing to do with coffee. (Duh, Ms. Obvious.) Instead I would include terms like #latteart, #barista, etc., that are directly relatable to your business and garner the attention of other people in your industry using the same hashtags. This is how you build relationships with followers as well as other businesses. (See Chapter 5 for more details.)

The next box marked "Tag People" is exactly what it says it's for. OK, not exactly. It's not like you are going to run around putting shiny gold gift tags on your peeps. This is all virtual and comes from the same terminology as Facebook and other social media profiles to indicate someone is included in your posts.

This is where you tag other users to link your media content with their profiles. As a business owner, the best use of this feature is to tag other independent businesses that you may be collaborating with or clients you might feature. This will provide a link for your followers to explore your business partners' pages, and it shows that you conduct honest business.

HOW TO MAKE WRITING POST DESCRIPTIONS EASIER ON MOBILE

I hate typing descriptions on my phone. Hate, hate, hate. I get spelling errors, write only really short ones because I get lazy, and tend to flub up the whole thing when I am typing on mobile. I have found a workaround, though—I write all of my posts in the Notes app on my Mac (which syncs with my phone in the iCloud) and then snag it from the Notes app on my phone to paste in. Other options include Evernote, Google Notes, or any other list-making app that can work on both your computer and phone.

If you don't want to include a tag within the actual photo itself, you also have the option of linking to another profile by typing a username within the caption section by putting the @ symbol before the name. This creates a hyperlink to the other user's Instagram profile.

Adding tags also directs user traffic to your page by linking your profile with the people or businesses tagged in your photos. Followers are able to see photos those users were tagged in by clicking on the tab for tagged photos. Basically, if a user follows a partner business that you've tagged on Instagram, chances are they are going to find you by association. That's a win-win for both you and the other enterprise you've teamed up with.

This is where some businesses will spam and spam some more by tagging other Instagrammers who have nothing to do with the post, just to get their attention. Once is fine if done with purpose. But do it all of the time, and you'll become an annoying gnat that will be swatted away, as you will deserve. (Can you tell I hate being spam-tagged?!)

Next is the option to "Add Location" if you desire to have your followers know where you're located. This is obviously not applicable if you run a business purely online or from your private residence. (Unless you want to be found, and that's your thing. If so, this feature is all yours.)

If you have a brick-and-mortar establishment, it would be wise to include your location in your posts so your followers can find you for services and goods. Adding your location to your Instagram post creates a link under your username that users can click on to find a pinned map of your location as well as posts you have either made or been tagged in. This is yet another way to direct online traffic to your Instagram page for more landings and conversions on your website and social media platforms. *Score!*

You can also link your other social media profiles with Instagram so you can simultaneously have your post show up across all your profiles. Currently, Instagram has the option to connect with Facebook, Twitter, Tumblr, Flicker, and Swarm. To link these profiles with your Instagram feed, go into the Settings tab and scroll down to Linked Accounts. From there, you can log in to your other social media platforms to allow them access to your Instagram content.

The accounts you select will now show up as sliders at the bottom of the photo information screen. Just tap the sites you would like Instagram to post on before you tap *Share*, and voilà! Now your filtered photograph from Instagram and all of those content-rich hashtags have posted to all your other social media pages. Your contacts and followers from those other sites will see you have an Instagram feed that they can start following and interacting with.

I am not a huge fan of linking all accounts because I find that my reach is better on each platform when I post directly, but if you are short on time, it might be best. But then I will mock you when I see you do that, so if you don't like being mocked, don't link. (Just kidding, I won't mock you. But you still shouldn't link. *Wink.*)

Adding Effects and Filters

Filters are about the best thing and reason why Instagram is so popular. With the click of a button we can apply the same filters that the media does to make our photos pop, skin look more even, or the sunset pinker. I know, I know—this is a distorted reality. All I am saying is that if I could apply these filters to myself in real life, I would in a nanosecond. It really would have helped my appearance while I was utterly sleep-deprived in the months that followed giving birth to each of my two daughters.

How Do I Apply Filters to My Photo or Video?

Once you've taken a photo or video, or selected one from your phone or tablet, you can edit it by applying filters:

1. Tap *Next*, then tap the filter you'd like to apply.
2. Tap the filter again if you want to adjust the filter strength up or down using the slider. Tap *Done* to save your changes.
3. Tap *Next* to add a caption and location and to share your photo.

Are There Personalization Options?

For the super users, I have a red cape for you. You can always personalize your filters by adding, hiding, and rearranging the ones you see when posting a photo or video.

Start by uploading a photo or video and swiping all the way to the right on your filters, until you reach the end. Then tap *Manage*. From there, you can:

- *Add a filter*. Tap the filter you'd like to add. You'll see ⊘ next to the filters that currently appear when you post a photo or video.
- *Hide a filter*. Tap the filter you'd like to hide. You'll see ◯ next to filters that are hidden.
- *Rearrange your filters*. Tap and hold the filter you'd like to move. Then drag it to the position you'd like.

When you've finished personalizing your filters, tap *Done* to return to your photo or video.

How Do I Apply Effects to My Photo?

You can edit photos you take or upload from your phone's library. Once you've taken or uploaded a photo, tap *Next,* then tap *Edit* at the bottom of the screen. Learn more about the effects you can create:

- Tap ⊟ *Adjust* to change the photo's vertical or horizontal perspective.
- Tap ☼ *Brightness* to make your photo brighter or darker.
- Tap ◑ *Contrast* to make the bright areas of your photo brighter and the dark areas darker.
- Tap △ *Structure* to bring out the detail and texture in your photo.
- Tap 🌡 *Warmth* to shift the colors of your photo toward warmer orange tones or cooler blue tones.
- Tap ◌ *Saturation* to increase or decrease the color intensity of the image (ex: adjust up to make the red more red).
- Tap 🎨 *Color* to add a color (yellow, orange, red, pink, purple, blue, cyan, or green) to either the shadows or highlights of your photo. Tap the color you want to use twice to adjust the strength of the color.

Tap ☁ *Fade* to give your photo an aged look.

Tap ⊟ *Highlights* to adjust the focus on the bright areas of the image.

Tap ⊜ *Shadows* to adjust focus on the dark areas of the image.

Tap ⊙ *Vignette* to darken the edges of the photo. Adding a vignette can direct the attention away from the edges toward the center of the photo.

Tap ▽ *Sharpen* to add crispness to your photo and make the photo appear clearer.

Frequently Asked Questions

I just applied an effect to my photo. How do I compare it to the original version?

Before posting a photo, you can tap on it anywhere to see what the original version looked like.

How can I tell which effects I've applied to my photo?

In preview mode, a gray dot will appear below each of the effects you've applied to your photo. For example, a gray dot below Brightness ☼ means you've adjusted the brightness of your photo.

How do I remove some of the effects I've applied to my photo?

You can remove any of the effects you've applied as long as your post is in preview mode and you haven't shared it yet. A gray dot appears under each of the effects you've applied to the photo.

To undo or remove an effect:

1. Tap the tool you used.
2. Adjust the slider back to 0.
3. Tap to save your change.

How do I turn borders on or off?

You can add a border to any filtered photo:

1. Choose the filter you want to apply to your photo.
2. Tap the filter again and then tap on the right side to add a border. Tap it again to remove it.
3. Tap *x* to cancel, or tap the checkmark to save your change.

How do I crop my photo?

After you've uploaded or taken a new photo, you can crop it. To crop a photo:

1. Tap ⬚ *Adjust*.
2. Touch the screen and pinch to zoom in. Then move the photo and adjust how it fits within the frame. Use the grid to help you frame the photo.
3. Tap *Cancel* to cancel or tap *Done* to save your change.

How do I straighten a photo?

When you take a photo using the Instagram in-app camera or upload a photo from your phone's library, you can straighten it with the Adjust tool. Once you upload a photo:

1. Take or upload a photo, then tap *Edit* at the bottom of the screen.
2. Tap ⬚ Adjust, then swipe the slider left or right to straighten the photo. Use the grid to help you frame the photo.
3. Tap *Cancel* to cancel or tap *Done* to save your change.

How do I rotate a photo?

You can rotate a photo after taking it or uploading it from your phone's library. To rotate your photo:

1. Tap > 🖼️*Adjust.*
2. Tap to rotate your photo.
3. Tap *x* to cancel, or tap the checkmark to save your change.

(*Source*: Instagram.com)

Now that you are all set up and know how to use the app, it's time to start using it to get a high ROI. In the next chapter we'll dive into creating your Instagram page's look and feel.

#INSTAGRAMFORBUSINESS POSTABLES

- Marketing should equal results. #InstagramforBusiness

- Everything in marketing is measurable. Everything. #InstagramforBusiness

- There should always be an offer. Or offers. #InstagramforBusiness

- It IS possible to sell directly to cold traffic on social media. #Instagramfor-Business

- There should ALWAYS be a REASON to RESPOND NOW. #Instagramfor-Business

- Brand is important, but it is just the FIRST step of a marketing and sales funnel. #InstagramforBusiness

- RESULTS RULE. Period. #InstagramforBusiness

Resource spotlight: Visit www.UGIGbook.com to download over 20 postable images!

Chapter 3

Putting on Your Fancy Outfit: Developing Your Instagram Brand

Let's start with a confession of sorts, shall we? Don't worry, you don't have to tell me anything. I am the one gabbing here.

The scoop is: I am a stalker. Or maybe it's more like a gawker.

When I am not traveling with my kids, I can get myself into trouble. You see, when I am with them, all of my time and energy are focused on making sure they don't knock someone over who is running to catch a flight while my girls are running around the airport for the sake of running; or getting them a snack; or arguing on why they need to take Dramamine before the plane takes off. (Yes, it is ironic that this family of travelers gets motion sick while traveling. But that's a story I will spare you from. *You're welcome.*)

When traveling for work, by myself, things are different. My eyes have time to wander and meander. They can scan the room without doing the "1, 2, OK they are both there" check 754 times. I can relax and observe.

The problem is, I tend to scan my surroundings and get myself into trouble because without meaning to, I often stare. What generally gets my attention is when someone is really pulled together and elegant when traveling. I am in awe and a little jealous, but more so, I stare because I am trying to figure out their secret. Being a chic traveler is something I aspire to do someday when I grow up.

Don't get me wrong. I am not a total schlep who only wears pajama pants and a stained t-shirt on flights. (When did flying like a hangover undergraduate become acceptable, anyway? *Said the all-of-a-sudden Etiquette Queen of fashion and travel.*)

I do put in effort when traveling, not for the betterment of those on the plane with me (no offense, 5A!), but for those I might see at my next speaking gig. Often, I am staying at the same hotel where I'll be speaking, so I try not to show up as a hot mess. But still, nobody's going to be staring at me as an example of having it all pulled together.

DEVELOPING YOUR INSTAGRAM PAGE BRAND

Maybe you've seen someone who just seems to "get it." They have the perfect proportion of accessories. The perfect match of pattern to solid. The perfect combination of formal and casual. Their brand proudly announces to the world that they care, but not too much. They personify visual branding at its best and are a walking billboard for success.

This should be your goal for your Instagram account. You should exude a brand that makes it clear who you are and what you stand for—quickly and succinctly. There should be consistency from post to post so that if someone picked ten random posts of yours, they could tell they were all yours.

I was *terrible* at this in the beginning as I was just figuring out what my posts should look like. Even though the design feels professional, they were definitely not putting out the overall vibe that is representative of my brand (see Figure 3–1).

FIGURE 3–1. Some of My Terrible Posts from When I Was Just Starting Out.

FIGURE 3–2. Now My Posts All Have a Unified Look, Feel, and Message.

There was nothing unifying about the posts, nothing visually compelling, and these posts were quoting all sorts of folks—none of them, however, being me. Thankfully, I eventually wised up and followed one of my favorite lines from the TV show *Mad Men*.

If you don't like what's being said, change the conversation.

And so we did. Now my posts are all unified in look, feel, and messaging. My follower count increases every day, and the post engagement has improved dramatically. Figure 3-2 provides a sample from my page now.

I only got there after receiving advice from a friend about Instagram. She suggested that I find ten Instagram sites with a look and feel that I loved—ten accounts that were telling the visual story that I wanted to tell.

I then took examples from those posts and made myself a brand board, using a very sophisticated method—I pasted them into a Word document. (I was kidding about the sophisticated method, in case you couldn't tell.)

I kept the branding page in front of me each time I created posts so that it was a guide to keep my look on-target for my visual brand.

Where I have settled is pretty simple. I use Word Swag—my favorite Instagram app of all time—to create all of my Instagram images and select the same font each time. It really is my true love. If I wasn't married to my wonderful husband, Ian, I might attempt to marry this app because I am so in love with it. (Don't judge until you've tried it.)

Word Swag offers variations within one font style, so my posts each look different but still unified. I tend to blur or soften the background image to make the text pop. Then I always add my brand stamp to the bottom (see Figure 3–3).

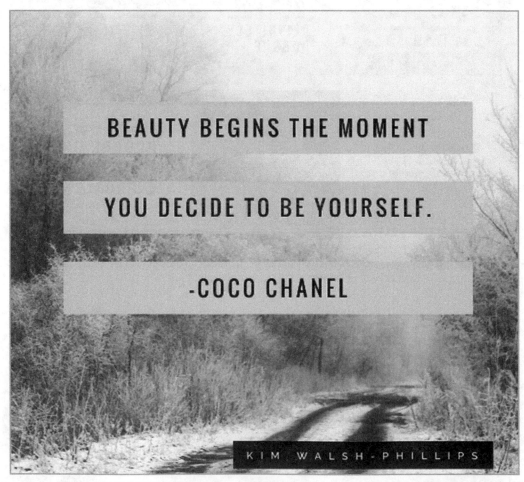

FIGURE 3–3. All of My Posts Have My Brand at the Bottom So People Can Identify Me with the Post.

FIGURE 3–4. I Like to Post Quotes Instead of Photographs.

Now, there are mixed opinions on doing that. A lot of social media gurus suggest that if you don't brand your posts, more people will engage with them. My philosophy is different: I'd rather have fewer people see my post but know that those who do can identify it with me so we can begin to form a relationship of trust.

I also tend to post all quotes, staying away from photographs (see Figure 3–4). Unlike photos on my Facebook page, when I run them on Instagram, they don't perform as well. But then I'm not selling something visual, I'm selling information and a marketing/life philosophy. Remember, each social media platform will have its sweet spot. On my Facebook business page, www.facebook.com/KWalshPhillips/, photos tend to get a better response than anything else.

If you are a retailer or in the fitness, wellness, or beauty space, then photographs will likely perform better than just quote images. Take time to figure out what the focus of your page should be.

If your brand were a person, how would you describe its personality? I mean, I know "awesome," but what is it you want to convey in each post? A photo to entice? An inspirational quote to motivate? A lifestyle to entice? What message do you want to share most with those who visit your page? The exciting thing about building your brand is that you have a chance now to make it into whatever you want. Start exploring options on Instagram, and then focus on your message and brand—it is going to be amazing. Because you are amazing.

In the next section, I interview a marketing expert who uses his Instagram page to recruit new hires.

CULTURE BRANCH WITH JOSH HARCUS OF HÜIFY

Josh Harcus serves as the head of inbound strategy at Hüify. He has consulted brands such as *Car and Driver*, Springer Global Publishing, and Compact Power Equipment Rental.

Harcus has a different take on building a brand on Instagram. He and his team utilize their page to showcase company culture as a tool to recruit new hires. It is less about the "likes" and more about showcasing who they are to outsiders who may be their future employees.

You've decided to focus your Instagram page around your company's culture. Why choose that instead of your company's expertise—outbound marketing?

Harcus: Our clients tend to be enterprise-level HubSpot users. These are very large companies, and we generally are landing them through channels such as speaking and referrals, rather than [through] Instagram. We have used our page more as a hiring tool.

Who is the voice of your page?

Harcus: I like to get all of our employees involved in the messaging of the page as a way of showcasing their love for the company. It makes a much better case for new hires because it isn't just me telling them this is a great place to work. It is our employees sharing it.

What is your posting strategy?

Harcus: To keep it simple, I show images from inside and outside of the office in a rather basic formula. We'll have two posts in-office of something with our team, and then I share something outside of the office, such as skateboarding, snowboarding, or another adventure sport. We've even featured one of our staff who is a Zumba staff instructor on the weekends. Or we'll post a professional development activity we just participated in. We want people not only to get a sense of our company but the types of people who work here.

Why have you invested so much in showcasing your company culture?

Harcus: We are in a very competitive marketplace in New York City for marketing staff. We have "fair market salaries," but we aren't going to wow them with pay as we are basically the same as everyone else, especially on the entry level. We leverage our company culture and our team as a way to recruit the best and the brightest to join us. Good applicants vet us like we vet them, and I want them to see what they'd be getting into. If it's a good match, I want our Instagram page to support our case for coming on board with us.

What's one posting hack you have implemented?

Harcus: We want it to appear fun at our company at all times to candidates, but of course we aren't going snowboarding every day. When we do an activity, we will take a ton of pictures but not post them all at the same time. Instead we will post a few on different days, so every few days you will see a picture of us having a good time. This way, whenever someone comes to our page, they will be able to see this is a fun place to work.

What's one thing you've done that would surprise people?

Harcus: We choose to be very transparent, and it works. One time, one of our bathroom pipes exploded and there was water *everywhere*. It was a mess. Many companies would try to hide this. We shared what was happening on Instagram, and it went viral. Everyone thought it was funny and so did we. It was a way to turn something stressful into a great marketing opportunity.

What is another marketing strategy you've put into place?

Harcus: Anytime someone has a microphone in front of them, we always get photo or video. This is the case even if doing a voice-over for a video; we will get a picture of it and share. We want to showcase that you can leverage your talents in an exciting way at our company.

What are some of your favorite posts?

Harcus: We include Darth Vader's head in a lot of pictures [see Figure 3–5, page 44]. It looks random, but this was very much staged and it came out perfect. It is a great

FIGURE 3–5. Hüify Likes to Post Pictures That Include References to Darth Vader to Show That They Have Fun While They're Working.

example of our company culture. We will do whatever we need to in order to get the job done well and will have fun in the process.

You recently released a book. How have you used Instagram as you brought it to market?

Harcus: For the pre-launch, I would leak random pictures of the book process. From writing to editing, I shared the journey. I followed Gary Vaynerchuk's process and kept building anticipation. Our goal was to intrigue them on what we were working on at all times. Like when I got a cover quote from Brian Halligan, the CEO of HubSpot. That was something that helped the project go viral.

What advice would you give others when it comes to their Instagram marketing?

Harcus: Track everything. Take time to create unique links with Bitly to track the ROI. Where you send people to your bio link has to be a great site for mobile. It should be an awesome mobile experience, not some janky site that doesn't work on the small screen.

What lasting impression do you want to give those who visit your page?

Harcus: When people look at our brand, I want them to see Darth Vader, Risk, and Catan lovers who work with developers. I want them to see dudes who are great to go out and have a beer with. More than just the stereotypical Ping-Pong table, I want them to see a culture of fun and loving what we do [see Figures 3–6, 3–7 (page 46), and 3–8 (page 46)].

You can find Josh's book, *A Closing Culture: Your Marketing and Sales Process Is Broken. Here's How to Fix It* on Amazon.

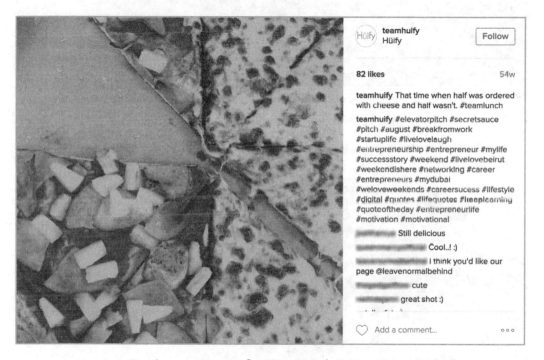

FIGURE 3–6. Posting an Image of a Pizza Lunch Is One Way Hüify Shows the Unity in Their Office.

FIGURE 3–7. Posts from Outside the Office Are One Way Hüify Helps Customers Get a Sense of Their Company.

FIGURE 3–8. Hüify Wants Their Posts to Show a Fun Culture and That They Love What They Do.

#INSTAGRAMFORBUSINESS POSTABLES

- You should exude a brand that makes it clear who you are and what you stand for—quickly and succinctly. #InstagramforBusiness

- Design your posts with the same look and feel each time. #InstagramforBusiness

- Your audience that is engaged isn't tired of hearing from you. #Instagramfor-Business

- There are enough others out there. Be you. #InstagramforBusiness

Resource spotlight: Visit www.UGIGbook.com for a branding guide for your Instagram posts.

Chapter 4

Starring You:
Leveraging Instagram for
Premium Positioning

Admittedly, I didn't even slow down.

She called my name and I ignored it because I thought, "That just can't be for me." When I realized she truly was talking to me, I almost did a happy dance right then and there. But that would have totally negated what just happened.

So the happy dance happened later when I was alone in my hotel room.

The first time I was stopped in an airport to have my picture taken with someone, I was *blown away*. And so ecstatic! And (I will admit), glad to have a witness. (See Figure 4–1, page 50, for the evidence!) Even though the witness was my driver for this particular speaking engagement, having a witness made the moment a little more scrumptious. Especially when he said, "Wow, I drove Rod Stewart's wife last week, and no one recognized her." (Rod Stewart's wife, if you are reading this, no offense intended, of course.)

For me, this was a fan-freaking-tastic moment of giddiness.

Now to be fair, this spotting wasn't random at all. It's not like I was traveling with the kids to Disney when a super-fan stopped me. I'm pretty sure that level of notoriety will only happen if I accidently join an international spy ring or pyramid scheme when I thought I was

FIGURE 4–1. The First Time I Was Stopped at an Airport to Have
My Picture Taken with Someone I Was *Blown Away*!

just getting a really good price on Prada shoes. ("But, they were tweed, and they were beautiful," I would say as the cuffs were placed.)

But no, there was no randomness about this "celebrity spotting." I was in an airport at the conference destination where I would be speaking, for an organization that features me in their content and social media a lot. The person who spotted me knew me from those promotions.

So it's not like this happens often, but that's the whole point. To leverage celebrity, you don't need to be famous worldwide. You only need to be a celebrity within the niche you serve. And that's a whole lot more obtainable than achieving Justin Bieber stardom.

THE POWER OF STARDOM: HOW TO LEVERAGE YOUR INSTAGRAM ACCOUNT TO STRENGTHEN YOUR CELEBRITY, AUTHORITY, AND EXPERT POSITIONING

Obtaining celebrity status is not about an ego boost (although I'm not going to lie, that was nice too). Instead, it is about premium positioning so you are magnetic to your target market. Your perfect prospects will line up to see you, and they will pay you top dollar as the celebrity expert you are.

For example, you would expect to pay Jamie Oliver a lot more money to cook you dinner in your kitchen than you would a random chef you found on Thumbtack (www.thumbtack.com). No matter what your niche, celebrity positioning is a powerful tool to grow your tribe quickly and convert them into top-paying customers for life.

Before you embark on a path to stardom, it is important that you set yourself up for celebrity success. Your profile must be on-point with your brand before you begin promoting.

GETTING READY FOR YOUR CLOSE-UP

How are you coming across? If someone were to visit your social media pages and/or website without knowing you or speaking to you first, what would they think about you or your company? Would your brand messaging communicate what you want the visitor to know?

If you are like most, you have some ways to go to tweak your brand message to be clear to your target market. Don't be ashamed. We all started with an embarrassing look at some point. Just pick up any *People* magazine and look at the "Who They Were Then" section to see a celeb's awkward moments. It's an issue for everybody, companies and individuals alike. There's a reason I'll never post a promo photo in a Throw Back Thursday #TBT post. And it isn't because of my date.

Being embarrassed of what your brand looks like today isn't reason to bury your head in the sand. You can develop celebrity positioning with just a few simple steps.

Get a Professional (and Recent) Headshot

This is the place to amp up your game and go beyond the selfie iPhone photo (ick!). Celebrities have good photos and so should you. To find an affordable one in your area, check out Thumbtack (www.Thumbtack.com). You can post the job there, and photographers will apply to take your photo, giving an estimate up front. You can get a good headshot for less than $100 using this service, and it goes a long way toward making you show up as a celeb.

And stop using that photo from 20 years ago, no matter how good you look in it! Those images are most likely hurting the trust factor with your prospects, as they look just as fake as a bad stock photo. (If you've done this, when you show up to your sales call, your prospect will feel like you started the relationship with a lie. Lying is lame, so get in the game with a current photo.)

You're cute—now smile!

Hire a Pro to Create Your Lead Magnet Cover and Landing Page Featured in Your Bio

Yes, there are great free template services like www.Canva.com and www.Leadpages. net, but when it comes to your main marketing funnel, do yourself a favor and use a professional. Just like your website, they will help you to show up looking pretty and professional.

One great resource to try is www.Fiverr.com. For $5 you can hire a graphic designer to create a Lead Magnet cover for you. Spend the extra few bucks to have this done the right way!

Make the Camera Your BFF, Seriously

Any time a microphone or professional camera is in front of you for *any* reason, have someone take your picture. And then share those photos sporadically online. From when you speak on stage, to being interviewed for a podcast, to simply getting an award at your local chamber of congress, leverage these photos as blog images and post backgrounds.

Celebrities are photographed often, so you should share your media coverage online as though you were your own paparazzi. (Hold your silly-meter—no matter how cheesy this may feel to you, celebrity positioning goes a *long* way toward getting you paid more.)

Feature YOUR Content in Your Posts

If you got a spot on *The Today Show*, would you use it to promote someone else's work? I sure hope not.

If you are sharing other people's content on your page a majority of the time, stop. This is your opportunity to shine and set yourself up as an expert in your industry, so feature your content and develop your own images and posts. Start with your blog posts—are there images and quote nuggets you can pull out to run on your Instagram page? (See Figure 4–2 and 4–3, page 53, for examples from my content.)

If you don't know where to start, begin by listing 12 questions your prospects tend to ask when you meet with them, and start by answering those. Turn them into image quotes and long-form comments on your Instagram feed.

Now it's time to share your message with the world. And thankfully you don't have to stand in line at 4 A.M. for 90 days in a row at *The Today Show* door to earn your publicity and celebrity status. (Although, if that's your thing, have at it.) Instead, you can leverage the power of your Instagram marketing and entire marketing funnel to establish your stardom.

The steps are rather simple.

FIGURE 4–2. Feature *Your* Content in Your Posts—Not Other Peoples'.

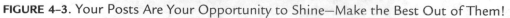

FIGURE 4–3. Your Posts Are Your Opportunity to Shine—Make the Best Out of Them!

Start Small and Then Go Smaller

It's easier to be well-known to everyone in a town of 5,000 than a city of 5 million, and you can't be all things to all people. Pick a niche and then a niche within that niche. Focusing on a smaller target market will grow your celebrity quicker.

Pick your target market and then zero in on a small portion of the group/industry/ subculture that you are focusing on, and stay focused on these individuals until you have achieved celebrity status. If you want to reach another subset of your audience, then once you have grown to celebrity status you can move on to the next niche.

Identify at least one group, association, or organization that serves your niche and make it your mission to dive deep and become a celebrity within it. Develop a relationship strategically and methodically with the organization that currently serves your niche market. This is a lot more effective than starting your niche from scratch, because you can leverage a group that has already brought members of that niche together.

Dive deep into getting to know the organization's members and leadership. Find a way to volunteer, such as joining a committee or advisory board or working at an event. Follow the organization's social media and begin to comment on its posts at least twice a week through your professional page. Make meaningful comments that show you actually read and connected with the content. (The worst thing you can do is post something meaningless and appear as Mr. Spam Man. No one wants that.)

And the next time you attend one of their events, use the Word Swag app to create posts from quotes you hear at the event, and post them on your page while tagging the other brand. See my example in Figure 4–4.

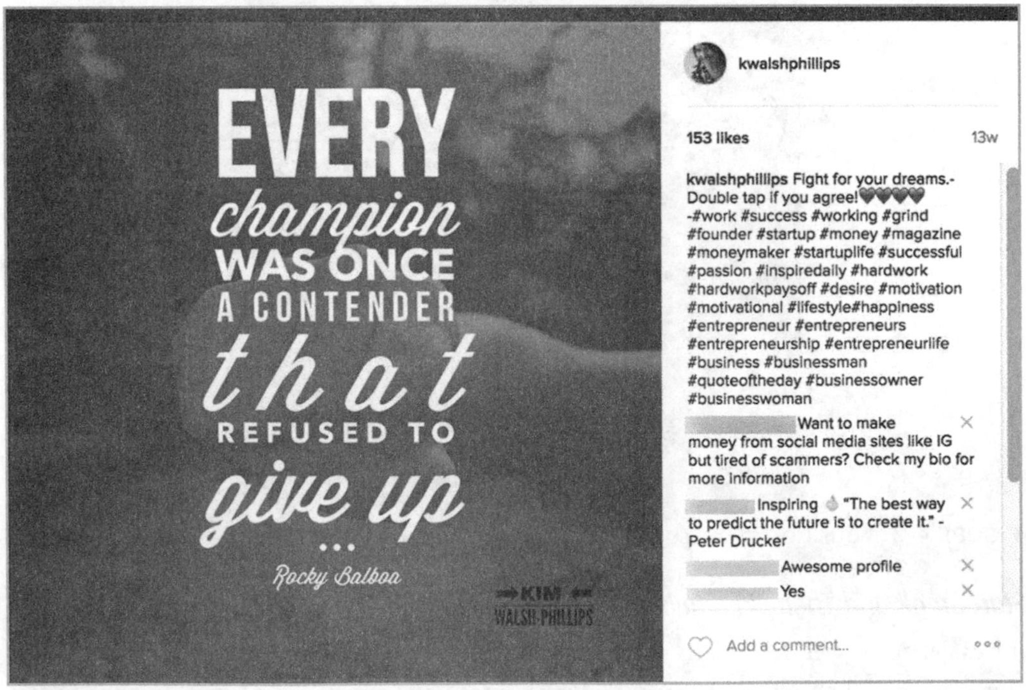

FIGURE 4–4. Featuring Someone Else's Content Is OK to Do Sometimes *If* It's Done with a Purpose and You Give It Proper Attribution.

The secret to getting in good is giving first and asking second. Even though this is in contrast to the recommendation I made earlier in this chapter—that you should feature all of your own content—this time it's done strategically and with purpose.

Keep the ratio at four posts of yours to one post of theirs, and you will be in great shape. Only use this strategy when you are aligning with an industry leader.

Give Social Clout Before You Ask for Anything

Post a couple of times a month tagging the other organization (meaning, use the @ symbol and list its social media username). This will not only distribute your post to more people (Instagram may show your post to some of its fans who aren't yours), it will also alert the organization that you mentioned it. If you take time to curate the content (meaning, you add commentary or questions to your post), it will begin to demonstrate how you are an expert in the subject matter. This helps to build a relationship with the organization and position you as an authority in your niche.

Leverage the Bazookas out of Photos

Celebrities are photographed often and so should you be. This means attending events in your niche, and going to meet-and-greets and having your photo taken with as many well-known speakers, leaders, or actual celebrities (depending on the event), as possible. You may feel like a complete tool for doing this, but this strategy is pure gold when it comes to positioning. Post these photos one at a time on your social media and tag the other person. This also means showing up to events well dressed and informed— meaning you know who the VIPs are, and you can talk to them intelligently about their work. Thanks to social media, this task has never been easier. Don't be lazy pants. Instead, do a little research before you show up. Others in the crowd won't bother, and this will help you get a little extra chat time with the VIP.

I did this at an event with Nido Qubein, president of High Point University, and was able to score a review and testimonial for the book I was writing at the time. (I was nervous to approach him, but the payoff was so worth it.) Live boldly, and you too can access thought leaders in your niche.

Feature Celebrities in Your Content

After you give value and develop a relationship with the previously mentioned celebrities, request to interview one of their key leaders who is well known within your niche and post it to your blog. Create valuable content to open and close the piece and well-designed social media posts to promote it. This will help to further build your relationship with the organization and establish your authority positioning with its members. You can then create Instagram posts using the celebrity's quotes and tag him or her in the image.

Get in the Spotlight

Well-known publications feature celebrities on the cover as a way to sell the magazine. It's time you were featured as well. After you have followed the steps above, seek guest blogging or guest columnist opportunities from the organization. Write content that is thoughtful and valuable, not self-promotional, and that meets the publication's requirements. (If you are unsure about word count or rules about picture inclusion, ask.) Once the article is published, promote it like your celebrity status and future autograph requests depend on it. First, give yourself a high five, and then, pull out quotes from the articles, turn them into Instagram post images, and tag the publication's Instagram account.

Once you have accomplished all we have just covered, the secret is to stay consistent—as in, don't give up! Continue to tag, post, photograph, interview, and guest post. Repetition is the key to establishing authority/celebrity/expert status. It generally takes me about one year to 18 months to conquer a niche. That may seem long, but the payoff could not be more worth it. A year of hustle for a whole lifetime of expert positioning and premium pricing? *Yes, please!*

CASE STUDY: GROWING AND MONETIZING YOUR INSTAGRAM MARKETING WITH ANTHONY CARBONE OF WWW.WOLFMILLIONAIRE.COM

Anthony Carbone has grown his Instagram accounts to 14 million followers over the past two years and currently earns six figures annually through Instagram ad revenue. He teaches others how to grow their followers and make money through Instagram at www.WolfMillionaire.com.

Anthony, your story is incredibly fascinating. Tell us about how you got into the field of Instagram list growth and monetization.

Carbone: I'm 38 years old and a computer engineer by education. I have a huge interest and passion in the automotive industry and created a hobby site about ten years ago called www.MadWhips.com—a photo-sharing social network, like Pinterest and Instagram, but just for exotic cars. I'd worked a stable corporate job for most of my life, though, spending nine years with a major corporation. I left that company a couple years ago to work for a small private company in the digital advertising space.

Shortly after I left my super-stable, comfortable corporate job for this smaller company, the new business laid me off as part of a company restructure. This was the first time in my life I was ever fired. Kim, I don't get fired! While I'm not an A-student, I'm that C-student who works his butt off for every grade, every dollar, and anything I've ever had in life. So it was pretty flooring to just simply get laid off.

That prompted me to take a good look at my life and what I was doing. After excelling online with MadWhips, and playing with Facebook and Twitter in the past, I had fallen behind on social media as I'd gotten older. Once I got fired, I started looking around and I decided for the first time in my life that I would do something 100-percent entrepreneurial.

I actually started to look for a couple jobs but couldn't find anything I really wanted to do, that married my passion for cars and technology and advertising. Again I started to look at the whole MadWhips equation, and I started to play with Instagram. I sold both the vehicles I owned at the time and had a little bit of money to get by for a couple months—hoping that things would turn around. I hired two developers who basically redesigned www.MadWhips.com, introducing an iOS app and an Android app.

While my team did that, I went to town playing with social networks, to see how I could growth-hack people's interest in joining and contributing to my website. At that time I had one account with 700 followers. That was my main @MadWhips account. It was very amateur. I posted just for the sake of posting because it was a new social network, and it didn't take me long to figure out the Instagram game.

I noticed what was going on with the larger accounts out there—especially in the exotic car niche—and saw the biggest car accounts (the ones with 100,000 to 150,000 followers) were charging $5 at the time to promote your Instagram account. So I thought, what better way to kick start my brand while the guys are recoding and relaunching the MadWhips website. I spent six or seven months growing the @MadWhips Instagram account.

In four months I took that one account from 700 followers and grew it to 100,000 by paying larger accounts to promote it. I quickly saw how much money was out there and how fast those other accounts were growing . . . simply by helping other smaller accounts like mine grow their following.

This was a little over two years ago. When I saw that, I thought, "Well, there's a huge demand." The exotic car niche on Instagram was by far the largest at the time—larger than travel, larger even than sports. At the time it was even larger than fashion and cosmetics, which are now the dominant forces on Instagram.

Even so, all the people I dealt with who helped me grow my accounts were amateurs. Given that I had corporate experience and a sales and marketing background, I figured I could spend time trading multiple accounts and running this Instagram game, charging other people for my help in growing their accounts just like I had been paying other people to grow my own.

These same accounts were also selling advertising space for stuff that would target the male demographic, not necessarily just automotive enthusiasts, but the male demographic who would follow these types of car accounts.

So within the span of the first four months of growing my @MadWhips account to 100,000 followers, I started a couple other accounts just to experiment. I literally bomb-tested Instagram to see how far I could push the different ways to grow an account, which resulted in a couple of my accounts getting blocked and banned.

When I did figure it out, I was able to very quickly grow a couple major accounts—@ Exotic_Performance—to 2.7 million followers. At the end of my first year playing on Instagram, I had created about 18 Instagram accounts with 5.4 million followers.

Wow!

Carbone: At that point, I was able to recoup the money I'd spent growing my initial account and was making about $5,000 a month, simply by providing the same service I'd paid others for. I shouted out other smaller accounts who wanted to grow their fan base. At the same time I was also promoting products.

In that first year, about eight months into the Instagram game, I launched my own e-commerce store selling carbon-fiber phone cases, because I saw how many people were successfully selling all different kinds of phone cases. There were a couple companies selling knock-off automotive cases and being taken down by the major companies, so I launched a carbon-fiber product for the iPhone and Android phone and I started to sell this online.

In the first month of launch, I did about $7,000 in sales, which showed me there was a huge market and high conversion rate for people following my Instagram accounts who wanted to buy phone accessories or automotive-related products.

That was my first year playing with Instagram. When we ultimately relaunched www.MadWhips.com I had a very healthy Instagram following. It was an easy fit for me to then ask my users—who all wanted to have their photos posted on my Instagram accounts—that if they wanted me to feature their photos, they had to upload them to www.MadWhips.com, no longer just a hobby site but now my full-time employment, in conjunction with the Instagram piece.

I actually have seven co-op students running my Instagram network now—I'll get to that in a second—but I hired my very first co-op intern after I grew my Instagram network to 18 accounts and 5.4 million followers.

I worked from my couch for about three months, and we finally got accepted into Canada's largest business incubator, the DMZ at Ryerson University, right downtown in Yonge-Dundas Square. Super cool. From there I received specific business venturing advice from the entrepreneurs who are part of that space, and I was able to quickly scale my company from just me and one employee up to seven interns.

So now I employ seven co-op students every semester who basically run my network of Instagram accounts, which I've now grown to over 30 accounts with 18-plus million Instagram followers. And our team basically sources all the photos from www.MadWhips.com. We're an automotive-based social network for photography enthusiasts, so we have an unlimited draw of photos flowing into www.MadWhips.com, which is same-day content that we get to feature from all over the world on our 30 Instagram accounts.

We post close to 220 photos a day across my network, all exotic car photography, all giving credit and promoting the amateur or professional photographer who contributed the photo. On top of that, I have a handful of clients in the non-automotive space who I help promote and help them gain awareness through caption advertising or photo or video advertising on the myriad of accounts that I have.

Can you give us some strategies on how to grow an Instagram following?

Carbone: Content is still king and on a social network that's photography- or video-based like Instagram, I can't repeat enough how important it is to share high-quality, unique content.

Now, not everybody can go out and start creating sure-fire awesome content that other people want to consume, but if you're a brand or a business, it's imperative that you keep your eye and focus on the type of content you're putting out there. You want to give a glimpse or a background view of your company or products or personnel, to allow others who want to engage with your brand to consume that media.

So, whether you're creating it yourself or curating someone else's, the number-one thing you need to remember is to always give proper credit. That's the biggest thing that I see people don't do.

And they also don't realize how important of a strategy it is, not only to give credit so you don't infringe copyright (which may cause your page to be disabled by Instagram), but by engaging and tagging and giving credit to the actual photo or video owners, it is likely they will like and comment on your photo, because it's a big compliment to them. If you can use someone else's photo and tag them and they thank you and like it, that's going to go a long way in making sure Instagram awards your page favorability.

Can you give an example of what a caption might include if you're posting somebody else's picture?

Carbone: The general consensus or standard is to put, "Photo by:" and then list the person's username. A lot of people confuse photo credits with citing the page where they found the photo or video versus giving credit to the actual owner. There are many pages out there that just regurgitate content from other accounts, and the proper photo credits get lost in transition. That's the biggest mistake people make. In the long run, giving proper credit will help your post go further in [Instagram's] Explore page, getting you more likes and thus attracting more followers.

How about another strategy?

Carbone: Hashtags. There are between 500 and 600 million Instagram users in the world, so the number of hashtags is abundant. It's important to use targeted hashtags that really fit with the content you're posting. Don't use irrelevant hashtags—especially spammy ones like #follow-for-follow or #like-for-like.

If you were to post a photo of a red apple, instead of using the "#red" and "#apple," you're better off using a hashtag that's two words "#redapple," because it's more targeted to the photo you're posting and thus more likely someone who's looking at the hashtag called "#redapple" will stumble upon your page. If you instead use hashtags like "#red" and "#apple," because there are so many of those hashtags out there, your content's just going to get lost. No one's going to discover it. I call these two-word hashtags "long-tail hashtags" because they're very specific, and it'll help you in the long run to really attract the right people to discover your content.

Would you still recommend people use paid shoutouts to grow their accounts? And if so, how would someone find accounts that offer this service?

Carbone: While it's not required to pay other accounts to grow, it's the brute force method. If you really want to jump-start and accelerate the growth of your brand new account—especially if you have an offering or a product—then it not only helps you attract new followers but gets your voice out there quickly in the marketplace.

From there I would do a lot of research. You need to identify your target audience, find out where that audience is and what other pages they follow, and then find the bigger pages among them—whether they're fan accounts of conglomerate postings in a high-level niche, or from specific influencers. An influencer is someone who has a personal brand online with a large amount of followers. You can reach out to them and say, "Hey, I've got this brand or this page I'd like to grow. What does it cost for you to promote it and what does that look like?"

Perhaps you'll give them a caption to be cut and pasted into one of their posts, or perhaps they'll write something clever that's in line with your caption and brand. But the first step is to identify who your audience is that you want to target and locate the large accounts and influencers.

Obviously pricing is going to vary, so you want to reach out to at least ten or 20 accounts in your niche, if you can, and ask people what their pricing is for advertising your account. A lot of them will be open to that. Some accounts might not, but for the most part anyone who has an account with an email in their bio or a little message in their bio that says, "DM for shoutouts," or "DM for business," it means they're definitely open to your request.

That's awesome. So once you are growing your follower base, you have found it's not only good for building your business, but your Instagram page can become a business in itself. Can you talk about how someone might make the transition when they think they're ready to start monetizing their page?

Carbone: The biggest thing I always like to reiterate is that every page, every niche, is going to grow differently. If you have a high-level account, like @exoticcars, you're going to appeal to a wide range demographic, predominantly male, versus if you had a more narrowly focused page like a BMW page or a specific model of BMW page. This will nail down the size of audience you can target. You have to remember that an account with 100,000 followers in a big niche is pretty much the same as an account with 10,000 followers in a tight niche.

In order to grow your account and monetize it, you really need to understand how engaged your followers are, what type of audience you have, and, most importantly, make sure the product or service you want to sell or advertise is something they're going to want to buy.

Instagram is a huge, huge, huge marketplace. I would almost argue that it's a billion-dollar marketplace where money is exchanged for service, products, reviews, and shoutouts. The biggest thing you need to understand is that fine balance of starting to advertise on your account—whether it's for yourself or someone else—and how hard to push it. It really all depends on how long your account's been out there, and the frequency of your posting.

If you're just starting out, then I suggest—whether you're a brand, a personal influencer, or anything—that you don't really push a hard sell until you have a meaty following. [And again, what constitutes a meaty following is going to depend on the scope of your niche. If you have a really high-level niche, then you might want to wait until you have 50,000 to 100,000 followers, whereas if you have a very specific niche you can start monetizing at 5,000 to 10,000 followers because you know that the people following your account are there for the specific reason that your niche services.]

When do you recommend adding a product into the mix?

Carbone: For me, I saw a lot of people in my space advertising phone cases, which meant there was a healthy marketplace for it. I did my research and crunched the numbers to find that because I had this massive following, my margin retainment would be fairly high, simply because I didn't have to pay for the advertising. So when you have a following base you can sell to, you can also start selling third-party affiliate offers—if it matches with your brand and your audience. Or if there's some sort of accessory you can test your market on that doesn't require a lot of capital outlay, then I'd suggest you test it out. It's really up to you.

But first you have to grow a bit of a following, validate that your following has a need for the product, and then test it out to see if there are sales. If there are, you can then scale the offer because you can basically go after those bigger accounts you've either identified as an influencer or a page in your niche and pay them to advertise your product.

So now you are not only selling a product directly through your Instagram page, but you're doing it through others as well. Again, crunch the numbers and make sure the cost versus margin ratio makes sense for what you're selling.

So what are some of the mistakes you see businesses make as they try to grow their following and/or monetize it?

Carbone: The biggest one is not keeping the account 100-percent business. The brand needs to exist on its own as a business or as a product. A lot of people will kind of blend their home/family life with their business account. And while that might be fine in terms of showing that you're human—that there's a person behind the brand—the quality of those photos frequently doesn't match up with the page's brand image.

I find it detrimental to the brand when you post something that's not really related. A lot of people really, really miss that mark. So if you're growing a company page on Instagram, whether it's a small business or a big business, just start out keeping it all about the business, your products, your services. Keep the home and family life out of it, unless of course you're selling a service that directly correlates to those images or the human element of it. If it doesn't, then just keep it strictly business.

One of your students, Tim Sykes, has a lifestyle guide he gives as part of his business. So for him it makes sense to showcase his lifestyle. But if somebody's going to focus specifically on paddleboards, let's say, they should just promote the paddleboard. It's not about them; it's about the product. I guess it matters what niche is your focus.

Carbone: Yeah, and again, content is king. So we can take awesome product shots of our paddleboards. If you're going to use a photo of you using the paddleboard, it needs to be inspirational. It needs to be very, very well curated. It doesn't have to be DSLR-quality, though. You don't have to hire a photographer or a DOP to do this. It just takes a little bit of trial and effort with your standard smartphone to create truly beautiful photos that amplify and highlight your brand. This is where a lot of people miss the mark—taking the proper photos. It's a bit of an art, but it's very addictive and can be learned quickly.

If folks want to find out more about you, or how they can learn from you about Instagram, where should they go?

Carbone: Visit www.WolfMillionaire.com. Readers can download my free 20-page *Instagram Guide*. It's filled with tips, tricks, and strategies you can use right away to start growing your account faster, lock it down so that it's secure, and see better engagement.

#INSTAGRAMFORBUSINESS POSTABLES

- Positioning yourself as a key expert drives prospects to come to you and gives you the leverage to get paid what you are really worth, which of course is a lot. #InstagramforBusiness

- Get ready for your close-up—the payout is marvelous. #InstagramforBusiness

- Find out how Anthony Carbone created his celebrity brand using his Instagram account. #InstagramforBusiness

- Being embarrassed about what your brand looks like today isn't reason to bury your head in the sand. Take action. #InstagramforBusiness

- You're cute—now smile! #InstagramforBusiness

- Give social clout before you ask for anything #InstagramforBusiness

Resource spotlight: Visit www.UGIGbook.com for "12 Ways to Pose to Improve Your Photos."

Chapter 5

Sometimes It Is a Popularity Contest: Growing Your Instagram Following

Kristen Ruby is the CEO of Ruby Media Group, a full service public relations and social media agency in Manhattan. A pioneer in the world of social media and tech trends, she is a frequent contributor on *FOX Business* and *Good Morning America*.

What's your business strategy behind your Instagram page?

Ruby: I think the most important thing I've learned on Instagram is that you really need to be focused on one specific thing. That's the best way to grow followers. For example, I was interested in health and wellness and sharing content around that. I opened a separate Instagram account, @WallStGirls, so anything related to wellness can be found under that account. In that space, my wellness content always gets a lot of likes. But if I tried to put that same content on 'Krisruby' people wouldn't be as interested. Those followers are more interested in TV appearances and other media. You can create totally different brands, even though it's the same person on each of the accounts, but you'll grow different followings around those distinct vibes [see Figures 5–1 and 5–2, page 66].

So you're not trying to make one page about multiple things.

FIGURE 5–1. The @WallStGirls Brand Focuses on Holistic Wellness and Nutrition.

FIGURE 5–2. The @Krisruby Brand Focuses on Behind-the-Scenes Interviews and TV Appearances.

Ruby: Absolutely. They literally look like two separate brands. The biggest mistake business owners are making is by trying to be everything to everyone. Instagram doesn't work that way. If you look at people who grow the fastest, they are seen as one specific thing.

I recently read about some guys who started a business called 'Men with coffee." They literally only post images of men with coffee cups. They have a huge follower base because they a very specific niche. They know who they are.

Another issue is branding. On Instagram, all your images should look somewhat alike. They should use the same filter. If your images don't look uniform, that's when people start unfollowing you. They should be able to look at your images and know who you are.

What are you trying to project on the @Krisruby Instagram account?

Ruby: @Krisruby is really about me, behind the scenes as a commentator. I utilize Instagram stories to showcase my business appearances. For example, if I'm at *Fox Business,* I'll post a quick Instagram live video or photo, updating people with #behindthescenes. On Instagram, you don't need to be sucked into updating all the time. You can definitely do just one great photo a day, or even one a week.

Are you seeing a direct ROI from the content you post? Can you track back sponsors or potential clients who have found you on Instagram?

Ruby: I think of it as brand building in a longer funnel, over time, since I'm not specifically selling anything on my pages. However, I recently posted about drinking tea. If my business was selling tea, those products would definitely see a higher ROI.

You mentioned that one of the mistakes businesses make is that they aren't consistent with their messaging or branding. Are there other mistakes you see?

Ruby: Businesses don't need to feel like they have to keep up with the social media rat race. I would rather see ten great posts over a month than a series of daily posts that don't have anything to do with the brand identity you worked so hard to build over the years.

If a business is just getting involved in Instagram, do you have any strategies you would recommend?

Ruby: First, you need a strategy of what you want to be putting out there. For instance a lot of people use a professional photographer to take photos of their day. What kind of background do you want your photos set against? White? Marble?

Next, research the hashtags because those are how people will find you. Be very specific about the hashtags you are using. For example, if I was posting a photo of my dog, with hashtags #cute or # adorable, and my business was selling insurance for dogs, no one is going to find me. You want to make sure your images show up where your target market is already searching. For local businesses, you should also be tagging the location.

Finally, consider your content scheduling. How often will you post? Once a day? Or will you partake in Instagram Live stories? Will you create your own posts, or hire people to post on your business' behalf?

When someone has engaged you for media placement, do you suggest they start incorporating more Instagram Live stories? Is that part of your media strategy?

Ruby: Depending on your business, this may be part of the media strategy. Just like with Facebook Live, there's a "land grab" now for Instagram live stories. These networks have invested their marketing dollars behind making these features successful. That means their algorithms are going to favor people who are using whatever is new. This is really important for small business owners to know, because it means you are more likely to be seen through an Instagram Live story than in the clutter of someone's Facebook feed right now. If you want to stand out, you absolutely want to be using these new kinds of features. Once everyone realizes their potential, the networks will monetize them and they won't be as easy to do, or as cost-effective.

Your main account, @Krisruby sends people to your website www.rubymediagroup.com. What clickable link do you use for @WallStGirls?

Ruby: I don't have a clickable link there, and I did that intentionally. I had purchased a link and then took it down because I decided I just want to build a community for @WallStGirls. That in itself is a strategy. I wanted to see if just focusing on one thing truly works better. That account's growth has been exponential simply because its content is highly focused on the same type of thing.

What's your long-term intention for @WallStGirls?

Ruby: Ideally I want to connect with other brands, whether it's a smoothie company or a new vegan drink or almond milk. I want to connect with those brands so I can build a community of people who know about those things. It's essentially microblogging without a blog.

Do you have any great client case studies you can share?

Ruby: A dentist client did a behind-the-scenes series with an Instagram Live story. Viewers could see all the plaques on the wall and her terrific Chanel boots while she was sitting in the chair. That was exponentially different than her other shared images. The difference in engagement was profound. You wouldn't think a dentist would show photos from the perspective of a client or someone walking throughout the office. It was a really cool way to market.

We also did a Facebook Live with the dentist talking about teeth whitening. When we looked at the stats, it was the highest-performing organic post they had ever done. The difficult part is getting clients to understand the importance of "Live." Most professionals are so into what they are doing throughout the day—whether it's surgery or typing—that it's difficult to stop the daily flow and put a camera up in front of them. There is definitely a learning curve and an educational process to using Instagram live for business.

Right. It's not like a paid ad that you're going to run that day and hope to see ROI.

Ruby: Really you can't escape Instagram Live anymore. It's changed the feel of social media for brands who only wanted to do static posts. Now they want to be visible for their clients, and they're able to leverage it with Instagram Live stories.

The old way of doing it doesn't work. I recommend you have a social media person, or someone at least designated once a week. Otherwise, you are losing out on a market opportunity that is already there.

It's the difference between *creating content* and *documenting*. Gary from Innotech says too many of us are focused on creating content. Instead, we need to focus on documenting as a form of creation. Most people think their lives are not interesting enough, but I say they really are. Documenting what you do is the best way to reach new people—showing rather than telling. People want to understand the culture behind what you are doing. Any of these "Live" feeds allow you to do just that.

Where can readers get to know more about you?

Ruby: You can find out more at Rubymediagroup.com, on Instagram @Krisruby, or Twitter @rubymediagroup and @sparklingruby.

THE POWER OF THE HASHTAG, AND HOW TO MAKE YOURS COUNT

You can't use Instagram for business without the almighty hashtag.

Wait, what is a hashtag? A hashtag is the # symbol followed by a word that describes the post or who it is for. Hashtags are a controversial topic when it comes to Instagrammers. Some despise their use, while others overuse them.

Here's my take on it—when it comes to using Instagram for business, it would be foolish not to use hashtags. According to Simply Measured, using even a single hashtag increases post engagement by 12.6 percent. Hashtags are an effective way to drive organic traffic to your content.

The most popular hashtags are general words like #love and #summer. (See a list of the 25 most popular hashtags on page 74.) However, these really don't do anything to drive engaged, quality traffic, as they are not specific and just attract numbers instead of potential tribers (cool-kids jargon for those who use Instagram).

The more specific you can get, while still staying with a frequently used hashtag, the more successful you will be at attracting an engaged and on-point audience. So how do you find the right hashtags to use?

Start by reviewing 20 of the most popular brands/companies in your niche and check out the hashtags they are using. For example, I searched on *#Entrepreneur* (see Figure 5–3). Make a list of these and start to test them on your posts. You will quickly determine what works and what doesn't and varying degrees of each. Remember, the more specific, the better.

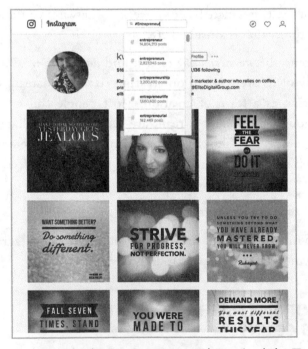

FIGURE 5–3. I Searched #Entrepreneur and Received the Top Posts Using that Hashtag.

FIGURE 5–4. Top Posts Using #Entrepreneur.

I then went through each and made a list of the hashtags. I was able to find 15 that were used on each of the profiles (see Figure 5-4). I made a master list of those and started to test different combinations of them on my posts. A few seemed to garner many more followers and likes while others didn't seem to make a difference. Keep track of each of yours while you are testing.

Also, it may be super frustrating to type all of these in each time—don't do it! Instead, create an Instagram post signature and save it in an online list keeper—like Apple or Google Notes or Evernote. This way, you only need to select and paste. Plus, you can first type out the hashtags on your desktop so you can work seamlessly between desktop and mobile. That is my jam.

The most hashtags you are allowed to use is 30. If you use more, Instagram will delete your comment. Start slowly, and as you find hashtags that work, build on them.

Beyond Growing Followers

Besides using hashtags to grow followers, categorizing content using the # symbol can be a powerful marketing tool. Among your list of hashtags, include a signature one that is just yours as reinforcement of your brand. For example, when I launched my last book, *No B.S. Guide to Direct Response Social Media Marketing: The Ultimate No Holds Barred Guide to Producing Measurable, Monetizable Results with Social Media Marketing* with Dan Kennedy, we used the hashtag phrase #NoBSsm (see Figure 5–5). This not only created a brand for the book but also built a tribe around it (see Figures 5–6 and 5–7, page 73).

Finally, a very popular use of the hashtag is to run contests, and we will dive down into contest ideas and how to make them work for your business later in this chapter.

Whether to grow your followers, launch a contest, or build your brand, hashtags remain one of the most powerful tools of the Instagram network. Leverage them to grow your following and online authority.

FIGURE 5–5. We Still Have People Posting Images of the Book with the #NoBSsm Phrase to This Day.

FIGURE 5–6. Another Image with #NoBSsm Phrase.

FIGURE 5–7. More Images with the #NoBSsm Phrase.

THE 25 MOST POPULAR HASHTAGS

According to Post Planner (www.postplanner.com), they are:

1. #love
   More than 696 million Instagram posts have the #love hashtag. Everybody say "aww."

2. #instagood
   This hashtag has appeared on about 314 million posts and counting.

3. #me
   More than 297 million posts have the #me hashtag. (Could this be more general?!)

4. #tbt
   This is a popular hashtag for those learning how to market on Instagram or for "Throw Back Thursday" where you post a picture of the past on—you guessed it—Thursday.

5. #cute
   This hashtag has appeared on more than 258 million posts: anything with puppies and babies wins!

6. #follow
   The #follow hashtag has appeared on more than 258 million posts—again, who doesn't want followers?

7. #followme
   Another hashtag all about follower growth. As in, I want you to follow me. And I am obvious about it.

8. #photooftheday
   Reserved for your best pictures—only one per day that you call the best, or any picture you put this hashtag on.

9. #happy
   Not related to the Pharrell Williams song, "Happy," although that one is smile-worthy. It does get the happy hashtag. So perhaps it is related?

10. #tagforlikes

    This popular hashtag asks people to tag them in posts so they can get more likes. I think this is crazy pants; I mean it's kind of like a business standing on the corner and begging folks to "Like me! Like me!" Not very good for premium brand building.

11. #beautiful

    Instagram users have typed this hashtag more than 250 million times.

12. #girl

    Again, I'm not sure you can get more generic, but good to know my gender is often featured in Instagram. "I'm very surprised," said no one. Ever.

13. #like

    Not sure about any ROI here, but again, it is very clear what people are going for with this hashtag.

14. #selfie

    There is nothing like a good selfie angle to make one's photo unrealistically gorgeous, which is why I love a good selfie! If you want to laugh for a minute or two, check out this hashtag.

15. #picoftheday

    Similar to #8 (#photooftheday), these are for some of your best pictures, or the ones you apply this hashtag to.

16. #summer

    No matter what time of year, this seasonal hashtag rules. I get it. Being warm and in sunshine is kind of awesome.

17. #fun

    Where photos are marked with things that are not awful.

18. #smile

    This sunshiney-day hashtag has been used millions of times.

19. #friends

    Helpful if you have a friend with long arms for group selfies, this hashtag is used for gatherings of people you like to associate with, or at least pretend to for the purpose of using this hashtag.

20. #like4like

This "I'll scratch your back if you scratch mine" hashtag does work to get more followers—quality followers, I am not sure about, but followers nonetheless.

21. #instadaily

This hashtag says, "Hey, it is today, and I am on Instagram!" A bit obvious, yes, but many people use it.

22. #fashion

This hashtag is where you start to see niches, with fashion being one of the most popular.

23. #igers

Sounds bizarre, but this hashtag—short for "Instagram Users"—has been used hundreds of millions of times. You'll have no problem finding photos with #igers.

24. #instalike

Another "please like this post" hashtag. Hey, if it works . . .

25. #food

Another very popular niche filled with yummy pictures of melted cheese and recipes I will never make but will save in a denial-like insistence that I will create this culinary masterpiece for my future imaginary dinner party (#InstaDelusional).

SPIN THE WHEEL! RUNNING A CONTEST ON INSTAGRAM

When it comes to social media, the number-one reason most use it is for entertainment and a momentary escape from reality. To tap into this audience behavior, try gamification. Getting your community involved in a contest is an effective way to build your market and brand message.

From the *Oxford Dictionary*, *gamification* is: "The application of typical elements of game playing (e.g., point scoring, competition with others, rules of play) to other areas of activity, typically as an online marketing technique to encourage engagement with a product or service. 'Gamification is exciting because it promises to make the hard stuff in life fun.' "

Getting your community involved in a contest is an effective gamification of your marketing and brand message. But it comes with pros (yay!) and cons (boo). It's best to know both sides before you launch yours.

Gaming It Good on Instagram

Instagram contests don't have to be as extravagant or budget-busting as a trip to Disney World to catch the attention of casual browsers, especially those who may already have an interest in your brand or what you have to offer. Instagram contests can be as simple as posting pics and asking for caption suggestions. The key to having success with whatever contest you run is to have a good idea and a solid implementation plan.

Instagram Contest Ideas

Start by getting an idea of what type of contest you want to run. You can make it as simple as clicking to enter. Get creative or use variations of reliable concepts like tagging friends or posting theme-related pics. (We need a selfie stick! Stat!)

Contests you can run on Instagram generally fall in the following categories:

- *Like to win*. These are contests where all a participant has to do is follow you on Instagram and like one of your posts to be entered to win. All you need to do is post an image or an update to announce the contest.

  Pros: Easy to setup, easy for visitors to enter.

  Cons: Engagement is low, little brand association.

- *Hashtag-generated*. Participants are asked to respond with a contest-specific hashtag when sharing a video or photo to enter, with all images/videos with that hashtag in one stream.

  Pros: Establishes emotional connection to your brand, creates common viewing area to increase engagement.

  Cons: Creates a barrier to entry by asking for content; complicated instructions (i.e., upload a pic, get your friends to tag it) can discourage participation, aka, this one is really rewarding when it works well, but pretty risky until it does.

- *Email-requested*. Often combined with a request to become a follower or submit user-generated content. Instagram contests of this nature require participants to give up their email address to enter by clicking on the link in the bio.

Pros: Builds reliable email lists and is a possible source of more content.

Cons: There is a barrier to entry, and prizes usually have to be something enticing enough to be worth giving up the email address.

TEN STEPS TO YOUR INSTAGRAM CONTEST

Once you have an idea of what type of contest you want to run, the next step is to actually run the contest. Determine when it will start and end since even a highly successful contest has to end at some point. This creates a sense of urgency or an added incentive to participate. Running a contest on Instagram also involves:

1. *Tell Me What You Want, What You Really, Really Want: Establishing Your Objectives.* Set your objectives and know what you hope to gain from the contest. Do you want to get more followers? Build brand awareness or create brand loyalty? Do you want a specific number of mentions or a certain amount of user-submitted content? The more specific you are with your objectives, the more likely you'll see positive results.

2. *Bam! Hashtag It Up.* Create a new hashtag for your contest, or use one that's also being used by one of your competitors or a popular national brand. See what contests your competitors are currently running to get an idea of what seems to be resonating with your desired audience. Take a look at other Instagram contests to get a feel for current trends.

3. *Seniors with Unicycles? Define Your Market/Audience.* Tap into your demographics to get a better idea of who is likely to participate in your contest and whether Instagram is really the right social platform for your contest. Ninety percent of those who use this platform are under 35 years old, with most users falling within the ages of 25 to 34, followed by those 18 to 24 years old. Further define your target audience so you'll have a better idea of what type of contest to present.

4. *More Cow Bell! Come Up with a Theme That Works for You.* Whether it's seasonal, topical, or something specific to your business, have a clear theme for your contest.

5. *Give It to Me Baby—Your Prize, That Is.* You might be able to get away with "bragging rights" for some contests, but you'll need something more substantial to encourage significant participation. Prizes can come from your inventory of products or be something a little more attention-getting like concert tickets, gift cards, or a trip. Whatever the prize, clearly state it upfront, and use it to promote your contest.

6. *First Stop, Instagram. Next, World Domination.* Decide if you want to limit your contest to Instagram or include other social platforms. If Instagram isn't your most popular platform, running a parallel contest on other platforms can have the added benefit of promoting your Instagram account and attracting more followers.

7. *No Playing Ball in the House! Establish the Ground Rules.* An effective Instagram contest needs clear ground rules. Post the rules to avoid any confusion or potential issues when winners are selected. Other than a clear start and end date, you'll want to determine:

    ■ Eligibility requirements, including any age requirements
    ■ How many winners you plan to have
    ■ Whether or not you'll announce the winner or just state that a winner has been chosen (which may be a good idea if you're going to allow participants under 18)
    ■ Prize or prizes to be awarded
    ■ Requirements for entry

8. *What Shall We Call This Thing? Title Your Contest.* Keep your title simple and descriptive of what the contest is about, such as "Holiday Photo Contest." If you're going to title it with a hashtag, check on a site like www.hashatit.com to make sure your preferred hashtag is available.

9. *Shout It from the Rooftops! Promote Your Contest.* Get the word out about your contest with a post on your Instagram account along with your other social accounts, website, and blog. Make the announcement post visually appealing, because Instagram is a visual social platform and this is what will attract browsers sorting through their latest posts. Further promote your contest with:

    ■ Your email newsletter
    ■ A well-crafted press release
    ■ Personalized email messages
    ■ A mention in your regular ads or in-store ads if you have a brick-and-mortar store
    ■ A QR (quick response) code on your ads to allow mobile users to instantly enter

10. *C'mon, Don't Stop There! Follow-Up.* Announce the winner and promote their winning entry with a post on Instagram. If it's just a "like-to-win" contest, you can still spotlight the winner in a post. Send out thank-you emails to all participants or post a "thank you" on your Instagram account to everyone who took the time to enter your contest.

CONTEST INSPIRATION FROM BIG BRANDS

Find some inspiration for specific Instagram contest ideas by taking a look at some of the social contests that have already been successful endeavors for bigger brands. Granted, these guys also have more to spend, but you can use a similar idea and tailor it to your available budget.

■ *Pepsi—PepsiSelfie Contest.* By offering tickets to the VIP party at PowerFest—a popular local summer concert event being hosted by the co-sponsor, radio station WCKX—as the prize, Pepsi generated a lot of social buzz with this Instagram contest. In addition to promoting the concert, it also gave Pepsi's brand an added boost.

■ *Starbucks—Red Cup Contest.* Using the hashtag #RedCupArt, Starbucks asked customers to draw something on their cups and submit the photos with the designated hashtag. The prize was a $500 e-gift card. In less than a week, the holiday-themed contest generated nearly 25,000 entries.

■ *Better Homes and Gardens.* This company has a fairly broad brand in terms of what it offers and the audience it targets, which is why an Instagram contest asking participants to submit photos of themselves enjoying summer in relation to the brand was effective. Eight different prizes were awarded to entice participation. Apply the same concept to your contest by offering multiple prizes to a handful of winners.

■ *Valpak—Submit a Photo with Mom Contest.* The popular direct-mail coupon company simply asked followers to submit a photo with mom with the hashtag #MomMomentsSweeps. It resulted in nearly a thousand unique entries and generated a lot of interest and engagement, which is definitely a payoff you want to achieve with your contest. (File that under "things that are obvious.")

■ *BabyCenter—Summer Photo Contest.* The website dedicated to providing info on parenting and pregnancy got plenty of attention with a summer photo contest. Users were asked to submit summer photos of their babies for a chance to win a gift card. Based on something a lot of mothers already do anyway, it perfectly targeted the same audience who was likely to be visiting the site.

APPS YOU CAN USE TO RUN YOUR INSTAGRAM CONTESTS

Apps can help with some of the technical contest stuff beyond what you can get through Instagram support. If you're running a like-to-win contest, then you can skip this step and run your contest without using any apps. Just post an update on Instagram to show that you are running a contest. Otherwise, consider the following third-party apps:

- *Votigo* (www.votigo.com). Run and track your user-generated content contests, including photo contests, enter-to-win contests, and video contests, with this full-service app that includes an assortment of analytics tools.

- *Piqora* (https://app.piqora.com/). Track participant eligibility, engagement, and influence when using this app for your Instagram contests. You can also use it to identify top photos and videos to determine what your audience is checking out while content is uploaded for your contest.

- *Wishpond* (www.wishpond.com). Use this app to collect your photos by specifying the hashtags necessary for contest photos. You can collect up to 5,000 entries. You can also use it to create voting galleries for contests where you want to let your followers pick the winner.

- *WooBox* (https://woobox.com/). If you're going to run a multiplatform contest, install this app on your Facebook page to collect participation information directly from Instagram and other social sites to better track results. You can also use it to fine-tune your galleries and integrate your brand image.

- *Shortstack* (www.shortstack.com). You'll gain access to more than 30 widgets and another 30-plus themes and nearly a hundred templates you can use for your contests; its detailed analytics provide real-time results.

- *Binkd* (www.binkd.com). Use this app to define your contest requirements, attract participants, and track your results based on your specific preferences and requirements. You'll have access to an easy-to-use tool to help with set-up.

- *Iconosquare* (https://pro.iconosquare.com/). Customize your galleries by adjusting colors and gain access to advanced metrics with this app that tracks such things as daily engagement rates and participant location. You can also embed the landing page or photo gallery for your contest.

Use your available stats to gauge how your Instagram contests are doing. Instagram has plenty of metrics available, or you can enhance your stats with some free analytics tools. Regardless of what you use, you'll want to see if you're getting a spike in traffic during your contest and, more important, whether you're meeting the objectives you determined prior to the contest's launch. If you're planning to repeat your contest, compare results of prior efforts to your current results. Successful contests can easily boost your brand image while providing a fun way for your audience to stay engaged with you.

To sum it up, gamification = awesome.

GROWING YOUR FOLLOWER BASE

Ah, you've finally found it! The Easy-Button chapter of this book. Just say a few words, spin around twice, and you will instantly have 1,000 new Instagram followers.

Or not.

Unfortunately, there is no magic potion or spell you can use to instantly get new followers, but as someone who has experimented and grown her account herself, I know firsthand the good, the bad, and the ugly. And I'm spilling all of the beans. Even the pintos.

I read all that I could, tried all that I could, and documented everything. Some of the advice was totally and completely awful—like the ideal number of hashtags to use—just wait until you see. Some advice was fantastic, like how to engage your audience. You will love the double-tap magic (Instagram lingo for "liking" a post).

What worked best, however, is a little embarrassing, but I'm going to share it anyway. And then on page 94, I'll give you a blow-by-blow 21-day formula for growing your tribe while maintaining your sanity.

THE REAL DEAL: A SAD LITTLE START

I only became serious about growing my Instagram in the beginning of 2016. Up until then, most of my social networking time was spent on Facebook, Twitter, and LinkedIn. Those channels have been nurtured and cared for and had flourished, each with thousands of followers. This is an important tenet in business growth: Go deep before you go wide. Spread too thin and none of your social media marketing will be effective. Since Facebook, Twitter, and LinkedIn were smooth sailing for my company, it was time for me to dive deeper somewhere else.

At this point, my Instagram following was loyal and engaged but teeny tiny. The reason was simple. Back when I started on Instagram, my first mistake was to have someone who had no track record of growing followers manage my account. He was great at posting and managing comments, but I was never going to get to big numbers unless I was willing to put on my big girl swim cap (don't want to ruin the blow out) and jump into the deep end.

I gave my consultant notice that he was delightful and did good work, but we had to break up. It was all me, not him. There were some tears, we did a photo montage of our time together, and we moved on. And with that, I started on my journey to grow my following and increase engagement. I started to figure out what worked and what didn't. Because on this platform, both engagement and follower size are majorly important.

Dubbed the "king of social engagement" by Forrester Research, Instagram offers top brands a per-follower interaction rate of 2.3 percent, which far surpasses the engagement rate these brands are seeing on both Facebook (0.2 percent) and Twitter (0.02 percent). With high engagement rates and over 500 million active monthly users, it comes as no surprise then that gaining more Instagram followers is a high priority for any business using the platform.

The social media site Hootsuite says, "Unfortunately, there's no magic formula on how to get more Instagram followers, but there are ways of improving your Instagram strategy so that more of your ideal audience can find—and follow—you."

Doh—again with the no-magic-formula!

Some Advice Stinks

Seeking what would work best, I read a lot of books on Instagram, checked out blogs, and listened to podcasts. If I could find it and it had the word "Instagram" on it, I consumed it. It was there that I found the magical formula that works every time.

Bah! You know this isn't true. (But you were secretly hoping it was, weren't you? I don't blame you. I was, too.)

I followed almost every tactic I read about and a lot of them didn't work at all. My numbers actually went down when I tried some of them, which was (if you are keeping track) the exact opposite of what I wanted to happen.

But some of the advice worked incredibly well and allowed me to grow from just a few hundred to thousands of followers in less than 30 days. So this is possible, but it isn't magic. Specifically, some of the strategies I share may have worked for me, but they may not for you. It is all about trying and experimenting and doing what works best for you.

Hashtag It Up Baby—Or Not

Hashtags are really important when it comes to Instagram. The problem is, there are *huge* discrepancies when it comes to the "Here are the # of Hashtags You Should Use to Get the Most Followers" debate.

Am I the only one who pictures a bunch of hipsters hanging out in a dark coffee shop arguing about this? They are sitting with flat whites and soy chai lattes, and one is arguing that hashtags will ruin the authenticity of Instagram, and the other is like, "Ruin what? I just want to sell more of my photography, dude." I guess maybe it is just me.

When I searched for "How Many Hashtags Should I Use," my search came up with 3,450,000 search results! Good grief, Charlie Brown! On the positive side, it means there is no shortage of ideas.

A sampling of the different advice I encountered included advice by Buffer (https://blog.bufferapp.com), sharing that "When you use more than two hashtags, your engagement actually drops by an average of 17 percent." So one might think less is more? This is great news as there is very little work to do in research and typing. So this is sounding good. But not so fast!

Sprout Social shared, "Since Instagram is less strict about the number of hashtags you can use in your posts than Twitter, it's easy to go overboard. Instagram allows users to post up to 30 hashtags in each post, but it's common practice to keep it between 5 to 10." So, keep it nice and simple with five to ten hashtags? Au contraire, mon frère.

The more I read, studied, and researched the more confused I became. From "don't use any," to "use a couple," "use all 30"—there are even two articles from Buffer that gave the exact opposite strategies from each other. The advice I read was almost as contradictory as the advice I got while pregnant, and in that same way, it is frustratingly exhausting enough to make me want to eat cheese and nap.

The best advice I found was to check out how many hashtags people in your own industry use. Then experiment and see what works best for you. There is no reason to get stressed out. In fact, every post is a chance to experiment—and experiment I did. I started out with just a few hashtags and tried all the way up to the max of 30. (Reminder, don't go higher than 30. If you do, Instagram will delete your comment and that would stink.)

I have found the "use 11 or more" to work best for me (see Figure 5–8, page 85), but after that, there is no exact number.

Also, if you write your image caption in a Notes app and then paste it in the comment on your phone, it is so much easier. You can add a series of periods and hard returns after each line so your hashtags won't even show up unless someone opens up the comment. Most don't.

By the way, don't put a space after any of the "." If you do, Instagram will squish all of your copy together. And then it looks like a hot mess. No one wants that.

FIGURE 5–8. Using 11 or More Hashtags Works Best for Me.

Tag Someone—Or Don't

In the next section beginning on page 97, I interview Nathan Chan of Foundr. Nathan successfully grew his following to over 10,000 in just a few weeks.

This is from Foundr's free *Marketing 101 Instagram Guide*:

Think of every post to your account as an opportunity for your followers to engage with you. With very few exceptions, every single post we add has an opportunity or invitation for some kind of audience interaction. We do this either in text we overlay on top of the image or in the post description (or both!). Give your fans something to do, and watch your account spread like wildfire. Please, don't mistake this to mean you should ask your followers to do something for you every time you post. [See Figure 5–9, page 86.] This is important. Engagement doesn't mean "buy our thing," "give us your email," or "share our account with everyone you know." It's much lighter than that. You're asking them to do something that makes them feel good, helps them to engage with their friends, or reaffirms their beliefs or goals. [See Figure 5–10, page 86.] In other words, engagement should be something they enjoy. Most of the time, this will be as basic as asking people to "like" if they agree, or asking them to tag a friend to share the post or their own thoughts about it. We frequently will ask our followers questions related to the post. Our posts that contain questions drive 300 percent more interaction than those without a question.

FIGURE 5–9. This Is an Example of a Post That Asks Followers to Tag Other People.

FIGURE 5–10. Another Example of a Post from Foundr That Asks Followers to Tag Someone in the Comment Section.

I have tried asking for the tag multiple times and have not found it to work. Maybe my audience is different, so I have decided to give this technique a break for a while. But that doesn't mean you shouldn't try it. See what works best for your account. Your people might like tagging more than my people. Then maybe they can tag my people. And then we can have a good old-fashioned game of tag. Wouldn't that be lovely? *Sigh.*

Emojis

This is one of those little ninja tricks for creating a *pattern interrupt* in your post. A *pattern interrupt* is a technique to interrupt what your audience is doing—a behavior or situation. Behavioral psychology and neuro-linguistic programming use this technique to interrupt and change thought patterns and behaviors. It is meant to make your post stand out in a crowded Instagram thread.

You can use emojis to bring attention to your call to action, such as when you ask them to share the post with others or to comment, or simply to bring visual attention to your photo description. I have found this easiest to do by using an emoji search site. I copy the image into my notes when I write the full caption, and then copy it on my phone for the post itself. One of my favorites at the time of this writing is www. Emojipedia.org. Emojis are broken down into categories:

- Smileys and People
- Animals and Nature
- Food and Drink
- Activity
- Travel and Places
- Objects
- Symbols
- Flags

According to Emojipedia, the most popular are:

- Face with Tears of Joy
- Heavy Black Heart
- Smiling Face with Heart-Shaped Eyes
- Smiling Face with Smiling Eyes
- Face Throwing a Kiss
- Smirking Face
- Pistol
- Face with Rolling Eyes

A few ways to use emojis include:

■ Using them while commenting on another user's post (see Figure 5–11).

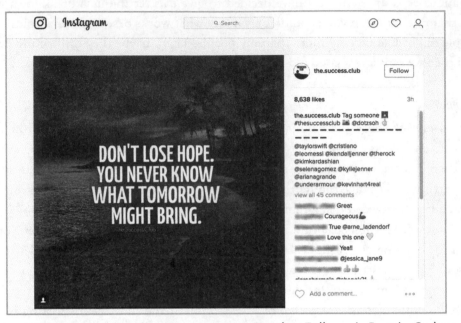

FIGURE 5–11. Use an Emoji to Comment on Another Follower's Post in Order to Draw Attention.

■ While tagging someone else in a comment (Figure 5–12).

FIGURE 5–12. Using an Emoji to Tag Someone Else in a Comment.

- Engaging your audience by asking it to pick an emoji to complete a sentence or to complete a post (Figure 5–13).

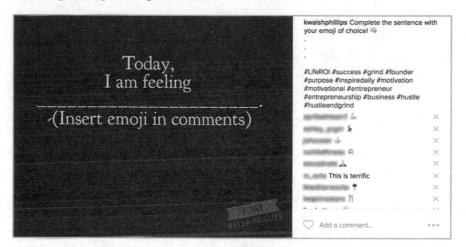

FIGURE 5–13. Using an Emoji for Engagement.

- Creating more visual interest for your post (Figure 5–14).

FIGURE 5–14. Use an Emoji to Create More Visual Interest for Your Post.

I have not had enough results to say whether it helps, but it does make the posts more visually interesting. I use them most of the time, so I give this one a thumbs up.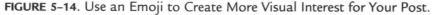

Post Frequency

This is another area where I have found a lot of different opinions. My research varied to once per day to four times per day to 11 to 20 times per month. This is as clear-cut as most elections in Florida—as in, not so much.

I have found you should post at least once per day, and whatever speed you choose, keep on keeping on with that speed for consistency and engagement. If you go up and down in frequency, it does seem to impact your reach and engagement. (Kind of like a favorite show being on once a week, then every night, and then once a week again might get irritating.)

Timing

This topic was a bit nuts. I mean, I found every answer possible. According to HubSpot, "The best times to post on Instagram are Mondays and Thursdays at any time except between 3:00 and 4:00 P.M. in your target audience's time zone." Spark says "Posts between 1 A.M. and 5 A.M. receive the highest engagement." Um, that's totally different. Yup. And there's another: "If you want people to like your Instagrams, the most ideal time to post is at 5 P.M. EST on Wednesdays," per ShortStack.

Easy, right? Wait, not so fast!

Following a request from *The Huffington Post*, Latergramme (a service that lets users manage and schedule Instagram posts) ran an analysis of over 61,000 posts to determine when photos received the most "likes" and comments. The Latergramme team also broke down the best times for each day of the week. According to the data, the most "engaged" time on Instagram shifts from day to day: On Monday, for example, 5 P.M. is actually a pretty crummy time; engagement is highest at 7 P.M. and 10 P.M. On Friday, 1 A.M. and 8 P.M. are apparently the sweet spots.

And yet another piece of advice from ShortStack says, "Before you post your photo to Instagram, there are two things to keep in mind: your audience's time zone and what time they're most often checking Instagram. Most Instagram users log in in the morning and in the evening, on their way home from work or school. According to analytics company Simply Measured, the best time to post on Instagram is on Wednesdays between 5:00 P.M. and 6:00 P.M. For brands, the least favorable time to post is in the middle of the night because an Instagram photo typically has a life of only around four hours before it gets buried in followers' feeds."

Here's the scoop with this one: I post when I can post. I don't get bogged down with times and you shouldn't, either. You have more important things to worry about. Like planning your world domination, and when the next season of *Orange is the New Black* is coming out.

Follower Software

There is a little-discussed truth around growing followers on Instagram. Many brands have used it, but few have spoken about it publicly. I was impressed with Foundr, who openly shared how a significant portion of their followers were earned:

> *When it comes to Instagram marketing, it is no different. With the right tools, we can replicate the success, down to the users, another brand has had. In order to help us do this, we found this super cool, super powerful tool called "Crowdfire." Crowdfire allows you to see which people follow a specific brand, and then follow those users. It also allows you to unfollow those who have not followed you back.*

> *The reason this tool is so valuable is that it allows you to find large groups of people who would be potentially interested in your brand. For us, we looked up other brands such as Fast Company, found out which people followed that brand, and started to follow those people via the "Copy Followers" function. Following someone on Instagram gives them a notification that links them to your own page and gives them a chance to follow you back, so following a lot of people allows you to pique the interest of many others.*

> *Another feature of Crowdfire shows you which users you follow but don't follow you back. This allows you to quickly unfollow those who are uninterested in what you do. We got a paid account for $9.99 a month, which unlocked the ability for us to hide which users we had followed and then unfollowed in the past, preventing us from following the same person twice.*

> *Keep in mind due to Instagram restrictions, you are only allowed to perform 400 actions a day (an action either being a follow or unfollow). So make sure you max out the number of actions you perform every single day. We got into the routine of three days of copying followers, and then one day of unfollowing.*

Now before you run out and join Crowdfire (which I happened to do and paid for it, and it was a dodo), let me warn you that they no longer have the follow-back program, so this app doesn't work this way anymore.

Recently, I have been using Influx (www.influxsocial.com), which has worked very well. That said, I must also warn that Influx has suspended their Instagram services indefinitely. But they recommend a nearly identical technology called Stim (www.stimsocial.com) as a great replacement tool that has all the same follow and unfollow features. In about two weeks I increased my followers more than 190 percent (see Figure 5–15, page 92 for a breakdown of engagement data). The beauty of this service is that you can choose which brand's followers to target so you get similar and like-minded people. I have not found my engagement to go down during this process. In fact, I have found it to increase.

So if there is anything that comes close to being a magic formula this is it.

Sources	Actions	Followbacks				Ratio
		Commenters	Likers	Followers	Total	
👤 incmagazine	1526	1	5	312	318	20.84% 🗑
👤 bossbabe.inc	1574	9	45	165	219	13.91% 🗑
👤 foundrmagazine	1215	31	23	88	142	11.69% 🗑
👤 entrepreneur	1126	14	34	83	131	11.63% 🗑
👤 foundrmagazine	646	-	2	54	56	8.67% 🗑
👤 girlboss	413	4	3	25	32	7.75% 🗑

FIGURE 5–15. This Is the Breakdown of My Growth with Influx over a Period of 30 Days.

Share the Love

But I love him?! Why doesn't he love me back?!

Thankfully, this drama doesn't play out as much on Instagram as it did back when we were in school. Or when my single girlfriends still share their horror stories. (No offense to my sister currently fighting the fight.)

In general, liking other people's posts is a great way to increase engagement and your following. Find a bunch that you like, double-tap them (it is fun—really—that is why they did a double-tap), and enjoy looking at some fabulous posts. Don't worry, it isn't goofing off. You are building your empire!

Use the Right Filters

I noticed a distinct difference in engagement with certain Instagram filters. Turns out those filters aren't just vanity—they can dramatically change your results with engagement.

Researchers from Georgia Tech and Yahoo Labs analyzed millions of photos and corresponding data on viewing and commenting frequency to determine that filtered photos are 21 percent more likely to be viewed and 45 percent more likely to be commented on than unfiltered ones.

What kind of filter works best? After examining five different types, researchers found the top filters to increase chances of views and comments are those that create:

- higher exposure
- warm temperatures
- higher contrast

Higher exposure filters were tied to more views, and warmth had the biggest correlation with comments. Two types of filters had negative correlations: Saturation correlated to slightly lower views, and Age Effects led to lower comments.

So filter it up, Jedi.

Advertising

I came into Instagram having spent a lot of time on Facebook for my firm and for our clients. I was used to advertising for "likes" as a viable option. Advertising to build followers on Facebook is often the first step we take in creating an audience of qualified prospects. I had hoped that Instagram would be similar. It isn't.

Thankfully there are still options. You can advertise on Instagram with an awareness advertisement (see Figure 5-16) and link it with your Instagram account. I ran one of these and received a few hundred followers from it.

The ad cost us around $500 for the 200 followers. We were able to target our perfect prospects, so while costlier than grassroots efforts, you are building an audience of key prospects.

Depending on your budget, advertising can be a viable option.

FIGURE 5–16. You Can Advertise on Instagram with an Awareness Advertisement and Link It with Your Instagram Account.

Shoutouts

When it comes to Instagram, a shoutout is a mention of another person's account in your post image and/or caption. Some accounts will do this for free while others charge for it. My research turned up Shoutcart (http://shoutcart.com), which will help match you to someone willing to sell you a shoutout. I have not tried this strategy yet, but I know a lot of products and brands that have. I suggest keeping it on your radar, but start with the 21-Day Blueprint that follows first.

THE 21-DAY BLUEPRINT FOR GROWING YOUR INSTAGRAM FOLLOWERS

Day 1
- Research 20 brands in your niche, and write down the hashtags they use.
- Get a good night's sleep; you have an empire to build.

Day 2
- Develop a brand board with the look and design elements you want on your page.
- Take a nap. Because you can.

Day 3
- Write your posts for the month.
- Give yourself a hand massage. Your digits are likely tired.

Day 4
- Design your posts for the month using the Word Swag app.
- Buy an artist's smock because you are now officially a "creative type."

Day 5
- Post your first post, writing a good description and using the hashtags you found to be popular in your niche. Prevent yourself from cursing out your phone by typing the description ahead of time in your Notes app on your desktop and then paste it in on your mobile phone.
- Like the posts of ten followers of others in your niche.
- Do a little happy dance. You are on your way to more followers.

Day 6
- Post the second post, writing a good description and using the hashtags you found to be popular in your niche.
- Like the posts of ten followers of others in your niche.
- Keep on boogying.

Day 7

- Continue to post each day.
- Open up an account on www.stimsocial.com and launch your account.
- Resist the urge to bow your head in shame for using an auto-follow program. The end result is worth it.

Day 8

- Post and add an emoji to your comment.
- Like the posts of ten followers of others in your niche and comment with emojis.
- Pretend not to be super excited that you are getting more followers, but secretly do a little jig when no one is looking.

Day 9

- Post and add emojis to your comment.
- Like the posts of ten followers of others in your niche and comment with emojis.
- Dream of having an emoji created in your honor someday because of your Instagram awesomeness.

Day 10

- Post and add emojis to your comment.
- Like the posts of ten followers of others in your niche, and comment with emojis.
- Start a Facebook ad for Instagram followers.
- Pour a little of your mineral water on the sidewalk for the dollars you will sacrifice in the name of growing your Instagram following.

Day 11

- Post and add emojis to your comment.
- Like the posts of ten followers of others in your niche, and comment with emojis.
- Resist the urge to add emojis to every text and email you write for the day.

Day 12

- Do some additional research on hashtags, and test adding some new ones to the mix.
- Run a post and add the new hashtags to the post description.
- Like the posts of ten followers of others in your niche, and comment with emojis.
- Start making a hashtag symbol in the air when others high-five you. After all, you've got to be in it to win it and might as well start a trend.

Day 13

- Test running two posts in one day today to see what happens to engagement.
- Like ten other accounts and comment with emojis.

■ If Doublemint gum is still a thing, chew it in honor of doubling up your efforts.

Day 14

■ Analyze the double posts to see if that should continue or stop. Post accordingly.

■ Analyze your progress with your auto-follow program. Add or subtract the brands to target.

■ Smirk to yourself for how cool you are and how well this is going.

Day 15

■ Post and like as you have been doing.

■ Check out some of the leading pages in your industry to see which of their posts are performing best. *Do not get jealous.* This is research, not a comparison game.

■ Treat yourself to the beverage of your choice. You've made it two-thirds of the way through! Cheers!

Day 16

■ Post and like as you have been doing.

■ Write a few new posts based on what you learned from watching other accounts.

■ Daydream about being interviewed by Social Media Examiner for your Instagram genius.

Day 17

■ Post and like as you have been doing.

■ Design those new posts with Word Swag.

■ Wear your artist smock out to pick up an extra-customized obscure coffee drink. Resist the urge to order it on your mobile app so you don't have to say all of the bizarre ingredients out loud. You've earned this moment. Savor it publicly.

Day 18

■ Post one of your new posts.

■ Check on the progress of your Facebook ads.

■ Pour a little more mineral water on the sidewalk.

Day 19

■ Post another new post.

■ Like ten other people's posts.

■ Create your own touchdown dance when you check your follower numbers. You are a champion.

Day 20

■ Post another new post.

■ Like ten other people's posts.

- Schedule the stylist for your first on-air interview about your social media success that someday is surely going to happen.

Day 21

- Post another new post.
- Like ten other people's posts.
- Toast your success. You did good.
- Congratulations, you completed the 21-Day Challenge! Run a post with #21DaysDone #InstagramforBusiness, and you can win one of 100 prizes!

For more inspiration, check out the next section where I interview Nathan Chan of Foundr. He quickly grew his Instagram account to over 100,000 followers, and it drove thousands of customers into his business.

HOW NATHAN CHAN GREW FOUNDR TO MORE THAN 10,000 FOLLOWERS IN LESS THAN A MONTH

Nathan Chan is the publisher of Foundr (https://foundrmag.com), a digital magazine for young, aspiring, and novice entrepreneurs. He's had the pleasure of interviewing rock-star business leaders to find out what it takes to become a successful entrepreneur.

Tell us a little bit of background on where you started and how Foundr jumped in to Instagram as a growth opportunity.

Chan: We are a digital-only magazine on the iTunes App Store and Google Play store. For a while, we hadn't found a channel that could drive traffic and leads to get more magazine downloads. I tried many tools and marketing channels. When I shared with my entrepreneur friends that I was using Instagram, they all told me it was a terrible channel for business. They said that only fitness and fashion brands should be on there.

[I laughed a little too hard on this one. So hard in fact, I feared that Nathan would hang up because I was obviously off my rocker. Thankfully, he didn't.] The data speaks louder than any of our opinions, doesn't it? How long did it take you to see traction from your account?

Chan: We'd had an account for three years, set up and managed by an intern, with just a few hundred followers before I jumped in. I started by researching hashtags and even by just writing better captions. This landed us a serious spike in magazine subscriptions. Within a single day—after just 24 hours of testing—I could tell my techniques were working. I noticed an extra hundred downloads for our magazine. Better yet, we were making an extra $100 to $200 on subscriptions. I saw very quickly that I was onto something.

[Laughing again here. Embarrassingly so.] Did you send a screenshot of the sales to the naysayers?

Chan: [Laughing to be polite.] No, I didn't. I just kept growing. Actually, in the first two weeks we grew to 10,000 followers back in 2014.

That's amazing. Do you think that kind of growth is still possible today?

Chan: Yeah, it's definitely still possible. Whatever else you do, it all comes down to getting as many influencers or as many other accounts as possible to share your content, and getting your audience engaged. While it might be harder to get followers now, it is vastly easier to get engagement.

I've heard you've talked about the "s4s" model—share for sharing—or shoutouts. How did you use it to leverage account growth?

Chan: Essentially, all the top Instagram accounts support one another by promoting others' accounts. Even *National Geographic* has done this. It is an "I'll share your post if you share mine" concept. Alternatively, money can change hands. This is where you pay another person or account to share your content, or perhaps you send them free products. Either way, to get someone to share your content there has to be some sort of value exchange. All of the top Instagram accounts do this.

When you were first growing your account, you obviously didn't have as big a following as you do now. How can you get started with s4s if sharing a partner's content may not be as valuable as them sharing yours? How do you find folks who might be willing to get into a partnership with you on this?

Chan: Well, I was lucky at that time because one of *Foundr's* early readers contacted me and offered to help. She said, "I've read the magazine and absolutely love it. I have an opportunity for you where you can post your Richard Branson issue on my page with 20,000 followers and I can drive traffic for you." I thought OK, I'd give it a try.

She charged me $50. We posted an image of the Richard Branson cover with details in the caption to download the issue in the App Store. It didn't work, so I blew it off. I decided maybe Instagram just wasn't a good source of traffic. There was no increase in downloads or subscriptions.

What I later discovered was that I shouldn't have mentioned where they needed to go, because it looked like too much work. Instead, the caption should have tagged my Instagram account, and then in the bio link I should have linked directly to the Richard Branson article. People just aren't going to type in an address or go to another app. You have to make it very easy for them.

I later reached out to a friend who I knew was on Instagram. I had followed his account progress. In a very short time, he had grown it from 10,000 to 100,000 followers. He suggested I try the share-for-share method again, but this time ask the brand to tag my profile in the caption instead. It was very successful. I then offered to feature other Instagram profiles in *Foundr* magazine in exchange for shoutouts and it aided us to grow our account very quickly.

That's amazing, but if someone is just doing this for the first time, how should they approach it? They probably don't have a digital magazine they can leverage, or a lot of followers they can share the other brand to. How can they partner when they don't have the same assets you had?

Chan: There are a few things I'd recommend if you're just getting started and don't have as much leverage as I did. First of all, I challenge you to dig deep and think about what you can potentially offer to a partner. Maybe it's an ongoing promotion, like links in your blog articles or a link to their site from your website resources page. You can always find something worth trading. Or you can just pay for shoutouts like we did in the beginning. To find potential partners, check if they list an email address in the account bio. Often that is an indication that they are open for business. Start small and find a caption and/or image that produces results—and then find other potential partners.

You've also had a lot of success using hashtags. Can you share what you've done that has been successful?

Chan: When you are first getting started, you definitely want to add the hashtags that are used most often by those in your niche. Not just the brands, but by those commenting as well. You'll have to put more time into this in the beginning to research and test which ones work best for you and your brand.

You've mentioned before that you've utilized tagging. Would you recommend doing this in the beginning, to tag other folks with valuable content in your specific target market?

Chan: That's definitely part of the strategy. The best way is to tag the other account by mentioning their username. Then viewers can click on it and reach the other account's page. That account's owner then sees you've mentioned and recommended them.

So what would you say is the overall goal of your account? And how has it changed over time?

Chan: We're aiming to build community [see Figure 5-17 on page 100]. At the end of the day, that should be the goal of any social media—to build community. But then you need to move that community out of the social media platform, since you don't own that network. Instagram or any other platform could turn around and

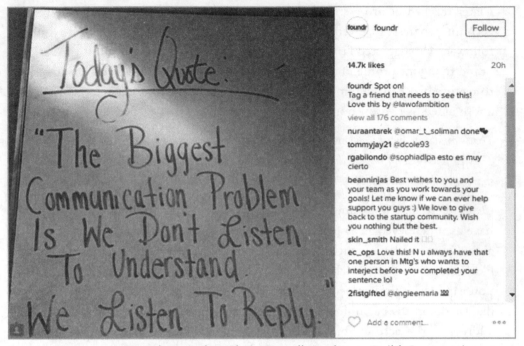

FIGURE 5–17. Foundr Says that Their Overall Goal Is to Build Community.

shut down your account. There's nothing you can do about it at that point. I don't think it's wise to rely solely on platforms you don't own.

So for us, the goal has been to build our own media base. We want to grow an email list, and a newsletter, as much as we can through any form of social media—whether it's Facebook, Twitter, Instagram, Pinterest, Snapchat, you name it—to drive people to our home base and capture their contact info, which allows us to stay in touch, build more trust, and provide more value.

In the early days when we first started the magazine, its subscription base was all hosted in the app stores. But those platforms are owned by Apple and Google. For us, it was very important to bring subscribers through a sequence to get to know us better, and to see what we are all about, and to learn about all the cool stuff we're doing that isn't just Instagram. We treat Instagram as a channel, just like any other channel (SEO, Google search, Twitter, Facebook). They're all marketing channels, which allows us to facilitate our relationship with the prospective customer and interest those who want to join our community.

Where do you go for inspiration for your posts?

Chan: When I first joined Instagram, I did a competitor analysis. I looked around for all the accounts that produced the best content in the startup motivational niche.

Then I started following them. We usually follow fewer than a hundred accounts and get enough inspiration and ideas for posts we can create or repost. We also have a lot of collaborative partners to help us grow rapidly, too.

So, not working in a vacuum, great!

Chan: Now more than ever, it's about relevancy. It's about posting the best possible content that your audience will love and triggering an emotion that makes them really want to tag their friends, mention their friends, like it, share it, screenshot it, repost it, or make it a screensaver. That's the whole goal more than ever. [See Figures 5–18, 5–19 (page 102), 5–20 (page 102), and 5–21 (page 103).]

How can folks learn more about Foundr?

Chan: We are a digital-only magazine on the App Store and Google Play, and we target aspiring and novice entrepreneurs. If you're thinking of opening a business but don't know where to start, or your business is just getting up and running, we provide in-depth how-to content to make your job easier. Find us at https://foundrmag.com/ or @foundr on Instagram.

FIGURE 5–18. Foundr's Posts Target Aspiring and Novice Entrepreneurs.

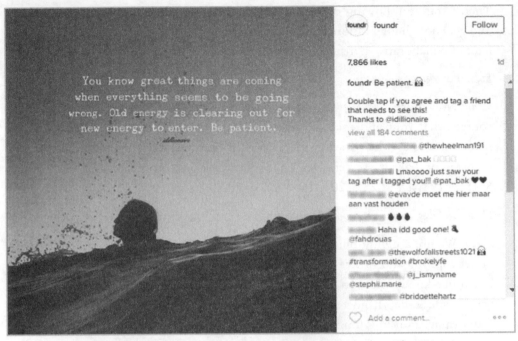

FIGURE 5–19. Getting Followers to Like a Post So Much that They Use It as a Screensaver or to Repost It Is One of Foundr's Goals.

FIGURE 5–20. Another Goal for Foundr Is to Post Content that Triggers an Emotion that Makes Followers Want to Tag Their Friends.

FIGURE 5–21. Foundr's Posts Are about Relevancy and Posting the Best Possible Content.

#INSTAGRAMFORBUSINESS POSTABLES

- Using even a single hashtag increases post engagement by 12.6 percent. #InstagramforBusiness

- The more specific you can get, while still staying with a frequently used #hashtag, the more successful you will be at attracting an engaged and on-point audience. #InstagramforBusiness

- Gamification is exciting because it promises to make the hard stuff in life fun. #InstagramforBusiness

- Toast your success. You did good. #InstagramforBusiness

- I did it! #21DaysDone #InstagramforBusiness

Resource spotlight: Visit www.UGIGbook.com to download your own "Instagram 21-Day Post Plan"!

Chapter 6

All About the ROI: Getting Superior Leads from Instagram

Imagine this:

You've been putting off going to the doctor for a while. Your spouse finally threatens a week at the in-laws if you don't go soon, and you don't generally see eye to eye with your mother-in-law since that time you accidently called her "Sir." (Never mind that the lighting was terrible inside the Elks Lodge.)

This threat of family awkwardness is all the motivation you need to finally get your bottom into the doctor's office. Literally and figuratively.

When you finally get into the paper-gown-of-embarrassment, your doc is swift but serious. "You know, I've known you for a long time," she says, "and I want you to take this seriously. Your heartbeat concerns me, and I want you to see a specialist. The good news is that I am friends with Dr. Thomas, and he is the best in the country. I've already scheduled you an appointment for tomorrow. He's expensive, but he's worth it."

"OK," you concede. "If he's the best, I'll go."

Oh crap, you think. *How am I going to explain this to my spouse? My kids?*

As soon as you get into the car you consult the number one source for all medical things—Google. You immediately start Googling everything around heart disease, heart palpitations, heart origami, even, by accident, and all about your doctor-to-be, Dr. Thomas. What you find online is that he is definitely the leading heart specialist in your area. At least if you have to go through this, you are going with the best.

So, the next day, you arrive at your appointment and see a rather strange scene. The gentleman sitting at the reception desk looks an awful lot like the surgeon you saw in the photos online. Maybe a little older and a little grayer, but that's him.

He looks up and smiles and says, "Hello. May I have your name and insurance card, please?"

"Yes," you say confused. "Um, would you happen to be Dr. Thomas?"

"Why, yes, I am," he answers. He goes on to explain that he staffs the waiting room throughout the day to save money on receptionist costs. This world-renowned heart surgeon cuts costs by answering the phone and helping patients fill out paperwork.

Maybe you are asking what this has to do with getting subscribers through Instagram. I'm getting there, I promise.

Answering the phone is the least profitable way for Dr. Thomas to spend his time. He should be spending 100 percent of his time meeting with patients and in surgery. If possible, someone should even cut up his food for him and feed it to him while he continues to meet with patients. Every minute he can spend performing his main skill of medicine is the most profitable way to spend his time—not at a receptionist job.

PROSPECTING WISELY

So how does this relate to your business and Instagram?

If you are spending time prospecting in person, you are no different than Dr. Thomas. If you are developing leads one to one, spending time going after the next sale personally, attending networking events looking for your next sale appointment, you are no different from Dr. Thomas working the reception desk. You are wasting time and your valuable skill set doing work below your pay grade. Instead, use your Instagram account to drive leads into your business.

Or maybe you rely upon your sales team to generate leads. Your sales super stars are tasked with not just closing deals but with bringing deals to the table. You have the top, highly compensated, uber-valuable team members spending time in low-value activities, with the hopes of generating high-value clients—being the doctor at the receptionist desk.

Instead, design your marketing tactics to develop your leads. Use your marketing to bring those high-value sales to the table and allow you and your sales team to spend your days doing as many high-value activities as possible.

By focusing your marketing on lead generation, you can target the best customer, at the best time, for the best results. You can take time to develop dialogue with your target audience instead of trying to instantly make the sale. This allows your prospects to build a relationship with you before they are asked to buy anything, which in turn will put your company in a position of authority and your salesperson in a position as trusted advisor, the strongest possible way to start a sales call.

Of course, this means that your Instagram marketing cannot focus solely on generating awareness. It must focus on generating *qualified* leads. The most successful entrepreneurs and salespeople focus their energy on their best prospects who have the greatest potential for a high return on their time and energy. The same needs to be true for your marketing.

So, how do you turn your marketing from awareness to lead generation?

Research your prospects and focus your messaging on their pain points. Draw them to you with your initial messaging, get their contact information, and then monetize the audience.

COURTING YOUR INSTAGRAM FOLLOWERS INTO BUYERS

Before I met my husband, Ian, I lived for three years in Palm Beach, Florida, as a single woman in the dating scene. Child, that place is a bit crazy. And I have some stories.

But let's just focus on one for the purposes of this book.

One night I was at a party, and I met this interesting man with an enticing accent. We shared a lot of the same interests and had a lively and playful conversation with one another. When the night came to a "I've-got-to-get-to-bed-any-minute-now-moment-or-I-will-fall-asleep-in-the-crab-dip" time, he asked if he could take me to dinner the following week. He seemed nice enough and the offer of a good meal and good conversation were enough to get me to say yes. He was only going to be in town for a few days, so I didn't see this as something serious. Just a nice night out with a good conversationalist, who also happened to be cute and have an enticing accent. (A girl's got to do, what a girl's got to do.)

As I had assumed, he and I had a great meal and enjoyable conversation and the dinner went by quickly. When we were done, he asked if I'd like to go out for a drink at another location to end our night. Since it was early and I was having a nice time, I said yes.

Here's where it got weird.

We were at one of my favorite places in the area, "The Cottage," sitting outside having a drink. It was then that he started down a path that flipped the night. He first asked me if I'd like to visit him at his home in Boston someday. I thought this was just innocent dating banter of a future that would never happen, as Palm Beach men are somewhat infamous for. I replied with a light hearted, "Sounds like fun!"

He then asked me when I would like to go and pulled out his calendar. "Um, I am not sure of my schedule," I said starting to feel a bit uncomfortable. *OK, a lot uncomfortable.*

He then moved on to say, "And then I'd love to bring you to my home in Crete. We could live there and have children. You would be very happy there." He took out his phone and started to make a reservation for two first-class tickets to Crete.

Um, say what?

Starting to hyperventilate I said, "Um, we just met and although I think you are very nice and I've enjoyed tonight, I am not ready to go away with you on a trip—and especially not to decide to live in Crete *(I don't even know where that is?!)* and have children with you." All while speed dialing my BFF under the table with our 9-1-1 code for "COME GET ME."

I'll spare you the details, but let's just say the night ended with him yelling things about our future home as I sped away in my couldn't-move-quickly-enough M-2 Spyder convertible.

Now, I think it was highly unlikely that I was ever going to end up in Crete having this man's children, but there was no way it was going to happen from this type of courting. He wanted to skip all of the steps and go right to a commitment. What he got instead was me speeding away.

While it makes for a great story, the opposite—normal dating, between normal, rational people—does not include asking someone to have your babies and move to a foreign country on date one.

This is similar to your marketing courtship (see Figure 6–1, page 109).

Think of your Instagram posts as the hot outfit you put on before going out for the night. The correct use of hashtags is the mating call you send out, looking for the right partner. The link in your bio is the equivalent of asking your prospect to go on a first date. You bring the relationship out of Instagram to nurture it and build trust with engagement and eventually you get serious and the follower becomes a buyer.

Unlike many, I like to reverse-engineer the prospect courtship, first determining the sales funnel, then discovering the right hashtags to use, and only then creating a posting strategy for the page. This allows a brand to put out posts that help support the goal of making the sale.

In the next section, we will go through what constitutes a sales funnel and how you can create one for your industry.

Ready to put that hot outfit on?

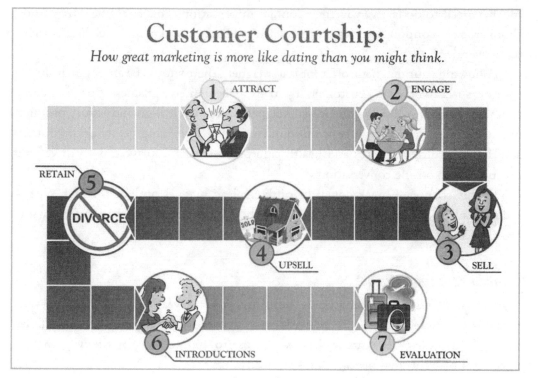

FIGURE 6–1. The Marketing Courtship.

GETTING YOUR INSTAGRAM ROI ON: CREATING YOUR SALES FUNNEL

One of my favorite quotes is from Og Mandino: "Always do your best. What you plant now, you will harvest later." This thought is certainly true for your Instagram account.

One of the most challenging parts of getting an ROI from Instagram is that you have only one link to use. The link inside your bio is the only spot you can use to actively drive a prospect into your sales funnel. This link should be used wisely and never simply as a link to your home page.

Since Instagram isn't a place people go looking for goods and services, to use this networking platform as a lead generation tool, you need to offer your prospects something of value in order to get them to click on your bio link.

Enter Your Magnetic Offer

The goal with your Instagram link is to provide something so valuable that the prospect would pay for it if it wasn't free. But of course, they don't need to pay you.

All they need to do is give you their contact information. This could be a free guide, ebook, report, coupon/certificate, video series, webinar, mind map, check list, or ticket to an event.

Following your magnetic offer (or lead magnet), there should be an opportunity for your prospect to become a customer. If you are an ecommerce business, this offer could come immediately following the initial magnetic offer, while high-end luxury products might use a few messages in between to nurture the relationship before asking for the sale. For consulting services and health care practitioners, your goal is to drive your prospect to an offline conversation.

In this chapter, I break down the different lead magnet options for each type of industry and niche as well as a quick-start method at the end of this chapter for my soul brothers and sisters—the impatient.

Creating Your Lead Magnet

My husband and I have been house hunting for three years now. Through several mishaps (or more likely Godly interventions), houses we have gone after have fallen through. In these three years we have seen close to 100 houses. (By the way, there is nothing fun about this—*nothing*. But, I digress.)

In many of the homes we have looked at, there is wallpaper that we know will have to be removed. I have done this job before, and if you have, too, you know that it *sucks*. If we did embark on such a project and I just happened to see two ads in my Instagram newsfeed that day, one for an "Ultimate Guide to Taking off Wallpaper" and one for "A Magic Wand That Will Take off Wallpaper as You Blink"—which do you think I am going to choose? (If you happen to have the second, I will gladly take it as a gift.)

The reality is, no one wants more information. Information itself is useless. What we all want is the outcome the information will provide, and if there is something else that can provide us with that outcome, such as an "Easy Button," we will take that over any guide, report, or ebook. We want to know that there will be transformative value for our lives in anything we spend time saying or doing.

The same is true for your platform tribe.

If you can help them solve their problem quicker with a tool, you not only have a new email subscriber, you have a new customer. I have split-tested the biscuits out of this, and tools beat information every time.

Tool Ideas for Lead Magnets
1. Checklists
2. Templates

3. Copy-and-paste scripts
4. Plans or programs

And then, there's another strategy that we've been testing for our own funnel and for some of our ecommerce clients that has been working better than anything else we've tried—ever. And that is attracting prospects with information laid out like above, and then offering an opportunity to purchase something for $1 afterwards that can help make their lives easier quickly.

My best-performing funnel of all time is one where I offered a free chapter of *The No B.S. Guide to Direct Response Social Media Marketing* (information), followed by an offer for 113 social media posts plus bonus images for a dollar. The first step is something with value (chapter of a book you normally have to pay for), and the second is a tool that helps you get something accomplished quicker. The tool also includes an option to take a 60-day trial of our Marketing Insiders Elite Club. This funnel rocks because it is focused around the interests and needs of my chosen tribe of fabulous get-er-done marketers and helps them get their job done faster. This funnel brings us members for less than five dollars each. And since our mission is to empower as many people as possible to get an ROI for their business, this helps us to go a heck of a lot farther with our budget. We have a similar funnel working for several of our clients with comparable results.

Here are some ideas for you to do the same:

1. Step one ideas:
    a. Chapter download
    b. Guide
    c. Blueprint
    d. Template
2. Step two ideas:
    a. Software program
    b. Copy-and-paste templates
    c. Done-for-you service
    d. Completed item you give them like a PowerPoint template or pop-up for their website, or something like our 113 posts plus bonus images

I haven't done a ton of testing of different price points for step two but have split-tested free-plus-shipping versus a straight one-dollar offer, and the dollar offer wins every time.

I know, this may all seem like a lot and be a little overwhelming if you are just starting out, but I know you can handle it. I would rather you take a little more time in this step and really develop your offer and get the most ROI out of it. However, if you are short on time, you may want to start with the next section.

A QUICK-START LEAD MAGNET BLUEPRINT

Here's how to do it:

1. Visit www.Quora.com.
2. Look up the top questions asked about your industry.
3. Record yourself answering the questions through the voice memo app on your phone.
4. Upload the recording to www.InternetTranscribers.com for a transcript (about $20).
5. Send the transcription to www.TextBroker.com to flesh out the report (about $10).
6. Request a report cover design from www.Fiverr.com (about $5).

You have your lead magnet for $35 in.
Sweet, no?

Tools to Get Your Lead Magnet Funnel Created Faster

- *Quora* (www.quora.com). Ask and answer questions, and collaborate with an entire community of online users.
- *BuzzSumo* (http://buzzsumo.com). BuzzSumo uses data from your own content to see what is performing well. Use it to help find content that influences and promotes your business.
- *Google Keyword Planner Tool* (https://adwords.google.com/home/tools/keyword-planner). A free tool that helps your business find popular keywords that would be beneficial for you to lead a successful campaign.
- *Facebook Audience Insights* (www.facebook.com/business/news/audience-insights). Use this tool to find the exact types of people who influence your business, like targeting specific demographics, purchase activity, geography, and more.
- *Fancy Hands* (www.fancyhands.com). It's your very own virtual assistant! Send a request to have them do research, make calls, and more to help you be more productive with your day!

Others to Write or Create Your Tool for You

- *Upwork* (www.upwork.com). Easily find freelance writers, artists, assistants, accountants, and more to improve productivity and your all-around business.

- *Fiverr* (www.fiverr.com). Find services from writers, artists, computer experts, and other professionals to get more done at an unbeatable price.
- *HireMyMom.com* (www.hiremymom.com). Hire talented, virtual freelancers who are also stay-at-home mothers!
- *Text Broker* (www.textbroker.com). Choose from thousands of qualified writers to create content for your business. Use new content to capture attention and to boost search rankings.

Platforms to Publish Your Resources

- *Leadpages* (www.leadpages.net). Use Leadpages to create a landing page in less than five minutes that is computer and mobile-friendly, and you don't have to mess around with coding!
- *WordPress* (www.wordpress.com). Choose from hundreds of designs to create a free webpage that can be used for websites, blogs, and more.
- *Squarespace* (www.squarespace.com). Create an eye-catching, professional website to sell your product, make an online portfolio, or even create a personalized website for your special event.
- *Unbounce* (http://unbounce.com). Use an existing template (or create your own) to build your own custom landing page.
- *CreateSpace* (www.createspace.com, Amazon's publishing platform). Publish your book through CreateSpace and make it available to millions of potential readers, without the hassle of navigating traditional publishing channels.

Miscellaneous Resources

- *For keeping ideas: Evernote* (https://evernote.com). Collect ideas from the internet, take notes, and convert your discoveries into easy-to-read presentations with just a few clicks.
- *For project management: Basecamp* (https://basecamp.com/). A "virtual office" that allows you to collaborate with team members and keep information all in one place online. Store files, create a schedule and deadlines, and converse with teammates with each "to-do" throughout a project.
- *For ideas, inspiration, and ROI: Marketing Insiders Elite* (http://marketinginsiderselite.com). This exclusive club gives information on how to manage campaigns, invitations to workshops, weekly newsletters, and much more!

In the next section, leading marketing funnel expert Oliver Billson shares the science and strategy behind effective funnels.

YOUR INSTAGRAM MARKETING FUNNEL, WITH OLIVER BILLSON OF WWW.OLIVERBILLSON.COM

Billson's superpower lies in strategizing and implementing cutting-edge, conversion-led, money-making sales and marketing funnels. It's safe to say that, unlike a lot of marketers, he makes more money actually practicing what he preaches than teaching it!

After starting his own business at the age of 15, his portfolio now spans four incredibly successful businesses, including information marketing, training and coaching, brick-and-mortar businesses, and his widely sought-after "done-for-you" marketing business. Billson is also an internationally recognized franchisor.

When he fancies it, Billson also spends time as a consultant to many other well-known entrepreneurs and business growth experts. In recent years he's been the mastermind behind lots of big launches and event promotions for other marketers, helping them grow and automate their businesses.

Tell us a bit about yourself and what a funnel expert is.

Billson: First, let's talk about what a funnel is. It's become a buzzword in the marketing community, but it's really just a process of driving people through a number of stages to become a customer who will buy a product or service from you. You're taking them through a predetermined series of stages to get to that point, and you are choreographing the journey of this potential customer before they make a decision to purchase from you.

So when it comes to Instagram, the reality is that you only have one link if you're looking to build organic traffic.

Billson: Some people might feel that one link could be quite limited, but the fact is, there's nothing wrong with having only one entry point. The first thing you want to do is to solidify your authority or celebrity expert status. You should do this immediately to differentiate yourself from your competitors and other brands your prospects may be looking toward to solve a problem. People prefer to buy from those they know, like, and trust.

So, the question is, how do we do that? How can you take someone from Instagram and begin to grow the relationship?

My advice to varying types of business owners and entrepreneurs is to move the prospect to some kind of ungated content (meaning no opt-in or other requirement for them to access it). [See Figure 6–2, page 115]. Usually it will be an article from the thought leader of the Instagram account. Give your audience the benefit of telling them who you are and why they should bother to listen to you. Tell them how you

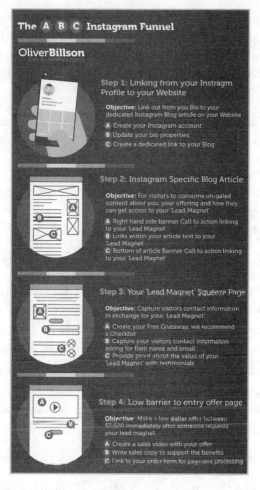

FIGURE 6–2. This Is "The ABC Instagram Funnel" by Oliver Billson.

started your business and how that relates back to them. And then give them some really good tips that share value right away.

How much space would you suggest for that background, personal stuff?

Billson: There are two different ways to do that. The first is to put together a bio at the bottom of your blog. This bio elaborates more on you and your interests and what qualifies you. The other way is to begin the blog post with an intention of solidifying who you are and what you do.

I think it's important to remember though, at this point, people are probably going to be more interested to learn what's in it for them than in learning about you. You have to be conscious of that because we want to be respectful of the person's time. We are going to take them through a series of steps I call micro-commitments to move them toward you. Be respectful of each step in the process. At this stage, consider using the article or blog to congratulate them for reading and welcome them to the next content they are just about to read. I think that's really key to kick things off on the right footing.

Should you link your bio to your general blog or create a blog post specifically for your Instagram followers?

Billson: Since you have the ability to craft a specific page from Instagram, you should do that. You can make it relevant with the posts on the page and the exact copy on the bio link. You can even welcome them from Instagram, letting them know they came from the right place. This is really powerful.

So after Instagram traffic comes to your blog post, where should they go next?

Billson: Provide them further value by offering something free in exchange for contact information. Take those people to a squeeze page or another landing page that's external from the blog post. This page should be dedicated to capturing their contact information in exchange for the item you are giving them. The value you offer will differ depending on the business you're in. It might be a free [estimate], a free report, or a giveaway, or free guide. It might even be a checklist. It needs to be something they can consume quickly, and ideally it's congruent to what they came to you for in the first place.

What have you found to be the most effective giveaway that your clients have used?

Billson: We really like checklists. They provide immediate value, are easy to create, quick to consume, and allow you to see good conversion rates. If your followers see they can get a quick win, they will be likely to opt-in for other content. It helps establish that you are going to give them value from the very beginning.

To get them to opt in, add graphics to your blog post that encourage them to click through to the squeeze page and take that next step on that journey. You may want to place an exit pop-up so that if they try to leave, they are encouraged to first opt in for the lead magnet. At the very least, make sure you can retarget the lead down the road with future marketing. This way, all is not lost if they don't take the step you want them to take at first.

Once they do give you their contact information, what should you have them do next?

Billson: Once they enter their information, don't get in the way of that motion. When they are at the highest point of taking immediate action, provide them an immediate offer that allows them to take a further step to change the relationship from lead to buyer. Usually this should be a very low-ticket item. A reasonable sum would be between $7 and $20, and something that offers a passive solution to one of the problems congruent with the free opt in they downloaded. Congruence between what they requested and the offer you're making is key to maximizing the conversion on your blog.

How can you test to see if your offer is congruent with the message or the funnel they've been coming through so far?

Billson: One of the ways we can do that is to profile an audience. We should understand their wants, and different needs and desires. Not everyone needs the same products, programs, or services. All that you offer might not be a fit for everyone.

So how do we do it? We take them through a survey. A survey is a very effective alternative to providing a checklist as a giveaway. If you don't know the intent of the traffic moving toward you, then a survey is a good way to capture the contact information of your target market. We can ask a series of questions in exchange for that contact information to be able to profile that person's demographic and psychographic information, in order to channel our offers more appropriately. It is also good to test different types of people so we can refine our offers in the background, and learn who to go after and what each prospect is worth.

I've seen you have a lot of success using surveys in the past.

Billson: Yes, it's been very effective. In broader markets, we have found that offering a quiz works great. A quiz is a type of survey where you offer some kind of results based on the information they provided. We've tested these in lots of different markets. Really, it's just a case of thinking out of the box to create something that will allow someone to give you the profile information you need. We can then provide a very tight solution that's completely aligned to the problem you are hoping to solve.

Once they have given you their contact information, where do you take them next?

Billson: Begin to present your key offering to them. This is the thing you would usually sell to the majority of people who come to you. Now you are changing the relationship from prospect to customer. It is also important to evolve that relationship into one that becomes a repeat customer. Because we know they bought from us once, they have a need. It makes sense now to present your core offering to them so they can take advantage of it. It may not just be on the landing page, either. You may want to take them into a webinar or a video series.

Obviously not 100 percent of prospects are going to link all the way to your core offer. How do you handle folks who slip out of the sequence?

Billson: There are two ways to do it. One is to think ahead of time about what those contingencies might be. You need to build in steps to be able to bring people back to continue to that critical path. Follow-up is the real key. It is so important, not just online with email but also in some cases creating an experience where you communicate with them offline so there are different modes and medias to get back in front of them and get them back on track. You can even contact them through mobile marketing. In fact, SMS is equally important in the mix of mediums you can use. To get people back on track, you have to prepare. They might need to buy but just aren't in the right place yet or at the right time to make the purchase. By adding different mediums into the follow-up, you give them a chance to purchase in whichever channel works best for them.

Maybe they're just not ready to buy yet. Not everyone who wants to buy is ready when you want them to be. They will only buy from you when *they* are ready. So what we need to do is to be able to stay in front of them on a regular basis by sending further valuable information that nurtures the relationship to the point when they will be ready.

Many studies have shown that it can take seven or more touches before a prospect is ready to buy. We need to create a long-term lecture campaign. This can be a series of 52 emails for a whole year that can go out to those leads to keep ourselves repeatedly in front of them. We mail to both unconverted leads and customers who haven't engaged with our splinter offer to get them back to us. This helps re-engage leads and customers and to get them back on track.

If someone is just starting out, 52 weeks of nurture emails can seem incredibly overwhelming. Could you share advice for someone who's just starting in this journey? Where would be that 80/20 rule—the 80 percent of results from 20 percent of the labor that they should start with?

Billson: Great question. First, have ready a short series of emails, probably three for each step of the process to be able to drive people to where you want them. This is what we call the short-term nurture process. It's really just educating people over the first 28 days. Compose emails you know are going to educate them.

The simplest way is to put together some recent case studies or testimonials into one email. I suggest creating one email for testimonials and case studies and one email for frequently asked questions. Perhaps use another email to give them an overview of the offer you are trying to provide to them. You can give an additional bonus for those people who act within a certain period of time and then a countdown series of emails—maybe three—saying, "Hey, in five days this offer is going to expire," "In three days . . ." and, "The offer expires today."

Just by having those emails scheduled in this way, you will overcome objections, challenges, and any concerns the prospect might have had when first coming to you. It's really just a case of mapping out those concerns and slotting them into a series of email communications without needing to create a whole year's worth of content at once.

Unless you're willing to build out some of this, there's not much point in doing the funnel. In essence, you're wasting all that traffic if you don't do something to nurture prospects into a later sale.

Billson: Exactly. Actually one of the most fundamental parts of the funnel you'll create is a longer-term plan for communicating with the lead. That's what builds real value for them, and your continual engagement brings them back when they are ready to take action. The real key is to make sure there's a choreographed set of contingencies to get people back on track.

What are some of your favorite tools that you suggest to others when they are building their funnel?

Billson: There is a whole heap of tools out there. They don't necessarily cater to different types of business but rather for different budgets.

I think what's important is not to get bogged down on tools or platform delivery. Building out the right offer, establishing your message, and knowing your target market—along with creating a long-tail nurture campaign—is most important. Start with strategy first. The tools can come second.

First you need an email system. You can start basic with MailChimp or AWeber, or go for a more sophisticated system like Infusionsoft or Active Campaign. For all of these, you can set up a predetermined set of messages so your target market goes through your entire campaign.

You also need to be able to take payments. This is where a lot of people get bogged down. But you don't need to be. If you have Infusionsoft, you can quickly turn on their payment feature and open up a Merchant Services account. If you don't, you can use Stripe and still take credit cards right away.

The third thing you need is a way to capture leads. On the basic side, I suggest Leadpages. It is simple and optimized to get leads. On the more sophisticated side, ClickFunnels works great because you can customize all of your pages and campaigns. Again, this is a very effective tool for bringing people through your marketing funnel.

For your website, WordPress is the way to go. Use a prebuilt theme and customize your content.

Would you mind sharing one more tool? What do you suggest for lead collection?

Billson: There are a lot of different lead, survey, and quiz programs out there and many are hosted solutions. I prefer to build my own. What works easily is something called Gravity Forms. It's a plug-in for WordPress, which allows you to integrate and link with most email autoresponders.

How can readers connect with you and find out more about the services you offer?

Billson: Visit www.OliverBillson.com for ungated, free, valuable content on the blog, where you'll find lots more about marketing and sales funnels and how you can implement them in your business to achieve success.

And they'll see firsthand how sales funnels work by following along on your site!

Billson: Precisely!

To connect with Billson or read more about your marketing campaign path to purchase, visit www.OliverBillson.com.

#INSTAGRAMFORBUSINESS POSTABLES

- Allow your marketing tactics to develop your leads. #InstagramforBusiness
- By focusing your marketing on lead generation, you can target the best customer, at the best time, for the best results. #InstagramforBusiness
- The most successful entrepreneurs and salespeople focus their energy on their best prospects who have the greatest potential for a high return on their time and energy. #InstagramforBusiness
- "Always do your best. What you plant now, you will harvest later."—Og Mandino #InstagramforBusiness
- People prefer to buy from those they know, like, and trust. #InstagramforBusiness

Resource spotlight: Visit www.UGIGbook.com to download your Instagram sales funnel template.

Chapter 7

Building Trust with Your Instagram Tribe

Pink. Orange. Yellow. All blending into each other with fiery tones and tenacity.

The sunsets are amazing. Stunning, really. I remember the first time I saw one, I was dumbfounded for a moment.

The view from my husband's family's cabin on the U.S. side of Lake Ontario is magnificent to any of us lucky enough to visit there. The somewhat rustic structure that is his cabin isn't what's valuable, though. It is the place where it is located. If his family had built the same cabin on rented land, then the generations who have come to enjoy this place might never have had the chance.

Long ago the landlord would have called in their property to sell it for millions, uprooting the life and moments built there.

Never. The land must be owned, cherished, and cared for. For many generations to come. (You can almost see an American flag rising in the background, can't you? Funny, because one time my cousin-in-law painted one on the cabin's roof, but that's a story for another day.)

The concept of building on rented land is one that too many companies forget when it comes to building their business. If you are reliant on Google traffic, Facebook ads, your Instagram audience, or any one media channel to reach your audience, then you are playing a daily game of Russian roulette.

If you aren't diversifying your traffic sources and capturing contact information quickly, you are risking losing your business every single day. At any moment the social media channel may shut down, may kick you off, or may change format. If you rely on one traffic source, at any one moment your whole business could be demolished.

When speaking of the one-source traffic issue, Dan Kennedy says it best, "One is the loneliest number." (Yes, Three Dog Night said it first, but Dan made it about marketing, which is my jam.)

First, resolve to use more than just one media source for traffic. Just using Google AdWords? Expand to Facebook ads, guest blogging, networking, and/or public speaking, for example. Make sure there is more than one way for you to acquire new customers so if any of them disappear tomorrow, you haven't disappeared as well.

Second, quickly obtain your prospects' contact information and move the conversation outside of your lead source. Once you know who they are and how to reach them (mailing address, email address, and/or phone) you own the contact, you no longer have to pay to access them, and you aren't at risk each time your lead source changes.

Third, use more than one media source for communication. Don't rely on just Instagram posts, emails, or a monthly newsletter. Effective marketing is multichanneled for saturation of your market and protects you if there is ever a drastic change to your marketing platform (such as being locked out of your email provider; it can happen easier than you think).

You have the link in your bio as step one, but where should it go?

Reinforcing what Billson shared at the end of Chapter 6, the next step after your Instagram page is to give value to your prospects through ungated content. Send your audience to an article that is useful. Share a piece of content that is relevant and congruent with what you will be selling down the line.

One of our private clients, sales coach Stephanie Chung, blogs about selling when you aren't the cheapest option. Her blog posts alone have resulted in high-end clients from around the world and even a column in *Inc.* Sharing relevant content with your audience is a profitable way to grow your business.

BLOGGING TO CONVERT INSTAGRAM FOLLOWERS TO CUSTOMERS

If you don't yet have a blog, make sure to create this asset immediately. It doesn't have to be complicated. In fact, I put together a ten-minute blog plan below so you can get started fast. No excuses.

No longer do you need to get on Oprah to get your message out. No longer do you need to get a spot on *The Today Show* or win a big award to dominate your market.

Now, you can reach people around your neighborhood, country, and world with your messaging. You can take them seamlessly from Instagram to your blog and effectively build a tribe of loyal followers.

Stephanie Chung shared with me what has organically come to her because of her blog. "A company recently hired me to do a few coaching sessions for their U.S. sales team due to the blog [post] that you had written for me ["How to Close More Sales Even When You're Not the Cheapest"]. That same [post] also caused a gentleman from Slovenia to reach out to me to inquire about my training services. Slovenia! *Wha, wha??*

I only share this story because I know how committed you are to results, so I wanted to make you aware of the "results" my blog has produced. Bravo!"

With a blog, you are able to position *yourself* as the authority and expert in your market. This allows you to increase the attraction to your perfect prospect, decrease the time needed to close a sale, and increase the amount of money you receive from each customer.

According to HubSpot's "The Science of Blogging," over 409 million people view more than 22.2 billion pages each month. In fact, 46 percent of people read blogs more than once a day.

As I wrote in the Introduction, over the past six years, my business went from bankrupt to booming and one of the biggest factors was writing my weekly blog posts. Without fail, I post at least once each week. Not only has it helped build our email list, I receive client inquiries each month and comments and messages reinforcing the power of this medium.

Ready to Begin Your Blog?

Here's how to get started quickly:

1. Open up a Leadpages account. While you will eventually want to build out a full site, gives you the chance to get started in a matter of minutes so you can post right away. Use this special link and receive a lot of special bonuses, including a free giveaway you can use to build up your email list: https://my.leadpages.net/wl/elite-bonuses/
2. Choose "Use Template" and choose the "Native Ad Landing Page" from Charles Kirkland.
3. Now it's time to update the page.
   a. Change the "Your Logo" to your logo if you have one. If not, you can hide that spot.
   b. In the upper-right-hand corner, describe who your blog is for.
   c. Change the title to the name of your first article.

d. Change the date to today's date.

e. Write your article or post in the space where there is text.

f. For the image, I love using Word Swag. It is a $4 app for your iPhone or Android and is full of stock photos for no extra charge. Make one with your title on it, again to make the page look even more professional (see Figure 7–1).

FIGURE 7–1. Here's an Example of a Post Created Using Word Swag.

g. Add a link at the bottom for where to go next. If you have a Contact Us page or giveaway to get opt-ins, that works great. If not, you can simply send them to your Facebook page or LinkedIn profile. Just make sure you always give them a place to go next because if they get all the way to the bottom, that means they are interested, and you want to be sure to leverage that. See Figure 7–2, page 125.

h. Then save, and publish.

i. When you do, you will get a URL (see Figure 7–3, page 125). This is where your blog post now lives.

You can share the link with friends and family to start gathering readers, or you can even publish right to Facebook using the Facebook button—a fantastic option if you are just starting out. Eventually, if you open a WordPress site, you can repost this article to that page. See Figure 7–4, page 126, for a completed Leadpages project.

Use an assistant to contact the prospect on your behalf and schedule. (People in demand are busy!)
Two options for those on a budget:
1. Fancy Hands: For as little as $29/month, you'll have an assistant who can schedule your meetings.
2. Virtual Staff Finder: You contract them to find you a support person in the Philippines who can work as little or as much as you like. With this service, you can get 10+ hours of service a week for less than $100.
In our next post, I will review what the scripting and marketing plan should be before the sales call takes place.
Connect with Me on Facebook

FIGURE 7-2. Here's a Post with a Link to Facebook.

How would you like to publish this page?
Leadpages
WordPress
Facebook
Your own server
Share Page Configuration
I want to use Leadpages to immediately obtain a URL for this page
https://locreative.leadpages.co/five-ways-to-close-your-next-sale/
View Page
Activate Leadpage Redirect
DONE

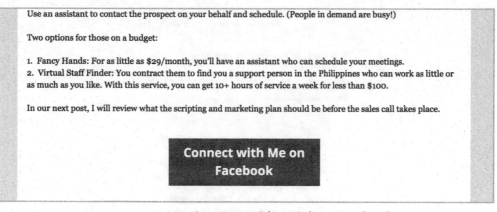

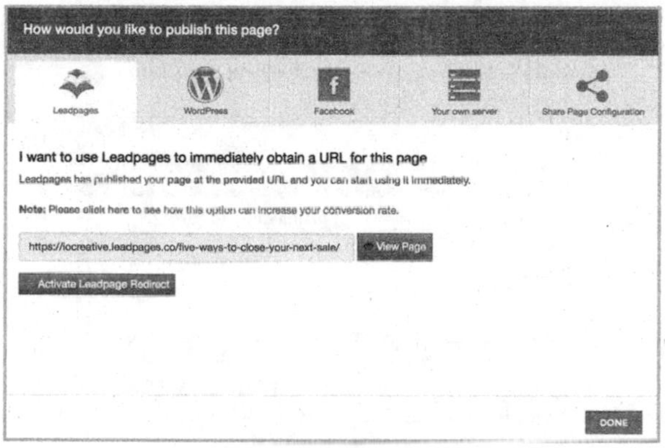

FIGURE 7-3. Once You Get a URL Similar to This One, You Can Begin Using It Right Away.

What to Write About

Not sure how to structure your blog? Here's my formula for successful blog writing:

Establish the Problem. In this step you need to establish the problem your target market has. This is where you want to reference those pain points so your reader understands that your article pertains specifically to them and solves their problems.

Teaser. This step is crucial and one that most people miss when they are writing their blog post. Here you want to hint at "the better way." This is where you give a hint at the problem's solution but not give it away.

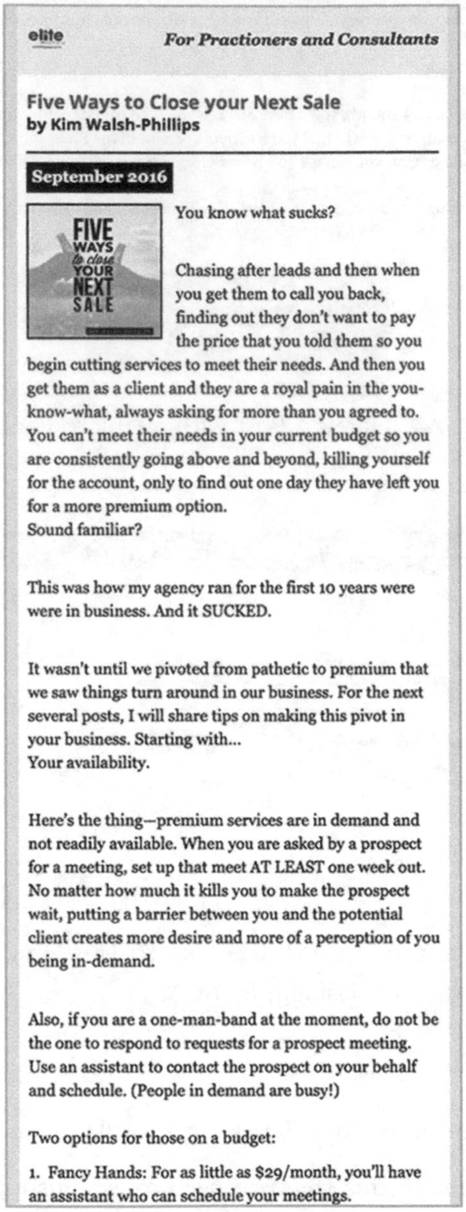

elite For Practioners and Consultants

Five Ways to Close your Next Sale
by Kim Walsh-Phillips

September 2016

FIVE WAYS to close YOUR NEXT SALE

You know what sucks?

Chasing after leads and then when you get them to call you back, finding out they don't want to pay the price that you told them so you begin cutting services to meet their needs. And then you get them as a client and they are a royal pain in the you-know-what, always asking for more than you agreed to. You can't meet their needs in your current budget so you are consistently going above and beyond, killing yourself for the account, only to find out one day they have left you for a more premium option.
Sound familiar?

This was how my agency ran for the first 10 years were were in business. And it SUCKED.

It wasn't until we pivoted from pathetic to premium that we saw things turn around in our business. For the next several posts, I will share tips on making this pivot in your business. Starting with...
Your availability.

Here's the thing—premium services are in demand and not readily available. When you are asked by a prospect for a meeting, set up that meet AT LEAST one week out. No matter how much it kills you to make the prospect wait, putting a barrier between you and the potential client creates more desire and more of a perception of you being in-demand.

Also, if you are a one-man-band at the moment, do not be the one to respond to requests for a prospect meeting. Use an assistant to contact the prospect on your behalf and schedule. (People in demand are busy!)

Two options for those on a budget:

1. Fancy Hands: For as little as $29/month, you'll have an assistant who can schedule your meetings.

FIGURE 7–4. This Is an Example of a Piece Completed with Leadpages.

Reveal the Solution and Why They Should Care. After you have given a teaser of how to solve the problem, you want to lay out the solution and why they should care.

Social Proof/Case Study Story. This is another one of those components that most people leave out of their posts, but it's one of the most important to include because it's where you build credibility and position yourself (or the author) as an expert. This is where you want to include an example, story, or case study you're involved in. This builds trust because it's social proof.

Call to Action. This is the most important part of the whole shebang! At the end of your post, you want to give the reader a call to action. This is where you tell them exactly what to do. This should relate to the overall sales goal you listed. For example, if your overall sales goal is to have someone claim membership, at the end of the post you should prompt them to claim their membership (see Figure 7–5).

FIGURE 7–5. Offering Value-Driven Content.

On average, your prospects see 3,000 messages a day. Cutting through that clutter can be tough, especially when your prospects are prone not to believe you. Research shows that only 14 percent of your audience believes the messaging you put out. In good news, however, is 78 percent believes anonymous peer reviews. (Think Hotwire user reviews on a hotel's website.) And in even better news, you can use this statistic to your advantage.

One of the best pieces of content you can put out is content about your clients. I don't mean sappy testimonials that just tout how awesome-sauce you are (you and I both know this is true, but your audience doesn't believe it). Instead, post editorial-style Q&As with your clients and then showcase these in:

1. *Your printed newsletter each month* (see Figure 7–6).

FIGURE 7–6. We Publish an Interview with One of Our Marketing Insiders Elite Members Each Month in Our Newsletter.

2. *Facebook Live Video.* Talk-show style, interview some of your best clients in quick segments on Facebook (see Figure 7–7).

FIGURE 7–7. Whenever We Are at a Trade Show and One of My Clients Is There, We Pull Them in for a Facebook Live Video.

3. *A social media post* (see Figure 7–8).

FIGURE 7–8. Highlight Partnerships with Your Clients in Posts That Celebrate Their Success.

4. *A premium opt-in giveaway.* Feature your success in your content giveaways (see Figure 7–9).

FIGURE 7–9. One of Our Best Lead Magnets, "7 Winning Facebook Ad Templates," Is a Showcase of Our Successful Client Campaign Work.

5. *Last step—get started!* You have all the tools you need, so set a timer for ten minutes, and write your first blog post!

Please don't skip this step, OK? When you have launched your blog, Tweet, Instagram, or Facebook a link to your post and hashtag it #InstagramforBusiness. I will re-share your link with my audience and enter you to win one of over 100 prizes we will give out to readers. So get writing and posting—I'll be watching for your blog and rooting you along. You've got this!

In the next chapter, discover how to take all of that traffic and your opt-ins and drive them to successful email campaigns.

THE DOS AND DON'TS OF EMAILING YOUR LIST

Cheap, quick, trackable, and easily measured: These are just a few of the reasons why email is the number-one marketing channel for most businesses. When it comes to making your Instagram marketing turn a profit, becoming more effective at email marketing is what lies between you and success.

The reality is you cannot copy what other people are doing. Not ever, because most of them are doing it wrong. And a duplicate of something that isn't working isn't going to magically start providing success.

Instead, apply effective direct-response marketing tactics to your email strategies to realize the highest ROI possible.

Effective email marketing starts with getting the voice, tone, and topic on-point. If you miss the mark there, you ruin your chances of turning your prospect into a customer for life. I like to start the process of creating an email campaign by thinking of my personal relationships. (Don't worry, this isn't another crazy dating story.)

I am blessed to have a few best friends for whom I would totally jump in the car for at any time of day or night with whatever supplies they asked me to bring, even if it included rubber gloves and a garbage bag, and would not ask any questions but would be sure to bring wine with me.

One of these friends is my girl Brittney. She and I were first introduced by someone else one night in Palm Beach, Florida. (This is when I actually used to go out past 7 P.M. and frequented places that don't give out paper menus and crayons.) When we were first introduced we didn't take a warm shine to one another. We totally didn't click.

But then after running into each other a few times and having more conversations—letting each other into our lives, seeing that we were on the same page for most things (except football—she follows it, I only watch it for the commercials), we became friends. We became closer over the months that followed, so much so that later that year when I met Ian and he went from a date to fiancé, I asked Brittney to be one of my bridesmaids. She is now an auntie to my girls and one of my dearest friends. We both know where the bodies are buried and nothing—no matter how gorgeous or delicious the bribes may be—will ever get us to uncover them.

Our friendship is probably very similar to yours in that the more we shared with each other and the more value we gave to one another, the more our relationship grew.

The same is true of the members of your tribe. Giving them value and opening yourself up to them over time will help you build a strong relationship of trust. It is through building this trustful relationship that you can move to the next step of making the sale.

So when you begin to create your email content, I want you to think of one of your best friends. If they had a need you could help them solve, how would you do it? What would you tell him or her? What might they ask that you could answer?

Begin to write your content as if you are helping that best friend with a problem. The draft should make sense if you sent it directly to him or her instead of to your entire list. Write with genuine authenticity and your messaging and its sincerity will come through to resonate with your target market.

Start by simply following these steps:

1. If (insert friend's name) has a need for (my product, program, or service), what questions would she ask me? How I would I answer them? Make a two-column list, one column for questions and the other for answers, of ten such questions.
2. Flesh out each of your answers into emails.

3. Pull out quotes from your blog posts and turn them into Instagram posts.

4. Use www. to have someone create the images for you, or use the Word Swag app to create them yourself.

Now you are ready to put out authentic and valuable content that is congruent from your Instagram account to email. You have authentic, engaging, and meaningful content for your target market to begin to nurture them and build trust. I even bet you will find this process easy because when you can just be yourself, help out with the thing you know well, and have a sense of purpose, things are just easier.

That being said, there are a few additional things to keep in mind when it comes to your email.

Personalize

The more personal your email can appear, the more effective you will be. Use personalization tactics, such as including the person's name in the subject line and a couple of times in the email. You can also mention the name of their town or company or spouse. Depending on the customer database and the email marketing program you use, personalizing an email is as simple as putting a few merge fields in before you send it out.

Recently I received an email from DigitalMarketer that was so clever (see Figure 7–10).

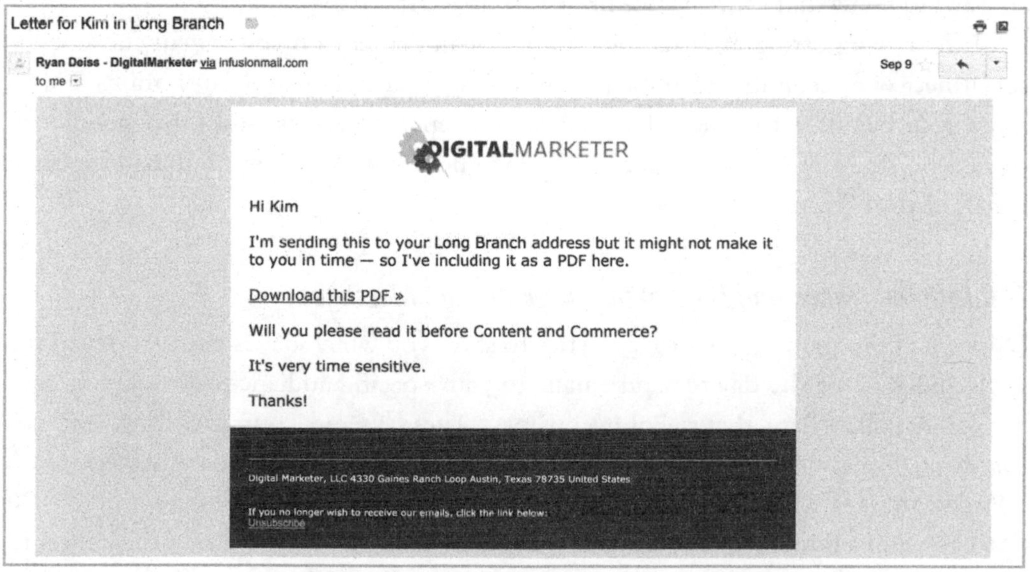

FIGURE 7–10. An Email from DigitalMarketer.

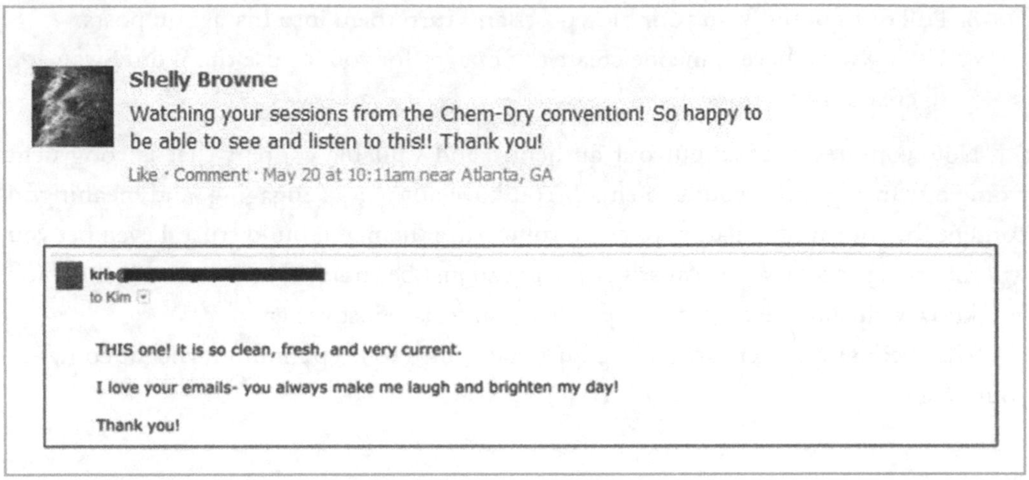

Shelly Browne
Watching your sessions from the Chem-Dry convention! So happy to be able to see and listen to this!! Thank you!
Like · Comment · May 20 at 10:11am near Atlanta, GA

kris[   ]
to Kim ⊡

THIS one! it is so clean, fresh, and very current.

I love your emails- you always make me laugh and brighten my day!

Thank you!

FIGURE 7–11. This Is a Screen Shot of a Subscriber's Complimentary Post that I Incorporated into an Email.

Check out how they personalized the subject line and the message. I mean, they probably should have had Ryan Deiss's name in the email, too, as a signature, but the short and sweet nature of this email and the personal touches certainly got my attention.

Are you getting complimentary posts from your subscribers? Snag screenshots of what they are saying and sprinkle them throughout your emails as social proof of the good work you do (see Figure 7–11). Nobody wants to be the first to work with you. They all want to know that other people like them have chosen to do so.

Incentivize posting and sharing of your email content on your email subscribers' social network accounts. Encourage them to use a hashtag or certain phrases and to share your emails with others. I give away free reports, ebooks, and other goodies to those who share emails, and you can do the same to create a team of ambassadors on behalf of your business.

Test Different Times and Days of the Week to Send Messages

Most email programs come with analytics to show you which day is the best day of the week and time of the day to send emails to your specific audience. Once you've sent enough to collect data, that is. For my business, Tuesdays and Thursdays work best, but that isn't always true even. *(Confusing?!)* One of my best-performing emails was sent on a Friday at 5 P.M. There is a data point going around that the best time to send is 4:30 A.M. CST, and a fast-track to deletion is from 1 to 2 P.M. CST. The truth of the matter is, there is no absolute. Check out your own numbers and go with what works best for you.

Formatting Hacks

We have tested this a bunch and a bunch more. The best performing emails are ones with images to a video with a play button on it. Second best are text-only emails. Also, a letter format versus a designed newsletter tends to do better. Really, anything that seems more personal generally outperforms a super fancy-schmancy corporate-looking newsletter.

Subject Lines

I think an entire book could be written about subject lines. There is incredibly fascinating psychology behind why some words move us to open an email and others don't. A few subject line ideas:

- *Numbers.* Try using unusual numbers, which seem more specific and come across as more authentic. For example, 743 pairs of shoes are better than 1.
  - 8,213 vs. 8,000
  - $3,218 for my first customer
  - How I paid 17 cents for my new car

- *Question marks.* Test ending your subject line in a question mark. Good idea? Yes, yes, it is. Curiosity and intrigue entice your reader to click open the email. In addition, it interrupts the pattern of other emails that aren't ending their subject lines with punctuation.
  - Black or blue?
  - Will this work?
  - Did you get your investor's funding kit yet?
  - Seriously?

- *Percentages.* Percentages versus absolutes help to make a fact more believable, 95 percent of the time. (Get what I just did there?!) Test putting a percent into your subject line.
  - Only 14 percent of your readers believe you.
  - 99 percent of people dieting need to do this.
  - 87 percent of business owners are doing this wrong.

- Video. Include a video image in your email and allow the reader to know that it awaits them inside your email. Placing "[VIDEO]" in your subject line is a great way to add interest and a visual interrupt to other emails on the page. Let's face it, we're all a bit lazy and most would rather watch a video than read a book. Even a book as awesome-sauce as this one.

- 7 Blog Ideas [Video]
- A 10-Minute Ab Workout That Is Actually Fun [New Video]

■ *Incentive.* Let your audience know something amazing is waiting inside the email for them. Drive their click by enticing them with value. (This is why I always get sucked into buying the foundation AND the eyeliner at the beauty counter. I covet the free lipstick. Never mind that I just spent $300. The free part and gift situation are what drive me forward.)
- 7 Deadly SEO Mistakes (Free Report)
- Facebook Live Video Template (Free Template)

■ *RE.* Use the Re: when you are following up with someone. This one is super successful, but should only be used sparingly or else your audience will catch on. (Kind of like my threats to my children that I will tell Santa not to come. Kind of.) This does tend to increase conversions when you send it, so pick your best time and fire away!

■ *Personal Pronouns.* As I shared above, the more personal you can make it, the better. Using "You," "Your," etc., creates a unique sense of speaking directly to the reader.
- Why YOU need to update your profile
- The mistake you are probably making with your budget
- Did you know this?

■ *Confusing, shocking, or just plain weird subject lines.* It is why the *Enquirer* or the even weirder *World News* still exist. I get some of my weird titles from. Current titles on this page include:
- The Perfect Hoodie for Anyone Who Just Can't Bear to Leave Their Cat
- Man Bitten on Penis by Spider for the Second Time This Year
- Woman Pays Through the Nose to Punch Martin Shkreli in Face
- Steve the Cat Has Achieved His Lifelong Goal of Becoming an Honorary Lamb
- This Piano-Playing Chicken Will Knock You Over with a Feather

■ *When all else fails, go negative.* This is why when there is a car crash on the highway, everyone slows down. We can't help but stare at the tragedy. This is not a statement on us as a population or culture. Just a reality of who we are.
- Things are bad—(maybe)
- Don't take it personally but—
- I hate technology
- I'm sorry

■ *Borrow credibility from another source.* Utilize something other people might know in your email subject line.
- What Mark Zuckerberg Knows
- The McDonald's Way
- Steve Jobs WAS WRONG and You WERE RIGHT

■ *Celebrities are killer for open rates.* My best-performing email open rate of all time came from, "What Oprah got wrong and Ashton Kutcher got right." My second best was, "How Obama did it." We as a population cannot get enough of celebrity pop culture. Use it to your advantage.
- Be the Taylor Swift of Your Newsfeed
- What Justin Bieber Just Bought
- Kristen Bell Wants to Partner with YOU

In the next chapter, we will dive into how to get our audience to the next step of the customer lifecycle—one I have lovingly come to know as my favorite—the sale.

#INSTAGRAMFORBUSINESS POSTABLES

■ Make sure there is more than one way for you to acquire new customers—so if any of them disappear tomorrow, you haven't disappeared as well. #InstagramforBusiness

■ With a blog, you are able to position yourself as the authority and expert in your market. #InstagramforBusiness

■ Formula for effective blog posts: Establish the problem, tease that there is a better way, reveal the solution and why they should care about it, offer a social proof/case study, and finish with a call to action. #InstagramforBusiness

■ Research shows that only 14 percent of your audience believes the messaging you put out. The good news, however, is that 78 percent believe anonymous peer reviews. #InstagramforBusiness

■ Begin to write your content as if you are helping your best friend with a problem. #InstagramforBusiness

Resource spotlight: Visit www.UGIGBook.com to see a training video with Dave Dee, sales and marketing legend, about the three headlines you need to use to get more opens, click-throughs, and sales from your marketing.

Chapter 8

Cha Ching!
Driving Sales from Your Instagram Page

I have a little secret. It is one that took me a while to figure out so I want to share it with you now in the hope that you will get this all nailed down quicker.

But first, let me tell you a little story.

I was doing a speaking gig somewhere about six years ago for a national association in Florida. I can still smell the room. There was only one motel in town, so I was stuck even though it smelled horrible, had obviously seen its fair share of illegal activity, and I was pretty sure my identity was about to be stolen by the front desk clerk who scanned my driver's license and credit card.

I knew I could never put myself through this ridiculous torture again. Something *had to change*.

Since I couldn't sleep for fear of my surroundings, I spent the night writing a blog post inspired by a recent reading about pricing yourself higher in your marketplace. My firm had begun to do that the prior year, but I still had older clients riding along with their old rates. That was because I was scared of what would happen if I raised them.

The problem was that we were spending so much time servicing those old accounts, we weren't able to focus on growing new ones. To supplement our income, I did speaking engagements like the one that took me to this "end of the world" night. (It was the only hotel I have ever stayed in where I wouldn't take my shoes off or use the shower. I still shudder just thinking about it.)

OK, so you've got the picture—shoes on, sitting on the bed, exhausted and scared, ready to send out a blog post about why my firm charges more than others, and giving an incentive to my list to book a prospect call with me that week so I could bring in some real money from doing work I loved, from my office, so I wouldn't have to travel to scary hotels anymore.

Just as I was about to hit send, I stopped.

I thought of a certain woman in my town who always talked badly of me when I positioned myself as an expert in my industry. She didn't take kindly to my premium pricing or elevated brand, and she was known to start trash talking the moment she saw me marketing.

Do you have that one person in mind who you think of that sometimes holds you back? Maybe it's a parent? A boss? A co-worker? Maybe it is that unqualified guidance counselor who said you wouldn't amount to anything. For me, it was someone I had volunteered alongside on a few boards. Someone who held some political clout in the small town where I lived at the time. True, it was just small-town clout, but to me, at that moment, it felt huge.

So there I was sitting on this gross bed in this gross hotel— and I was allowing the fear of a woman who was hundreds of miles away to stop me from improving my life. That's when it hit me.

What am I doing?

That woman wasn't going to get me out of this hotel. She wasn't going to pay my bills. She wasn't going to ensure my kids could experience a life without fear of lack. She wouldn't do one single thing to make my or my family's life family better. Only I could do that. And only I could share the message with the world that I was born to share (with God's help, of course). I couldn't let that woman stop me from taking action, because doing nothing wasn't going to get me anywhere.

That was when a verse came to mind: "He that began a good work in you will continue to perform it until it's complete" (adapted from Philippians 1:6).

God certainly didn't plan to keep me in that motel forever. So I hit send.

And you know what?

My firm got more prospect requests that week than ever before. And those folks were all coming to us knowing in advance that we charged premium pricing. And they were ready to pay it. We were able to work with those businesses and help them get their word out to those who needed to hear it.

HOW TO DRIVE PROSPECTS FROM INSTAGRAM FOLLOWERS TO CUSTOMERS FOR LIFE

So what I wanted to whisper to you at the beginning of this chapter?

You and I were created with a purpose. The fear of what others will think is just a roadblock to our final destination. We were created with majestic intentions, not mediocrity.

If you don't take action, no one will be blessed by what you were created to do. The product, program, or service that you offer will help those who need it so much, you have a divine obligation to put yourself out there so your audience can be reached. One way to make this happen? Start selling. Don't gloss over this chapter and focus solely on follower growth through your Instagram account. You have to get to a stage of selling so you can truly fulfill your purpose and, of course, receive an ROI from your Instagram marketing.

Here's the thing though: In order to sell, you have to do something most won't.

You have to be different.

You have to stop looking, sounding, and appearing the same as everyone else.

You are different after all, so stop appearing just as your competitors do.

Maybe you don't think you do. Most of our private clients don't realize it. When asked about their competitors, almost every new client answers the question, "We don't really have any."

Unfortunately, your prospects won't see it that way. If your marketing isn't showing up any differently, chances are you appear just like everyone else. That makes you a commodity. And commodities only compete on price. (Just ask Walmart how that's going for them. "Being the cheapest sometimes on most of the days" is not a great distinction. I'm in Target twice a week, but I refuse to step into Walmart after way too many bad experiences.)

What makes you different from your competitors? And how can you leverage that in your marketing so that you can excel at sales?

Offer Value in Your Instagram Bio

Tell your prospective qualified audience why they should like your page and how it will benefit them (see Figure 8–1, page 142). You can even offer a lead magnet to give them a quick win in their relationship with you (note the link in the bio in Figure 8–2, page 142). Make sure they know right up front what's in it for them if they decide to follow your page.

Fill Your Posts with Value

Focus on your unique selling proposition—that one big idea that makes you different— and post valuable content around that one thing. For me, it is that we connect marketing

FIGURE 8–1. This Bio Tells You Exactly What the Company's Page Is About.

FIGURE 8–2. Another Bio that Tells You Exactly What You Need to Know About the Company Up Front.

with sales, because you have value and deserve to be paid for it, and you have a unique purpose that should be shared with the world. All of my posts are in line with this big idea (see Figure 8–3).

FIGURE 8–3. Focus on Your Unique Selling Proposition When Posting.

Make Your Posts and Ads About Your Target Audience, Not You

Focus on their needs and how you can uniquely meet them. Most brands are focused on their products and services. Stand out by focusing on your target market instead (see Figure 8–4).

FIGURE 8–4. Focus Your Posts on Your Target Audience

Talk to Them

Ask questions and have a conversation around your one big idea. Engage with folks and build trust to let them know you are looking for relationships. Not sales. When you ask questions, they are much more likely to engage. Here's an example in Figure 8–5 on page 144.

Be Willing to Be Controversial

The most successful brands have raving fans as well as big detractors. Your goal through your posts is to attract exactly your perfect prospect and repel everyone else.

Be Authentic

One of my pastor's sermons focused on the masks we wear in different aspects of our lives. Wearing a mask is exhausting. It also creates a barrier to developing real relationships. Take the mask off. Stop trying to be someone else and instead be real with your audience. Different is good. Different stands out. People relate more to those they

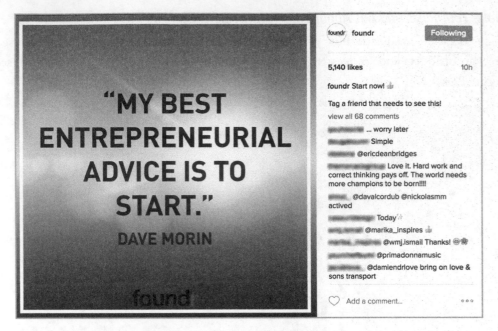

FIGURE 8–5. Keep Your Posts Focused on Things That Matter to Your Audience.

believe are being real. Occasionally let your fans in a little on your life, your family, and who you are as a real person (see Figure 8–6). People want to do business with people they know, like, and trust.

FIGURE 8–6. Occasionally Let Your Fans See into Your Life So They Feel Like They Know You.

Focus on Transformation, Not Information

This is the most important point to remember. Your competitors focus on their product and service features. If they are slightly more advanced, they also focus on their benefits. But you are better than that. You are advanced and will focus on how those benefits will impact their lives. How working with you will be the exact thing they were looking for to bring them peace, take away a pain, or bring them joy. This will not only help you make the sale, it will also position you as the leading authority in your marketplace. The transition from Instagram follower to customer for life can be seamless and fast. Simply focus on why they should pay attention and take action, and why it is the best decision they will ever make. (See the interview with Dave Dee on page 150 for more on transformative value.)

Are you ready to make the sale? In the next section we will dive into the different types of sales funnels to run and how to make it work for your Instagram marketing.

CHOICES AND MORE CHOICES: SALES CAMPAIGN IDEAS YOU CAN USE

"I go onto Instagram to read more about products, programs, and services."

Said no one. Ever.

A harsh truth—no one cares about your product, program, or service. No one.

What they care about is how what you have to offer will make their lives better. For most, the outcome should have something to do with saving time, saving money, or eliminating a pain or frustration your prospects are currently experiencing. What they don't want is more information.

So (warning, controversial statement here), I recommend that you forget "Blueprints and Checklists" as your lead magnets. When it comes to social media marketing, I have found the greatest success is in focusing on buyers instead of leads, skipping over giving them information, and instead offering them a low-cost tool for sale.

Because a buyer beats a lead or a "like" every time.

Selling something upfront allows you to:

- Obtain real contact information, because when someone enters their credit card information, they have to give you their correct phone number and will likely give you the proper email address so they can get the thing they just bought.
- Get more information than you could normally. When entering a credit card, your buyer will give you their mailing address, even if the item is just $1. If it was just a free digital download, there would be no reason to give that to you.
- You now have a buyer instead of a lead, developing a stronger relationship from the start.

- Your sales team will have higher-quality leads to follow up with as they come in, and something to talk about—the item they just purchased.
- You are filling your email list with more qualified leads, which increases email open rates and overall deliverability rating from Yahoo! and Gmail.

Here are some examples.

Brick-and-Mortar: Music Matters

Music Matters School of Music is located in Batavia, Illinois, and run by Jeff Matter. They were looking for a new way to get students onto their mailing list and signed up for classes.

Instead of running a "12 Ways to Pick Your Music School" cheesy report, we went right for those serious about coming in. We ran a coupon that required someone to enter their contact information in order to claim it.

We decided on an offer of 47 percent off your child's first month of lessons and, of course, ran the ads with adorable pictures of kids playing instruments that would make any mom swoon.

The Results

- Offer length: about 30 days
- Offers claimed: 41 (this does not include the folks who saw the offer and called the school instead of filling out the form)
- Cost per conversion: $18 to $25

Jeff Matter says, "Using the coupon offer instead of a free report, we achieved a significant increase in class inquiries and sign-ups. Through driving targeted traffic from an offer for classes, I can track each dollar spent on marketing and know the exact return it is giving me while staying true to my mission of spreading happiness and creating memories through music."

How to Apply This to Your Business

Is there a loss leader discount you can give up front to get people through your business door? Request contact information to redeem the offer, and follow up with those who don't respond on their own. Plan multichannel follow-ups including phone calls, email, and direct mail.

B2B: American Society of Tax Problem Solvers

Ever hear that social media marketing doesn't work for B2B businesses? That simply isn't true. We have multiple B2B client accounts successfully using social media to grow their businesses.

The American Society of Tax Problem Solvers targets accountants as their target market. Instead of offering "The Business Blueprint" or some other piece of information, we put together a tool that would appeal to their target. We developed a collection of five letter templates to use when contacting the IRS.

Results
- Total spend: $1600
- Buyers of their $1 offer: 298
- Cost per buyer: $5.29 each

How to Apply This to Your Business
Ignore those who say social media can't work for B2B. With their $1 sale, ASTPS acquired other businesses as *customers* for under $5.00 each. What template or tool can you provide your target market to collect leads while positioning yourself as the leading authority or expert for just five bucks?

Online Training: Ted Thomas
One of the best ways to build a list of buyers is to run a webinar. With a webinar, you are collecting the contact information for your lead, building trust, and ultimately making the sale during the training.

Ted Thomas had previously only sold through live and on-stage trainings. He wanted to scale his business with an evergreen webinar that would teach people the basics of buying tax liens as a real estate investment option. This allowed us to grow his email list while also bringing in revenue.

Results
- $614.21 spent
- 137 conversions
- $4.47 per conversion

How to Apply This to Your Business
Is there a topic you can share via a webinar to drive leads and sales automatically into your business? Could you leverage a webinar as a way to make sales automatically?

eCommerce: Stay Loyal Dog Food
A dog food manufacturer in Australia, Stay Loyal, sells its dog food via subscription. To increase sales, we created several funnels targeting different audiences. One of the campaigns offers a $1 sample of its dog food.

The top-performing image: Those interested in the topic are sent to a sales video and offered to purchase a $1 sample of the dog food.

Results
- $553.62 total spent
- 32 conversions
- Cost per new customer $17.30

How to Apply This to Your Business
Can you sample something from your business to get a buyer?

Marketing Agency

Our agency, Elite Digital Group, took information and flipped it on its head. We turned it into a tool. Our best-performing buyer funnel is a simple lead page and offers 35 ad templates and bonus training for $1 at https://elitedigitalgroup.com/adsbonus.

This allows us to add serious marketers and business owners to our customer base every day.

Results for a One-Week Period
- $428.69 spent
- 64 conversions
- Cost per buyer: $6.70

How to Apply This to Your Business
Ignore what the masses are doing and forget leads and likes. Focus on the best possible outcome from Instagram for your business: buyer acquisition.

Webinars

One of the most popular ways to move a prospect from Instagram to being a customer is through webinars. They are very common in online marketing funnels; companies get the lead first, then drive that lead to a webinar in order to make the sale. I've set up my webinars to be more like free trainings, and at the end, I offer our membership trial for $1 if they want the slides, recordings, and bonus resources from the workshop. Or we sell one of our other social media training programs from www.EliteDigitalGroup.com.

When I am running opt-in offers for a webinar or other promotion, I will change my bio link to the opt-in page and run posts promoting the event (see Figure 8–7, page 149). There's more on webinar and online sales in the interview with Dave Dee on page 150.

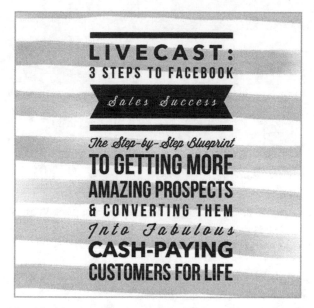

FIGURE 8–7. Use Your Instagram Posts to Promote an Upcoming Event, but Be Sure to Change the Bio Link to Drive to More Information.

Set up a marketing and sales funnel that first offers content and then remarkets to start a sales conversation. (See more on setting up your marketing and online sales funnel in my interview with Oliver Billson in Chapter 6.)

A Prize for Lead Generation

For many local businesses, we have run sweepstakes for lead generation and each person receives a prize of a gift certificate toward a product, program, or service (see Figure 8–8, page 150). It was a prize that would be fantastic to get and the perfect lead-generation tool for the business. For example, for a business selling a $10,000 product, a $500 certificate can be a great prize to the business's audience and fantastic lead generator. We have one client who gives away a day of handyman work to get contracting jobs. Think strategically about what your perfect prospects might want as a way to start the sales conversation.

Most Important, Start Selling!

In the next section, I dive into the number-one source of Instagram monetization—online sales events.

I don't know if that mean lady still talks trash about me. She very well may, but the thing is, I don't pay attention anymore. And you shouldn't listen to the trash any longer,

FIGURE 8–8. Offer a Prize Your Key Prospect Wants.

either. Start selling to those who need your products, programs, and services and fulfill the passion and purpose you were created for.

To help you along the way, check out my interview with the amazing Dave Dee, salesman extraordinaire, where you'll find strategies to take your sales to an unparalleled level.

HOW TO DRIVE MORE SALES IN ONE DAY THAN YOU DO ALL YEAR, WITH DAVE DEE, THE MONETIZATION MASTER

Dave Dee is the man who will "sell more of your products or services in a day than you now do all year." Previously, he was a struggling entertainer—a mentalist, to be precise. Then he discovered the power of sales and marketing, and his business skyrocketed from three shows a month to an average of 25 shows a month in less than 90 days.

Based on what he learned, and by incorporating techniques from his mentalism show, such as cold reading (the art of getting inside someone's mind) and hypnotic language patterns, he developed a bulletproof system for crafting webinars and online events that literally created buying frenzies.

Dave lives in Georgia with his wife Karen and their five children.

Tell us about your past, your celebrity, and all the amazing things that brought you to today.

Dee: I have a pretty diverse background. I always wanted to be a professional magician. That was my lifelong dream ever since I was three years old. After pursuing some jobs that didn't work, I finally got to pursue that dream. The problem was, I could only land about three shows a month, and I was deep in debt. I was about $80,000 in the hole.

My wife was working two jobs at the time when we found out she was pregnant. I had to figure something out fast. Fortunately, I went to a seminar and came across a marketing program. I never understood how marketing was the key to finding success. I thought I just needed to get really good at my craft. I thought to be successful I just had to work harder. Then I discovered it doesn't matter how good you are if no one knows about you.

I started implementing my new marketing skills in a big way. In less than 90 days, I went from doing three shows a month to averaging 30 shows a month. The very next month, I did 57 shows after tweaking my marketing further, and my life radically changed. In a year, I paid off all of my debts. I bought a new house. I bought a new car. And best of all, my wife quit both of her jobs.

From that success, I started speaking at events. Other business owners would ask me, "How did you do it?" Those were savvy business owners because they understood their business was not different. They understood that marketing is marketing is marketing.

So I started consulting and coaching other business owners, which then led me to teach them. I took my skills as an entertainer and marketer and brought them online. I believe in the power of selling online through live-streaming events for one important reason: They are one of the biggest breakthroughs for entrepreneurs and business owners that there is because we can sell to our prospects *en masse*. Without anyone ever having to leave their home, entrepreneurs can sell around the world.

I started doing online sales and really developed that skill. I mastered the system for selling online via webinar, webcast, and live-streaming events. The results are pretty spectacular, not just for me but for my clients and students. For example, we've done $272,000 in sales under three hours for a new client her first time. We've done $420,000 in one day. . . . one client . . . did $117,000 in just 57 minutes.

All of this took place online and all without ever needing to leave home. The beauty is that you can then put it on autopilot after doing it once live. At that point, you have a system for generating this kind of sales and paydays on demand and on a regular basis. I just love it.

I just recently interviewed the client who reached $420,000 in sales, and he was saying that it totally changed his life. It rebooted his business and self-esteem. It's such a thrill and an honor to work with entrepreneurs and business owners who get it, right? They see the vision—business is going online, marketing is moving online, and products are *selling* online.

And what's even better, we can sell more than one-on-one. We no longer need to send out sales people. We can sell *en masse* online, in addition to or in place of selling one-on-one.

That brings up a great point. Coming from a traffic source like Instagram, you only have one link, one option, and one place to send people. Or maybe you're running ads on the platform and you can send traffic to whatever landing page you like—why should I choose a webinar instead of funneling toward that one-on-one sales appointment?

Dee: Let's say you do have a one-on-one, and let's say that one-on-one is really your sales conversion mechanism. You're selling coaching or consulting, or you're a financial advisor or an attorney, maybe. You're probably not going to close that appointment through a webinar. However, what you will do is position yourself in the viewer's mind as an authority, celebrity, or an expert (the ACE formula).

By positioning yourself as an authority, celebrity, or expert, a number of things happen for you. That's why people will want to do business with you. They want to do business with the person they see as the authority, as the expert in the field, in the webinar, or live-streaming event. Whatever is online definitely positions you as that.

If you're perceived as the celebrity or expert, you will be more in demand, and it will separate you from your competition. But it also preframes the sale. When someone watches you on a webinar and then comes into your office, you are the expert, and they are predetermined to buy. They are presold. Even if it's on the phone or web consultation.

In a five-minute training, I'm probably not going to close an estate sale, but I can have someone watch my webinar in a nonthreatening environment and then when they come into my office they are much more likely to buy.

On the other hand for many other businesses, you can actually sell through webinars. Most of my clients sell right on the webinar in the live event. There are two differences. Most people think of webinars as just online events, but there are many ways they're even more powerful.

You can use your webinar as a lead generation magnet from Instagram. You can collect a prospect's contact information and then have them watch your webinar. Once you have made this an automated webinar, it can run 24 hours a day, 7 days a week. So your Instagram account becomes a 24/7 sales generation machine. This is how you use your webinar as what we call a lead generation magnet.

You are building your email list at the same time you are making sales!

Again, I'm not saying it replaces one-on-one sales. That is still very powerful. But, man! If I can sell to a hundred people or two hundred or five hundred people at the same time and not have to leave my house—and they don't have to leave their house—you remove all obstacles.

This is where we have headed. People aren't leaving their house. I mean, I get an Amazon Prime delivery every day, sometimes twice a day, right? I don't want to go to the store. You know where this is going. This can be applied to nearly every business.

What are some mistakes you see businesses make when it comes to online presentations?

Dee: There are three key elements. To run a successful event, I call it the online success event triangle. The first step is to get people to register for the event. That's really important. Whether they're coming from Instagram, Facebook, direct mail, or your own email list, you've got to have a way to make sure you're getting people to register. And, you've got to get people to show up for your event.

The second thing is creating your irresistible offer. What is your offer? Is it solving a major pain for them? Is it clear? Is it addressing something they want to solve? All of these things need to happen in order for our audience to take action.

The third thing is the actual presentation. Whether you're doing a webinar or a live-streaming event online, the key is the core presentation. That's where a lot of people go wrong. And one of the key areas where they go wrong is by building their presentation from the beginning until the end.

But as the late Steven Covey taught, you should always begin with the end in mind. Therefore, we should start from our irresistible offer. We need to know precisely what it is we are selling and we need to start from there. Build up your offer first.

Create an order form for your offering. That way your presentation will seamlessly relate to your order form and the product you are going to sell. If you do it the other way around, trying to structure your offer around your presentation, it doesn't work.

The second biggest mistake people make is overlooking the power of the structure—meaning they don't construct their presentation all around selling their offer. Every word, every slide, everything you do should be designed to lead to the sale. Everything you present should build up desire in your prospect.

It's a big mistake for you to teach, teach, teach, and then at the end, remember, "Oh, I need to sell!" This doesn't mean there's not really good content in your webinar or online event. You can have tremendous content, but if it doesn't set up the sale, it won't sell.

These folks wait until the very end and then add on the close or the sale. The truth is, your entire presentation is the close. And so is the way you deliver the information. It all needs to set up that sale.

One of the ways to do this is to tell people what to do—but not how to do it. For example, let's take estate plan attorneys. On a webinar, the attorney might talk about all of the documents you need and why a will is not good enough. It leads to the importance of having an estate plan. He's going to give you all the reasons why but not show you how to do it. Your goal is to educate on why the audience needs it—not on how to do it.

The second tip is to give useful but incomplete information. For example, let's say I'm selling a course on how to use Instagram, which obviously I never do, Kim, because I have you and you're the best in the world at it.

But let's say I created a course for Instagram. And let's say there are seven big secrets for getting results from Instagram. Well, I could say I don't have time to go over all seven of the big secrets for making Instagram extremely effective for you in this webinar. However, let me give two of the most powerful secrets in detail. Well, guess what? What does that do for the audience? It creates a desire to learn the other five secrets. Then when I get to my close, I say, "In section number seven of the manual we go over all of the seven strategies for making Instagram quietly effective." Right? So I set up the desire with the content part of my presentation, which then leads to that close where I present a method to get the solution. They buy the product, feeling completely fulfilled.

It's really about truly understanding your ideal prospect, your ideal buyer, your ideal customer, client, or patient. What makes them tick? Because before we can develop an irresistible offer, we have to know what our prospects want. Not necessarily what they *need* but what they *want*. We need to sell people what they want, while in the process, delivering to them what they *need*. That's a really important concept.

Here's a question you can ask to find that out. What keeps your prospect awake at night staring at the ceiling, unable to fall asleep, or just frustrated when it comes to the product or service you're selling?

For example, if I am a financial advisor, I imagine my clients wonder, "Am I going to have enough money for retirement? Am I going to be able to retire? Am I gonna run out of money?" That's something that keeps them awake at night. The reason we want to know these pain points is because people are more motivated to take action to get out of pain than they are to gain pleasure. We need this knowledge in order to develop our product offer—courses or products or services.

The next question you want to answer is: How does your prospect fill in this sentence? "If I could just (blank)?" Maybe the prospect says, "Man, if I could just have a sound financial plan. If I knew beyond the shadow of a doubt that I would have enough money for retirement, I would be happy!"

Now, when I know the answers to those questions, I can develop not just an offer but an *irresistible* offer that can fulfill precisely what they want, which moves them from pain into pleasure.

When you focus on looking at the offer, it reminds me of something you taught me, Dave—make sure everything in your presentation is about your prospect, and not about you. To me, people tend to focus way too much on themselves. Do you have any formula or checklist that you go through in order to make sure you're keeping the presentation on your prospect and not on yourself?

Dee: Yes, I call it my seven-figure template, and there are different chunks or sections of the presentation. I open my webinar or live presentation or streaming video presentation by telling attendees what they are going to learn. "In the next 60 minutes, you're going to discover a 1–2–3 step-by-step strategy that will allow you to . . ." Whatever the thing is they want. For example, "In the next 60 minutes you're going to discover a 1–2–3 step-by-step proven strategy for making sure you have enough money at retirement to live the lifestyle that you want. I can make a virtual guarantee that you haven't heard this exact strategy I'm going to describe to you. But it could be life changing." Notice, I'm not talking about me, I'm talking about what's in it for the prospect.

When I get to the section where I do have to talk about me—and this is really important, advanced information—I do it in a way that even while I am talking about me, I'm framing it in a way that I am relating to my prospect.

After I became a successful entertainer, I put together a marketing program that I sold to other entertainers. So I would tell my story about being a struggling entertainer, about being $80,000 dollars in debt (just like I did at the start of this conversation). I would share that I had a dream. My prospect who is watching can instantly relate, because while I'm telling my own story, I'm also essentially telling their story. I share with them that I had the same dreams, the same aspirations, and the same goals as they are having now while they are struggling.

But what if you don't have that kind of story? Then you want to tell your core business story.

Talk about why you got started in your business. Again, this should be all about the prospect. For example, "I became an estate-planning attorney because I really wanted to help people. I saw how the government was basically stealing people's money through state taxes, and families had been just devastated. I wanted to help those families for generations to come. So that's why I became an estate-planning attorney. And here's what makes me different . . ."

Next you talk about what makes you different, but phrase it in terms of how that difference is a benefit for the prospect. So first you tell a personal core story or business core story, but in either case you frame it as, "Hey, this is why it's important to you, Mr. Audience, Mrs. Audience Member." This is why it's important to you; this is what it means to you. When you do this, your presentation is always talking about the benefits and outcomes that your prospects are going to get.

When I go through my offer, and I mention a "feature," I always go beyond it. A feature is like an air bag in a car. That's a feature. But the benefit is that when you're in an accident, you're not dead. So whenever you explain the feature, you want to give the corresponding benefit—and of course it's the benefit that is what the buyer actually wants to receive.

There's a really important concept that ties us all together, and I called it my "hierarchy of persuasion." If you think of a sales letter, the lowest rung on the letter, which a lot of people operate from, talks about features, right? "Here are the features of my thing . . ." The next level up on the ladder are the benefits. "So here are what the features actually mean to you . . ." This is where probably 90 percent of all entrepreneurs and salespeople go wrong. They just stay at features and maybe benefits. But the next rung on the ladder, which is more persuasive and more powerful, is that of *outcomes*. "Here's the feature, here's the benefit of it, but now here's the outcome. Here's what will happen for you when you have this feature with that benefit." This is the rung, which almost nobody goes to. Most people never get to the outcome.

But let's say we do get to the outcome—there's a higher level still, and that higher level is transformation. Transformation is what those features, benefits, and outcomes are going to do for the person. This is how it's all going to affect their life as a whole. Powerful, right?

For example, when I was selling that program to entertainers, the features were that they got a binder of marketing material I used that was effective. That was the feature. The benefit was that they didn't have to create all of the materials themselves and wonder if they were going to work. That's the benefit. The outcome was that they would be able to send those materials, use those apps and letters, book more shows, and make more money.

But the transformation is that it means they were finally going to be able to live the life of their dreams. They would finally be able to do the things they're passionate about. They're finally going to prove to all of those people who said they couldn't do it, that it wasn't practical, that they were wrong. They'll finally be living their ultimate dream.

See the difference between just sharing features (that binder of stuff) and transformation (living your ultimate dream)? There's a huge gap there. That's the "hierarchy of persuasion." And if you keep focusing on that throughout your presentation, you naturally need to focus on your prospect. You're talking about what they're going to get, what they're going to receive, how they're going to be different.

Focusing not just on benefits gives you a competitive advantage because benefits is where most people stop. They don't move on to the outcome. And they almost never share the transformation step. By focusing on the transformation, you really are setting yourself up for sales. It gives you that expert positioning because your competitors are not doing that. They're simply focusing on the benefits.

Dee: Well, honestly, most presenters get stuck on features—a few of them on benefits. But you know, features and benefits are first grade. We've got to get out of the first grade. As the late Jim Rohn used to say, "That's why they make the chairs so small, so when you're seventeen and don't fit in the chair anymore, you know it's time to move on." You have to move on to more sophisticated selling. When it comes to persuasion—and make no mistake, that's what your webinar, live event, or webcast is—this is a sales tool that can later be automated, producing more money in one day than you do now all year, with paydays over and over again.

Would you mind sharing some of your client stories?

Dee: My very first private client happened to be an estate-planning attorney and we used a basic form of my seven-figure template that was nowhere near what it is now. But the foundation was there, and we used this formula to get her into a new business. At the time she had no list of prospects, no product, and no clue how to go about it.

She had earned $117,000 in her previous year of business. Within six hours of her webinar, she brought in $117,000. Then we automated it and within a four-week period she brought in over $250,000. I recall two vivid memories: I'm on the phone with her after we do the event, and she opens up her email to see the sales pouring in. (By the way, that never gets boring—waking up every morning and seeing how much your automated marketing made you the night before. I never get bored with that.) But she literally saw sales pouring in. I remember her just screaming, enjoying, laughing, and crying all at the same time because she was struggling and everything just changed for her in that one instant.

Recently, the same type of thing happened with a live video broadcast I produced. The client did $420,000 in sales. Right out of the gate, he sold 137 of a $1,500 product. His wife was there and we all just started jumping up and down, hugging each other and high-fiving. It was so phenomenal. Again, this is all following the template we just talked about here. Create your core presentation, and share not just the features and benefits but the outcomes and *transformation*.

It should also be noted that these clients were B2B. They were selling to other accountants and attorneys. Those are two industries you might think could not sell in an online presentation.

But it doesn't matter what the product or service is. The biggest mistake one can make is to think that "my business is different and that won't work for me." What I've found is that when the most successful people in the world hear a new concept, they immediately think, "How can I make this work for me?" That's what you should be thinking. And yes, this *will* work for you, almost regardless of what you're selling.

That's why I really love what I do. A guy came up to me at an event, just shaking with excitement, tears swelling up in his eyes. He said to me, "Thanks to your program, I'm a better husband. I'm a better father. And I'm happier than ever before, because now I actually have the business of my dreams, and I don't have to worry about money."

That's my goal—helping good people, good entrepreneurs who provide valuable products and services—to help other people. That's why I do what I do. It's really a blessing to be in the business that we're in.

To discover more about Dave Dee and his system for selling more in one day than you do all year, visit http://EliteDigitalgroup.com/DaveDee.

#INSTAGRAMFORBUSINESS POSTABLES

- "He who began a good work in you will carry it on to completion." (Philippians 1:6) #InstagramforBusiness

- We were created with majestic intentions, not mediocrity.#InstagramforBusiness

- The fear of what others will think is just a roadblock to getting to our destination. #InstagramforBusiness

- If you don't take action, no one will be blessed by what you were created to do. #InstagramforBusiness

- You are different after all, so stop appearing just as your competitors do. Be willing to be controversial. The most successful brands have raving fans as well as big detractors. Your goal through your posts is to attract exactly your perfect prospect and repel everyone else. #InstagramforBusiness

- A harsh truth—no one cares about your product, program, or service. No one. What they care about is how what you have to offer will make their lives better. #InstagramforBusiness

Resource spotlight: Visit www.UGIGbook.com to download your "Instagram Postable Power Pack"!

Chapter 9

Your Instagram Product Launch Formula

L et me in, let me in!

Remember back when Google+ first launched? They did an incredible job at building buzz for their social networking site. Only a few people were able to join at first, and then those people could invite others who would get an invitation to a waiting list. It created desire, interest, and frankly the belief that Google+ was going to blow us all away.

Of course, we now know it was kind of lame-mc-lamerson, but at the time we didn't—and that's the point. It doesn't really matter how good your product is—at least at first. Great marketing can make your launch successful no matter what.

The same goes for each and every iPhone launch. There is secrecy around the features, a release date announced ahead of time, and a limited supply available. As an admitted Apple junkie, I secretly/not-so-secretly want to get a camping chair and be first in line for the newest offering each and every time. Admittedly though, my love for sleeping in a bed and bathing win out, so I never do this. But I want to.

I did join the Apple program that lets me upgrade each year so I can always have the latest and greatest model. Because my current one is broken? Nah. It's because Apple's marketing is amazing.

And I'm not alone. Apple has sold more than 1 billion phones since its first release in June 2007. They've released more than 14 models and they sell more than 400 iPhones *every* minute. This is in spite of a continual increase in price by about 11 percent—even more proof that with great marketing, price isn't an issue.

This is incredible, if you think about it, because Apple used to be a hot mess. More than two decades ago they fired Steve Jobs for the abysmal failure of the personal computing systems he helped develop. Apple wasn't always the force to be reckoned with that it is today.

You could be the next Apple.

Leverage your launch well and you can increase your followers, subscribers, customers, and market share. You can create a tribe of loyal followers who maybe someday will get your logo tattooed on themselves, like the great brands of Nike, Harley Davidson, or even the aforementioned Apple.

But you must be strategic instead of sporadic, as most businesses are.

Businesses like Simple Green Smoothies are the exception. They have more than 400,000 Instagram followers and engage their massive community of loyal followers with 30-day challenges. They focus on one simple habit—drinking a green smoothie each day. At the end of each challenge, they offer a program for sale for a 21-day eating program. They have kept it incredibly simple, and it has paid off in spades. Jadah Sellner, cofounder of Simple Green Smoothies says, "I always encourage people to think about what was the gateway drug for you in your transformation. Because you're usually several steps ahead and several years ahead of the people you want to teach, you think, 'I want to teach you everything that I know,' but it's too much information in the very beginning. You're trying to basically just like open them up to want to learn more and so just really thinking about that is super helpful. Then think about what are the simple action steps that the reader can do to move them closer to that transformation. The transformation that we're promising with the 30-day green smoothie challenge is you're going to have more energy, you're going to crave healthier foods. That's the promise. It's like, how can we get them to that promise in the simple easiest most convenient way possible (SPI Podcast Session 205 on www.smartpassiveincome.com)?

This simple marketing and sales funnel, promoted primarily on Instagram with images of smoothies and recipes, produced more than $86,000 in sales the first time they launched it. It has generated more than $1,000,000 in sales since then. The Simple Green Smoothies Instagram page has produced a multimillion-dollar revenue stream for the two stay-at-home moms who founded the company. Plus, they are achieving their overall goal of better health for their followers. Jadah adds, "We just believe that every dollar we make means that someone said yes to their health. That's what really inspires us to keep going and grow this business. It's not just about us having freedom to spend more time with our families, but actually to be changing and transforming other peoples' lives is what really matters to us."

When it comes to launching your product via Instagram, there are four phases to any successful campaign. First, you have to identify your target market and their needs. Second, build desire through a buzz campaign. Third, get them to opt-in so you can move them off of Instagram. And fourth, get them to hand over the cash happily. (And better yet, invite their friends to come along!)

CREATING AN AUDIENCE AVATAR

Recently I attended a conference that was one of my favorite types—filled with data-driven strategies and marketing geeks like me. *Oh, the late-night conversations about conversions are almost too much. Almost.*

While there, I had the pleasure of hearing my friend Jason Swenk speak. Jason owned a marketing agency that he sold several years back for multiple millions. After he sold, he didn't just skip off into the sunset as many might. (Jason is like 8,000 feet tall, so the idea of him skipping into the sunset is quite funny, actually.)

Instead of retiring at 35, Jason launched a coaching and educational organization. And he showed just how smart he is. He didn't try to teach everything he knew to everyone. He was strategic and focused right away on other advertising agencies and their greatest pain points—how to get more clients and close more proposals (see Figure 9–1).

FIGURE 9–1. His Posts Focus on His Direct Target Market Niche.

His narrow focus allowed him to grow very quickly with members and garner the attention of some major industry players such as Leadpages (he was one of the first they contracted with to create a new template), Infusionsoft (he was a speaker at PartnerCon), and DigitalMarketer. If he had tried to be *for everyone*, this likely never would have happened.

Before you begin to market and grow your platform to launch your product, program, or service via Instagram, develop your perfect prospect "avatar." This is everything about your key, perfect customers who you want to flood your business and the group of people you actually want to work with.

Not sure where to start? Look at your sales numbers and choose from your top 10 percent of profitable customers. Or if you don't have customers yet, focus your business on the niche you are most passionate about. Targeting your audience to as small a group as possible allows you to offer content that is valuable to that group so you can build a strong relationship with them and increase your chances of brand conversion.

This can be scary because it means saying no to some people, but it is much better to have 500 raving fans than 10,000 tepid followers. You want to attract and engage exactly the type of person who will eventually want to give you money. Remember, someone already has the money that will be your next sale. Your job is to figure out who they are, and why they will give it to you.

Things to focus on when creating your avatar include: sex, age, profession, marital status, sexual orientation, location, native language, education, income, technological expertise, and family composition. Equally important to discover is what are their media-buying habits, interests, frustrations, and favorite brands. All of this research goes into the strategy behind our current clients' work. Most companies skip this step. Successful companies don't.

If you are unsure, check out some of your competitors' Facebook fan pages, Instagram accounts, and other social media networks. Explore those who are commenting. You can learn a lot from what they have listed on their public profiles.

Don't guess as to the demographics, habits, and pains of your prospects. You might think you know what your prospects want to hear and how they want to hear it, but assumption is a dangerous, foolish thing. Build out your profile so when you create all of your content in the future, you know exactly who you are talking to. Use the worksheet in Figure 9–2 on page 165 to work this out.

Your content needs to speak to your target market so clearly that to them it seems like you are a friend, not a business. The only way to do this is to get to know your target market inside and out.

I know research is the un-fun part for most. So let's do what we have to do in this step quickly, yes? Quick in and out and back to the steps that make most of our

---

Avatar Worksheet

Name him/her: _____

Age: _____   Gender: _____

Family composition: _____

Job: _____

Where does this person live: _____

_____

Habits, hobbies, and interests: _____

_____

Greatest pain point: _____

_____

FIGURE 9–2. List the Characteristics of Your Perfect Customer to Create an
Audience Avatar.

hearts swoon, like creating content and building promotions and putting together that
beautifully gorgeous gift for the world—your platform message—and turning it all into
fabulous sales.

Tactics to Research Quickly

When you are getting started, make a list of five of your top competitors or five other
companies your target audience might do business with (for example, Social Media
Examiner, Infusionsoft, and MailChimp are a few of mine).

Look up the link of each of their blogs, and paste that link into the search bar of
www.BuzzSumo.com, like in Figure 9–3 on page 166.

Visit the articles that are most popular and check out the types of content written
and the readers' comments so you can get a sense of what content is popular and what
questions these individuals have.

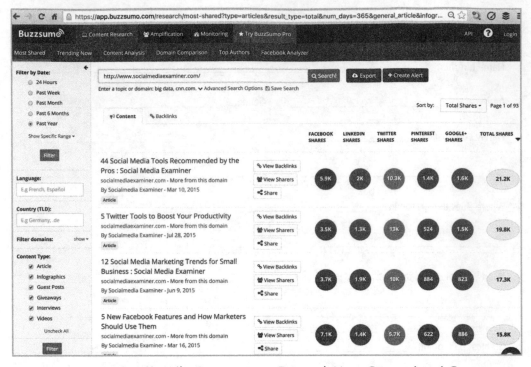

FIGURE 9-3. Use a Site Like Buzzsumo to Research Your Competitors' Content.

Then hop over to one of my favorite research ninja tools—Facebook's Audience Insights. Visit Audience Insights inside www.Facebook.com/AdsManager. See Figure 9-4.

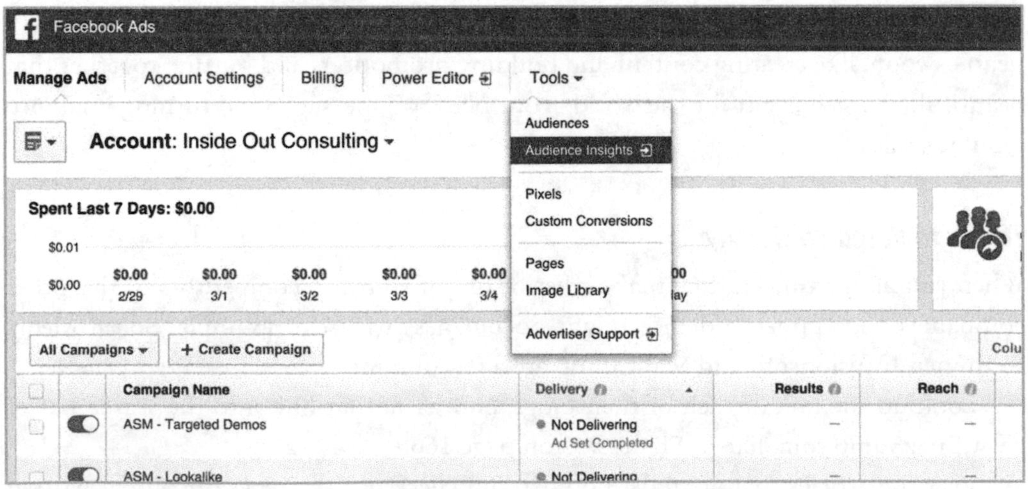

FIGURE 9-4. Audience Insights Offer Valuable Information on Demographics, Even If You've Never Run an Ad on Facebook.

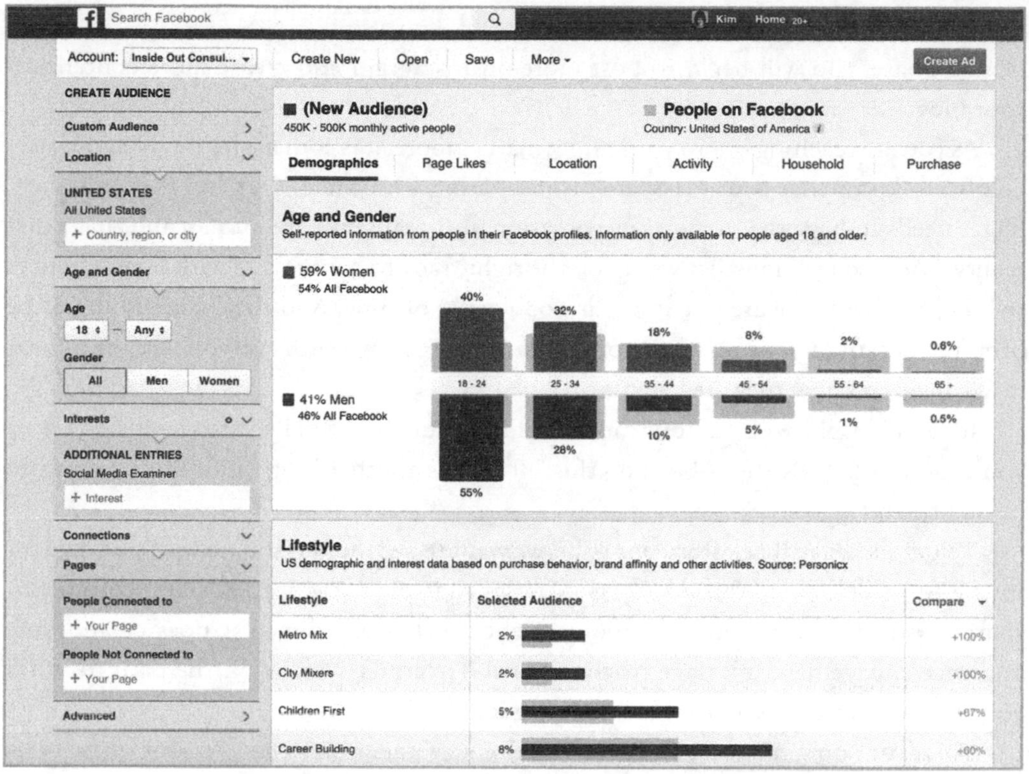

FIGURE 9-5. Inside of Facebook Audience Insights.

Choose "Everyone on Facebook," and then under the Interest box, type the names of the fan pages you have been researching, one at a time. See Figure 9-5.

Click on the Demographics tab and receive a full analysis of their entire audience. No, I'm not kidding. This information is 100 percent available to you for free inside Facebook right now. I'll wait while you go and check it out.

Good, you're back! Amazing, isn't it?

Use your findings on Audience Insights to list the topics your audience is interested in. Then, map out the following: the topics your audience is interested in, the questions they have, and their demographic information.

Following this feat of strategic greatness, take time to pour yourself a cup of tea or sip a glass of wine because you deserve a little break. You have effectively researched your target market and are ready to dive into the next step of creating content to reach your audience.

Once you understand who they are, it is time to build your messaging to resonate with them completely.

Creating Irresistible Content

In this phase, you will begin to post more on Instagram and create more content on your blog.

As you are reaching out to your target market more, it is sometimes (or, okay, always) helpful to know that your messaging is resonating with them. Our "do they love me?" meter needs to have the needle move occasionally because we are human and that's just reality. We need to know that we are on the right track to connecting with our audiences so all of this work we are putting in is not a waste of time. And that's something to be proud of because we are on a mission to share our message with everyone meant to hear it. We need to know they are listening.

It's kind of like when at four months of age your child finally starts smiling back at you—you think, "OK then—I can do this." It makes another long night of parenting go just a little bit easier.

To get some feedback from our tribe, we want to see them resonate with our content in the form of one of those successful posts that produces lots of likes, comments, shares, and private messages. While it might not be ROI direct, it does create more audience engagement, message reach, and tribe referrals, which—on the path to fulfill your purpose and monetize it—are all very good things.

There are some tricks I use to get higher engagement on posts. Try one or two this week and see what happens with your numbers.

Instagram Videos

Currently, Instagram video posts get more free distribution by Instagram than any other type of post you can do. I also get more interaction from my audience on these than any other type of content. Try this type of post for an immediate lift in engagement.

Word Swag

This iPhone app is the bee's knees. It creates gorgeous posts that always get more interaction than any other design software I use. Simply pull nuggets from your blogs or a sound byte from a speaker at a conference or a random idea that pops in your head at 3 A.M. (maybe that's just me?) and design it out in Word Swag (see Figure 9–6 on page 169). The app is $3, but it's the best $3 you'll ever spend.

Post Directly to Your Instagram Timeline

I love scheduling posts ahead of time so content is guaranteed to show up daily no matter how chaotic my life may get. But nothing gets as much reach on your timeline as posting to the page directly.

FIGURE 9–6. One of My Word Swag Creations.

Share Photos from Real Life That Resonate

Connect with your audience occasionally like you would with a friend. Let them know what is going on in your life to strengthen your relationship, just like you would do for someone you are close to. As you allow them to get to know you more, they will start to trust you more and grant emotional buy-in, which is required for a long-term relationship. My tribe has blessed me time and time again with encouragement and confirmation that we are a community with mutual understanding, and it is the exact boost I needed to keep going. See Figure 9–7 on page 170 for a post of me with some of my tribe members.

And don't worry about getting all of this on day one. Content marketing is a marathon, not a sprint. Put on your running shoes and take a nice brisk walk to get started. In the next section, we will dive into creating a whisper campaign to create buzz before you launch your next product, program, or service.

FIGURE 9–7. If You Share Personal Photos, Make Sure They Are Photos that Will Resonate with Your Audience.

DEVELOPING A WHISPER CAMPAIGN TO CREATE BUZZ

Want to creep out guests at a dinner party? Start the conversation with a sales pitch. I kid you not, I was at an event like this recently. I was invited to a luncheon only to discover it was a loosely veiled sales pitch. Not a great trust builder and definitely did not encourage me to attend something this "guru" put on in the future. It also might not surprise you that this "guru" ended up being a total fraud and was put under investigation by the FTC the following week. I don't wish ill upon anyone, but I can't say I was surprised. Going right in for the sale and trying to trick others into buying just doesn't work. Even worse, it can ruin your chances of ever selling to that prospect in the future. *Gasp!*

The thing is, the same dynamics are in play on your Instagram page. Lead off with sales, and you will not be invited to the party again. On the other hand, allowing followers just to "freeload" on content while never asking them to do anything will not pay the bills.

So, what's a savvy and successful marketer like you supposed to do?

The minority—those actually *making money* from their Instagram traffic—condition their audience to buy and stoke the fire of desire before they launch a product, program, or service. They are training their audience to be ready to pounce when there is an opportunity to buy.

BUILDING YOUR LAUNCH LIST

Here's how to stoke the fire of your fan page and get your audience amped up to buy.

Condition Them to Click

Offer relevant and valuable content that is not promotional. Encourage your fans to click through to your bio link for more valuable information. They will learn that clicking is good and valuable. When it comes to you, following directions means getting rewarded. Similar to when I was potty training my girls—good behaviors receive rewards. (Their reward of choice, diamonds on a paper princess tiara. Is there any question that they are taking after yours truly?!) Conditioning your audience to click when you ask them to is, of course, a very helpful behavior to have in place when you later want them to opt in to a webinar or other landing page.

Build Trust

Feature the "who says so" besides you by turning your clients, customers, or patients into content on your page. From Q&As to member spotlights, bring their faces into the conversation. No one wants to feel like they are the first to choose you to spend money with. Show them they aren't alone. We feature our clients and customers in our social media through client spotlights and links to their promotions.

It's one thing to like a post, it's a whole other jar of marbles to like a business enough to want to hand over your money. When it comes to marketing effectively on social media, the focus should be beyond individual "viral" posts and more to long-term relationship building—from follower to customer for life.

If they don't trust you, they won't buy from you.

One strategy that is quite effective but very few businesses use, is to use content from your clients or customers strategically in your posting action plan. This allows your prospect to discover who is the type of person that chooses to do business with you, it builds social capital, and moves your prospect farther along in their decision ladder, closer to the top to saying "yes!"

Instead of making all of your posts come from you, use editorial style Q&As with your clients, customers, or patients. Or feature them in your content (see Figure 9–8, page 172).

FIGURE 9–8. An Example of Using a Client in a Post.

Show Results

Use case studies and past customer experiences as the foundation for engaging your fans. Make sure not to be too promotional, but still share stories as social proof (see Figure 9–9, page 173).

Want even more social proof? Hold a contest with your audience where you ask members to share the positive results that they have had from your product, program, or service.

Share Some Behind-the-Scenes

Let your followers get to know you and your team better by building trust that then moves them closer to a yes to buy. It helps to show you are an actual person, not just words on a page. In Figure 9–10, page 173, we see an Instagram post of the Hüify team enjoying time together.

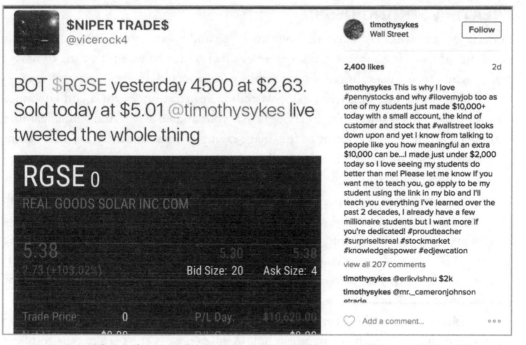

FIGURE 9–9. Share the Proof that Your Audience Shares with You, Making Them Part of Your Ongoing Marketing.

FIGURE 9–10. Hüify's Entire Instagram Page Is Dedicated to Showing Their Authentic Selves.

CREATE A STRONG DESIRE

These strategies will help warm up your audience and create strong desire. (Get your mind out of the gutter, we are talking *buying desire*.) And then when it's time to have a launch, you can strategically build buzz right up 'til launch day.

Two weeks before your webinar or workshop registration, begin a content series on your page. This is pure, straight content that your audience will find valuable. More than just the image, post content in the image example. Then in each post, direct them to check out the link in your bio that will send them to a lead magnet link where there will be even more value.

For example, two weeks prior to my last launch, I wrote content about Facebook Live and had a free giveaway of a Facebook Live Script Template. This type of giveaway made sense and was congruent, because it was relevant to the content and upcoming training. Make sure whatever you post during this two-week period is connected to what will come next. Your goal is to create buzz, so as soon as you open up registrations or sales, your audience cannot wait to buy.

After these two weeks, open up registration to your webinar with one post and change your bio link to the registration link. A video post is the perfect type to insert into the mix when registration opens. However, when you start going after registrations, try not to be too salesy. If you are, your audience may turn away from your posts and start ignoring you. That would stink, especially after two full weeks of giving them value.

It would kind of be like flirting just the right amount with a love interest—not too much, not too little—and when he/she finally asks you out, you say, "Yes! Let's Get Married!" (As I shared in Chapter 1, in case you didn't already know, this is not good.)

Once the registration period opens up, alternate one day with a "Register now" notice and the next with a piece of content. Content days will still have some kind of banner in a call to action to make sure people continue to opt in through the bio link.

Then, on the day of the event, run another video on your page. Encourage your followers again to opt in, and if they have already, encourage them to show up. Make sure to tell them how attending will not only benefit them but will *change their lives*.

The first thing in the morning, and right before they get on to the webinar, post on Instagram and email them as well.

A SEVEN-DAY SCHEDULE FOR PROMOTING YOUR LEAD MAGNET

To make things a little less overwhelming and make sure you take action, follow the instructions for each day, and complete all activities listed for maximum results.

Sunday

Sunday night, as the weekend is winding down, take some time to do a little research. This will set you up for success for the rest of the week. Make a list of the following:

1. Ten of the most popular blogs in your niche (use www.BuzzSumo.com as mentioned earlier to help you find that).
2. Ten of the most popular podcasts in your niche that are ranked 75 to 100 in popularity. You don't want to focus on the top ten as they are hit up for requests all day long. Start with the super strong but less popular shows to get your feet wet. (Visit iTunes, then Podcast, to get these.)
3. Make a list of all the people in your industry who you personally know who have a blog, podcast, or other platform.
4. Create an easy-to-give domain name for your lead magnet with www.GoDaddy.com (buy a domain), or use www.TinyURL.com to create one for free. I do this with all my lead magnets that I want to promote, the one I give out most often being www.nobschapter.com.
5. Now get to sleep: You have a busy week ahead!

Note: If you have a teeny-tiny list right now some of these strategies might seem pointless, but don't use that as an excuse not to do them. Even if you only have 12 people on your email list and eight Twitter followers (and some of them are family members and yourself), start with those 12 and run through these strategies. The more you do this step, the more your audience will grow, and you will grow more comfortable with self-promotion.

Monday for Video-Palooza

It's time to do your own self-promotion of your funnel to drive traffic and comments before you reach out to others to promote it.

1. Use Facebook's Live Video and Instagram Stories to share with your audience three bullet points or one main tip from your blog. At the end of the video, send them to the lead magnet web page to get more information. Also include a link to that video in the video settings and post description.
2. Download the MP4 from the Facebook Live Video and upload it to YouTube. In the description, first place a link to your lead magnet.
3. Share the YouTube link on LinkedIn. Include a link to your lead magnet as well.
4. In preparation for tasks later in the week, read the blogs of your top bloggers and make any notes about their blogging style that you can use later in the week.

Tuesday Was Made for Email

If you are a newbie, this step can be S-C-A-R-Y when you are just starting out, but rip off the Band-Aid® and email them. I remember how painful it was in the beginning, but I promise it gets easier and eventually even *fun.*

Yes, I am serious.

1. Send an email to your list with a link to your blog post. In the P.S. of the email and at the end of your blog post, include a link to your lead magnet.
2. Share a link to your blog post on all of your social media channels.
3. Listen to three of the podcasters you plan to reach out to later in the week and make notes about their podcasting style (so you can remember them when you reach out later).

Wednesday for Book-Me-Danno

In the early days, a lot of my list building started with me simply being willing to contribute content to other people's newsletters and blogs. At one point, I was contributing to 15 newsletters and blogs a month. Now that my audience has grown, and I am a columnist for *Entrepreneur* magazine, DigitalMarketer, and GKIC Insider's Circle, I have stopped writing for most others, but this still is a major component of my success in list growth.

Use this day to contact the people you know who have networks you can tap into by doing one (or both) of the following:

1. Send them a personal email to ask if they would be willing to share a link to your blog post to their social media followers.
2. Share a link to your blog post and ask if there might be an opportunity to guest post on their site or write for their newsletter about a similar topic.
3. Listen to four of the podcasters you plan to reach out to later in the week and make notes about their podcasting style (so you can remember them when you reach out later).

Thursday Is Perfect for Podcasting

Now it's time to venture out into the podcasting world to people you don't know and try to get booked on their shows.

1. Listen to the remaining podcasters you haven't heard yet and make notes about their shows.
2. Send an email request to be a guest on one of the podcaster's shows. Follow this formula for getting heard:

a. Use a unique subject line to grab their attention.
   - I'll promote our episode like my life depended on it.
   - You'll wonder what just happened but then smile.
   - No, seriously . . . let me tell you why.

b. Write a short but sweet email telling them how having you as a guest will benefit them. Do NOT make it all about you.

Here's an email I sent to Pat Flynn back in 2013 that landed me Episode #89 on his show that you can use as an example:

Subject: Because you rock (with beat boxing)

Message Body:

Greetings Pat . . .

I love the show . . . and not just because you beat box . . . something I can never seem to do without spitting . . . but I digress.

You bring so much value to us working our tails off today to live the lives we want forever.

You help me keep up the pace . . . you see, I have owned my company for 13 years and have had the ups and downs and roundabouts like the rest of them, but I really became an entrepreneur three years ago when my daughter was born and my back was against the wall. I discovered direct-response marketing and everything changed so much for the better. I still have the crazy scaling company schedule and lack of sleep from balancing a growing business and two kids, but it is now with joy and excitement that I face each day. In my long drives, I listen to your podcast for inspiration, education, and motivation. Through this year, my company has killed it, having taken on clients like Sandler Training, GKIC Inner Circle, Chem-Dry, and Ron LeGrand. My focus is bringing direct response tactics to social media . . . I monetize the fluffy stuff.

I don't suppose you would consider having me as a guest on your show? I am sure there is no room for me, but if I am wrong, I would come prepared to offer value with high energy and an occasional joke or two . . .

I am sure that you already have too many like me beating down your door, so even if you don't have the time to respond, know that you have a fan here at www.facebook.com/KWalshPhillips, and I am ready to cheer when you soon hit episode #100. (BTW . . . your recent one with Clay Collins nailed it. I have been a Leadpages customer for a while now, and it is off the chain.)

Focusing on the ROI,

Kim

c. Set a task reminder to follow up by "replying all" to your message, but change the subject line, trying something unique again, perhaps offering five reasons why they should book you as a guest. Make this again about them and not about you.

Friday for Blogging Fun!

Repeat the podcast step but this time ask bloggers if you can guest blog on their platform.

Saturday

A quick cleanup in the morning and you are done.

1. Thank anyone who shared your link or promoted your work in any way. (I like to send gifts as a thank you. It helps to show how much you appreciate their help.)
2. Post a link to your blog post again on all of your social media channels.

And you are done! Take a deep breath and get some rest because next week we are on to getting paid traffic.

In the next section, we will dive into Instagram ads and how they can support your overall marketing goals on the way to launch.

THE INSTAGRAM AD CAMPAIGN BLUEPRINT

If you want to amp up your game when it comes to Instagram marketing, then you may want to look into Instagram advertising. Later in this chapter, Lindsay Marder of DigitalMarketer will show us how they have successfully driven hundreds of thousands of dollars in sales from Instagram ads. The payout can be incredible. Of course, anytime you advertise, you are risking your money, so it's best to arm yourself with all the facts before diving in.

All Instagram ads are set up through your Facebook Ads portal so first, you will need to set up either Facebook Ads Manager or Facebook Business Manager.

Facebook Ads Manager is used only if you run ads for one Facebook Business Page and one Instagram Account. Facebook Business Manager is used if you run ads for more than one business page or account. To set up your Facebook Ads Manager, go to www.facebook.com/adsmanager. To set up Business Manager, go to www.business.facebook.com.

To add your Instagram account to your Facebook Ads Manager:

1. Go to your Facebook page.
2. Click *Settings* in the top-right corner of your page.
3. Click *Instagram Ads*.
4. To add an existing Instagram account to your page, click *Add an Account*.
5. Enter your Instagram account's *Username* and *Password*, and click *Confirm*.

To create a new Instagram account and add it to your Facebook page:

1. Go to your Facebook page.
2. Click *Settings* in the top-right corner of your page.
3. Click *Instagram Ads*.
4. If you need to create a new Instagram account, click *Add an Account*.
5. Select *Create a new account*.
6. Fill in the details of your new account and click *Confirm*.
7. An email will be sent to the email address specified. Follow the directions in the email to set the password for your new Instagram account.

To add your Instagram account to your Business Manager:

1. In Facebook, go to your Business Manager.
2. Click on *Business Settings*, then *Instagram Accounts*.
3. Click *Claim New Instagram Account*.
4. Fill in the username and the password of the Instagram account you would like to sync and click *Next*.
5. Select the ad accounts that will have access to this Instagram account and then click *Save Changes*.

Mission accomplished. Now it's time to create some Instagram ad magic.

Fail to Plan and You Can Plan to Fail

Before jumping right into the ad creator, it is important to decide how you're going to adapt your message to the crowd that follows you on Instagram. Every social media platform is used by fans for different reasons, so identifying what it is that appeals to your target audience is a key component in building out your Instagram ad plan.

Cold, Hard Truth Alert: There *will* be some strategic guessing in the beginning stages as you see what imagery resonates with your audience, so don't get discouraged if the icon ads that performed so well on Facebook don't give as spectacular results on Instagram.

Review your Instagram posts and consider what your audience engages with the most. Are you racking up page upon page of comments on photos of people using your product? Or does the perfectly positioned hero shot of your product standing tall in all of its glory steal the show? Or maybe your video posts are the favorite child? Make a list of what you see doing well in your Facebook ads and what your fans on Instagram love to see and start testing.

Test the Water

Now that you have your accounts linked and an idea of the direction you want to take, it's time to start creating the actual ads. Facebook has updated the system so that you can use your ad builder of choice (Ads Manager or Power Editor) to create your Instagram ads.

To use, Ads Manager, go to www.Facebook.com/AdsManager.

Click *Create Ad* as shown in Figure 9–11.

FIGURE 9–11. Click on the Create Ad Button.

Next choose your marketing objective from the categories shown in Figure 9–12. We'll look at each category in more detail.

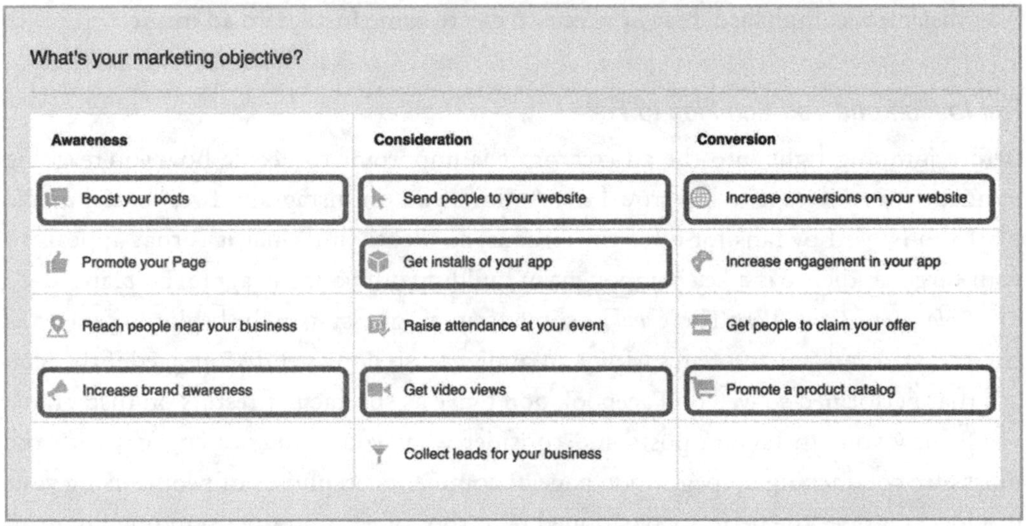

FIGURE 9–12. Selecting Your Marketing Objective from a Range of Choices.

Awareness

Boost Your Posts: Expose your posts to as many people as possible, expanding your reach and increasing your page engagement.

Increase Brand Awareness: Expose posts to audiences specifically targeted based on the likelihood that they will pay attention to your ads. The posts (see an example

FIGURE 9–13. This Is a Post to Increase Brand Awareness.

in Figure 9–13) can be used to expose more people to your brand and ultimately grow a larger following.

Consideration

Send People to Your Website: This option is to increase the flow of traffic on your site or landing page. In the ad-builder process, you have the options to make consideration and conversion ads clickable so that someone can be redirected to the site where you want them to go simply by touching the photo. This option is recommended when sending traffic to a piece of value-driven content that doesn't require an opt in, such as a blog.

Get Installs of Your App: Send viewers to the app store to encourage them to download and install your app.

For example, the goal of McDonalds' is to get people to take part in their app so they've included a sweet deal. In order for the viewer to get the free coffee with five purchases, they need to click the McDonald's bio link to download the app where they will be rewarded with the program. "I'm loving it!" (Not really, I am a loyal fan of the

Green Bean Roasting Company in York, Pennsylvania, [Hi, Jen and Vanessa!] for the substance that makes up 75 percent of my body mass, but I can't resist a jingle.)

Get Video Views: These videos can be testimonial based, product how-tos, behind-the-scenes clips, product launches, or just promotional videos designed to drive traffic.

Ruby Tuesday used this method by circulating a video of different clips of people enjoying the food and atmosphere at a Ruby Tuesday location. They also incorporated a variety of hashtags that made sense for their message. For many users, food porn is one of the best parts about Instagram, so this ad type does very well. Because if there is anything we like better than *pictures* of mouth-watering, juicy, and huge hamburgers dripping with cheese, it's a *video* of mouth-watering, juicy, and huge hamburgers dripping with cheese.

Conversion

Increase Conversions on Your Website: Use this when you want your customer to take an action such as entering their contact information or purchasing a product. Website conversions let you track the number of actions that are taken via Facebook through this option.

Here's an example from Facebook: An online dating service, Match, wanted a way to drive registrations among a new generation of people who are actively dating. Since Match acquires clients primarily on mobile, they decided to run a website conversion campaign on Instagram. During the website conversion campaign, Match increased registration volume by 20 percent.

"Our goal is to help singles of all generations find meaningful connections," says James Peng, head of Mobile App Acquisition at Match. "Through Instagram conversion ads, we were able to deliver a visually crafted message to a new age of dating-minded individuals at scale."

Promote a Product Catalog: If your business has a store or a catalog, this ad will automatically pull from that catalog to promote your products to your target audience. Add a new pair of kicks to your online selection? If you've set this up ahead of time, ads for that product will automatically start showing in the Instagram feed to those you are targeting.

Setting Up Your Ad

Once you have selected your objective and named your campaign, you are ready. Put on your big boy/big girl pants and create an ad. Start by setting the audience, placement, budget, and delivery schedule of your ad.

Select Your Target Audience

1. *Custom Audience.* If you have a custom audience, such as an email contact list, website traffic, conversion pixel, or lookalike of one of these, you are able to upload it here. The three categories are:

   a. *Custom Audiences.* Target your current customers by securely uploading a contact list of people you'd like to reach.

   b. *Lookalike Audiences.* Find people who are similar to your customers or prospects by building a lookalike audience from your Facebook page fans, customer lists, or website visitors.

   c. *Custom Audiences from Your Website.* Remarket to people on Facebook who've already visited your website.

2. Set your location by entering an address or town and selecting how many miles away you will allow this ad to expand. The options are:

   a. Everyone in this location

   b. Lives in this location (meaning they have a home there)

   c. Recently in this location (meaning this is their last tracked location)

   d. Traveling to this location (meaning they were recently in this location but their home is somewhere else)

3. Set age range.

4. Select your target gender.

5. Enter any specific languages.

Note: You do not have to set all of these up. They are *optional* and based on who you want to target specifically. See Figure 9–14, page 184. Notice the "Estimated Daily Reach" in the bottom-right-hand corner of Figure 9–14. As you manipulate the settings, this number will adjust to reflect the average number of people who will come into contact with your ad.

Set Your Detailed Targeting

Set your Detailed Targeting (see Figure 9–15, page 184) by including any interests, demographics, and behaviors you'd like to identify. To narrow a broad audience, try stacking interests. For example, if you are selling a gym membership that specializes in classes, you could target people who have an interest in yoga and Pilates plus the purchasing behavior of buying fitness equipment. Then you would know that these people have an interest in your product and are willing to spend money on it.

Set a Connection to Your Page

Setting a connection to your page (see Figure 9–16, page 185) will further narrow your audience to show your ad to the people who already have a connection to your page or other related categories.

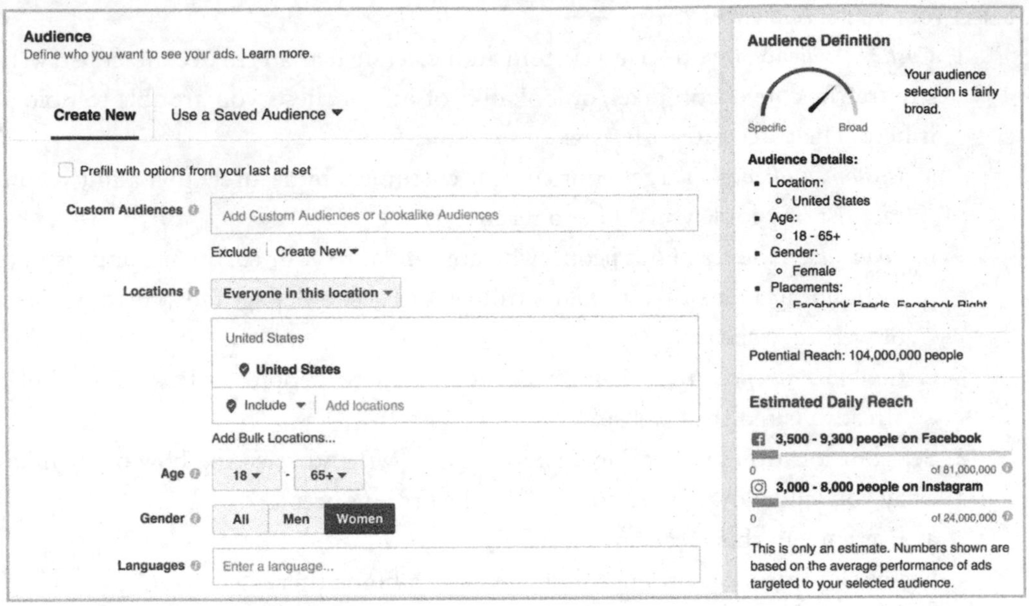

FIGURE 9–14. Selecting Your Target Audience.

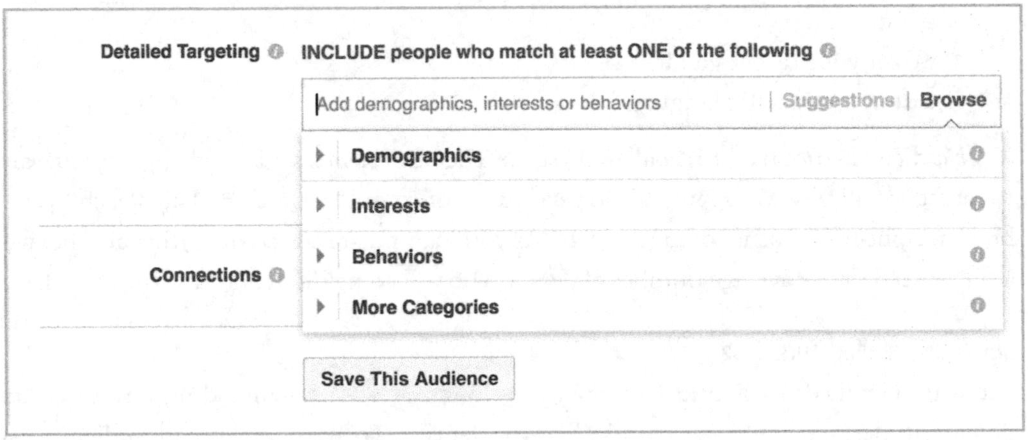

FIGURE 9–15. Setting Detailed Targeting.

Set the Placement for Your Ad.

This is where you select that you want your ad to circulate on the Instagram feed (see Figure 9–17 on page 185). Note: You can select more than one option and edit the images to fit both categories later.

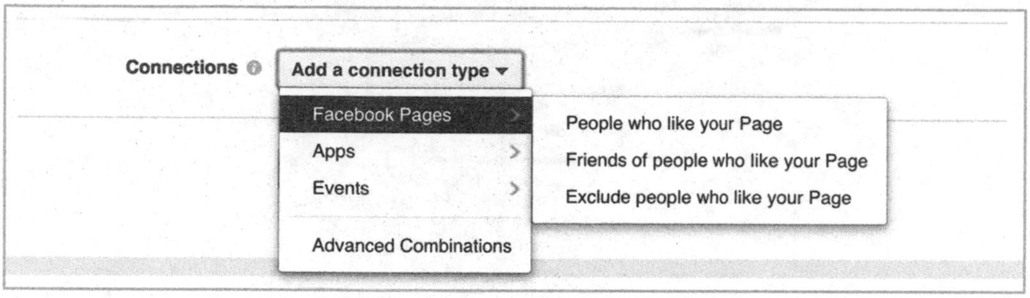

FIGURE 9-16. Further Defining Your Audience Based on Your Facebook Fans and Their Friends.

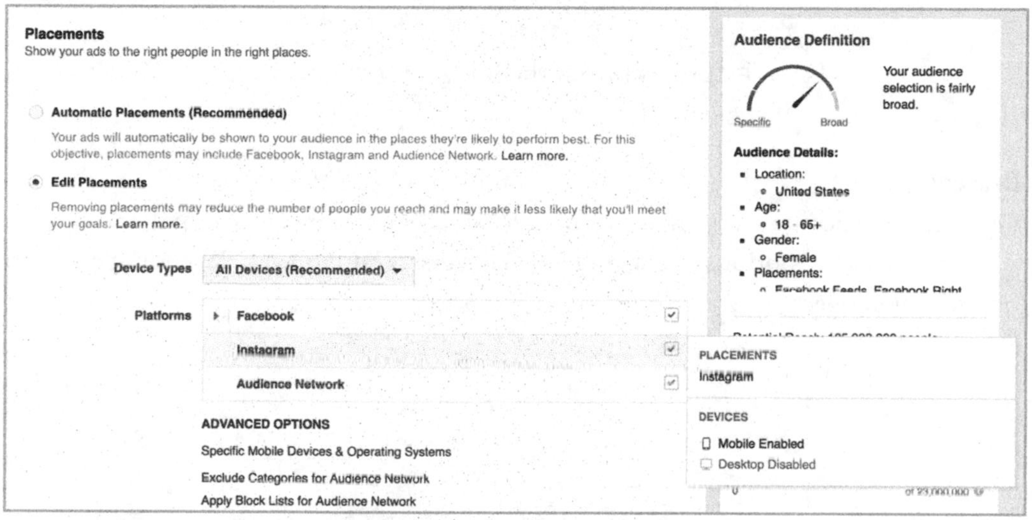

FIGURE 9-17. Selecting Your Ad Placement.

Set the Budget

Select either the daily or lifetime budget and how much you want to dedicate to the distribution of this ad (see Figure 9-18, page 186). The more money you opt to spend, the higher number of impressions you will receive, increasing the likelihood of reaching your objective.

Note: When optimizing the ad for delivery, check the manual budget to make sure that your daily ad spend is at least double the high bid. Return to the automatic option to allow Facebook to find you the best price.

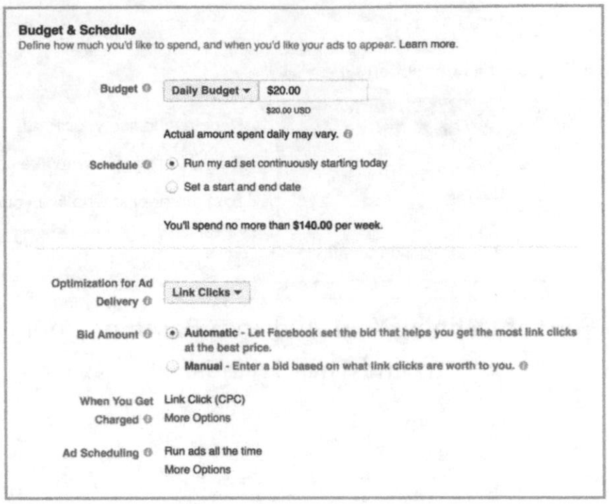

FIGURE 9–18. Set the Budget for Your Ad.

Delivery

Once the logistics are set up, name your ad set and click *Continue* to set up the ad creative.

There are four options (see Figure 9–19) for Instagram images, depending on which objective you select.

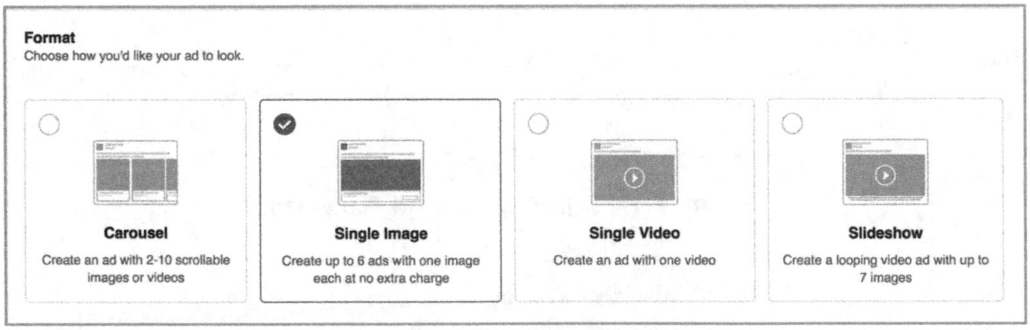

FIGURE 9–19. Selecting Your Ad Format.

Next, select the associated Facebook page and the Instagram account option. If you've synced your Instagram account with your Facebook in Business Manager or your Facebook page, your account name will appear in the drop-down menu. If you haven't, you can do so here (see Figure 9–20, page 187).

To add your Instagram account, click "Add an Account" and enter your Instagram login information (see Figure 9–21 on page 187).

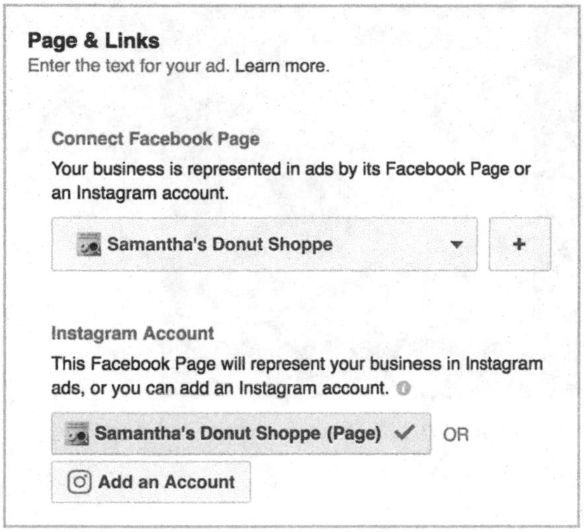

FIGURE 9–20. Linking Your Account(s) to Your Ad.

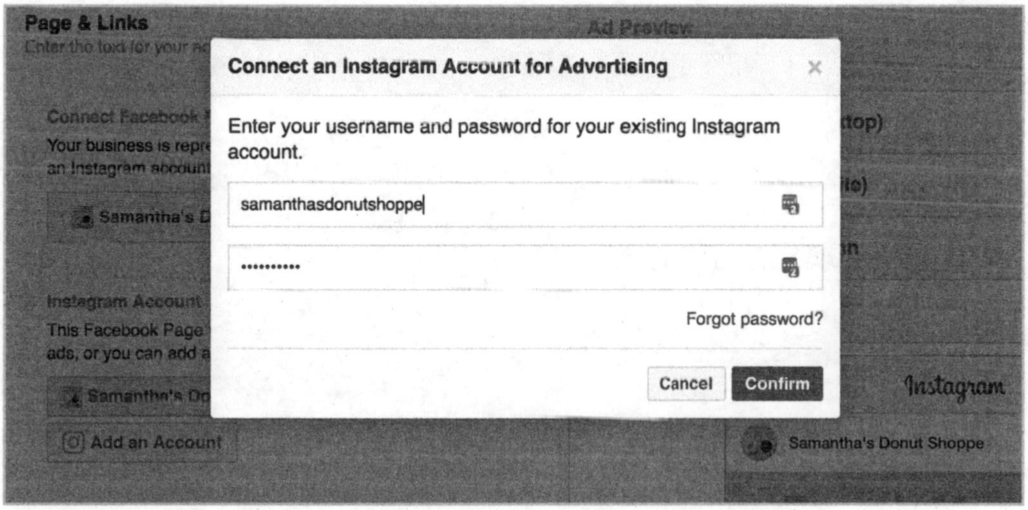

FIGURE 9–21. Adding Your Instagram Account.

Build the Ad Creative

Upload the ad images that you have selected, and using the Edit Crop button, Facebook
will allow you to alter the image so it fits appropriately in the Instagram feed. If you elect
to use the ad for Instagram and Facebook in the same campaign, it will give you options
to edit the size for both individually (see Figure 9–22 on page 188).

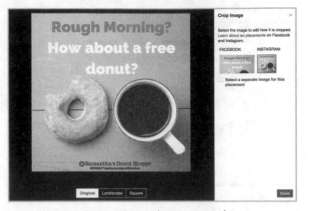

FIGURE 9–22. Cropping Your Ad Image.

Next, add in the text that describes the action you want the viewer to take. For this example, the Samantha's Donut Shoppe is encouraging people to stop in for a free donut with a large coffee (see Figure 9–23).

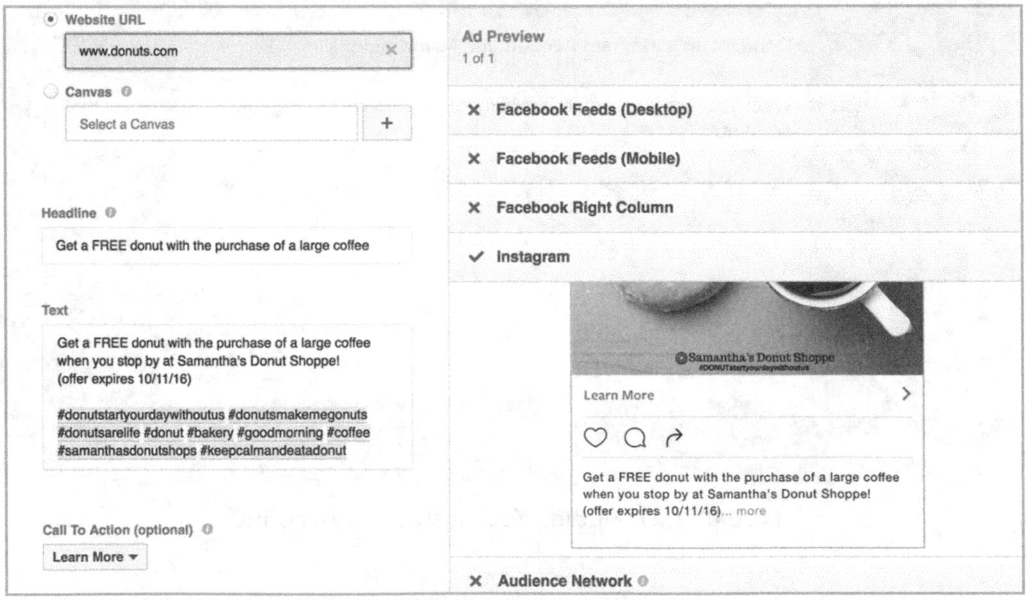

FIGURE 9–23. Adding Text to Your Ad.

This is an opportunity to utilize popular hashtags that you have found success with on your Instagram page (see Figure 9–24 on page 189). That way your ad will be shown not only to the people who fall into your target audience but also to people who search that hashtag.

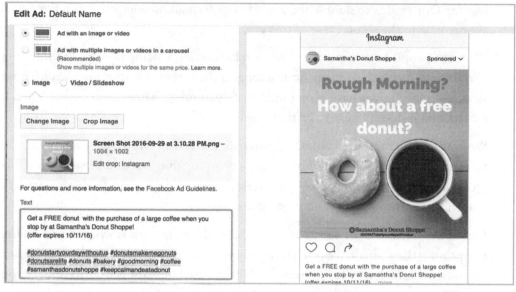

FIGURE 9–24. Use Hashtags to Broaden Your Ad Reach to Relevant Audiences.

And that's it. Review and click *Place Order*. Within 24 hours, Facebook will review your ad to make sure it meets all of the guidelines, and then begin circulating through the feeds of your target audience.

(One of my staff members put together the ad images. I had Samantha pick whatever industry she wanted, and she went with coffee and donuts. It seems I either hire people who have the same delicious obsessions as me, or I rub off on them over time. Either way, I'll take it. The coffee and donuts, that is. Especially if you are willing to throw in Pumpkin Spice, aka Soccer Mom Catnip.)

The most important thing when it comes to Instagram advertising is to track, measure, and scale once your data supports it. With that, you can achieve incredible results.

Business powerhouse DigitalMarketer uses Instagram every day to start prospects on their path to purchase. Check out my interview with editorial manager Lindsay Marder in the next section.

DRIVING SALES WITH INSTAGRAM ADS, WITH LINDSAY MARDER OF DIGITALMARKETER

Lindsay Marder is the managing editor at DigitalMarketer and was previously the publishing editor at Southern Yellow Pine Publishing.

Tell us about what you do at DigitalMarketer.

Marder: Our goal is to double the size of 10,000 small businesses within five years. We are now in the second year of this goal.

We teach people how to market their own businesses, sharing how to do things the correct way—because so many do it wrong in the internet marketing world. Those who advertise online have a reputation of spamming. They have a terrible track record, and it doesn't have to be that way.

We want to change the context of internet marketing—how you can follow the rules and still get results, and how you can provide value first and be very profitable second. We teach our audience to create dynamic, engaging, and valuable content and turn that into lifelong and profitable customers.

Our entrepreneurs learn how to drive traffic, and how to look at what they're selling to optimize their offers. We teach how to boost sales conversions and how to engage an audience and develop a community. Mostly we really want people to understand the difference between selling a product versus selling a brand.

Our market of college graduates have degrees but no tangible marketing skills. We teach them how to do content marketing and paid traffic and customer acquisition. Now they're going out and changing the way businesses do advertising and [get] customers.

You no longer need to re-invent the wheel every time you try to sell something. We want to teach people the process to do it—a repeatable process that works with everything, not a one-hit-wonder kind of campaign. We teach a process that is evergreen, and we're trying to change the economy while we are doing it. We put more money back into peoples' pockets, sell more, and give people better products. Really, we just do what we can to make things better for everyone.

I love that all your social media channels focus on that messaging, and that the messaging is on-point and focused on that overall goal. For your Instagram account how are you leveraging this?

Marder: A lot of people have been using Instagram for direct selling, advertising a product, and measuring success by purchases. When you're selling information or instructions, however, people need to get to know you first. So we follow a cold-warm-hot kind of process. We use Instagram for sharing content and introducing ourselves, so we can get them to listen to one of our podcast episodes or read one of our blog posts, giving value first and establishing the relationship over time.

We use Instagram to provide as much ungated (no opt-in required) value as we can up front, before we ask anyone to make a transaction with us. When folks give us their time on Instagram, that's a really valuable thing to ask from anyone who doesn't know you yet.

So what types of things do you share?

Marder: We share our podcast episodes. A lot of what our Instagram ads are right now are long-form descriptions, telling folks, "Here's what you'll learn in the content"; "Here's what you'll learn by listening to this"; or "Here's what you'll learn by reading this." We tell people everything to expect upfront and let them know what they will get out of it.

And what have you found that is working well on this channel in comparison to others?

Marder: We're definitely seeing that it's great for brand awareness. We use Instagram as a way to generate awareness for our company, its brand, and our customer-facing employees. For the longest time, DigitalMarketer was synonymous with Ryan Deiss since he was the front man. Ryan is obviously still very well known, but we're now in a place where we are establishing authority through other team members, too.

There's nothing wrong with having a team and establishing that your team has expertise on lots of topics. You'll see customer-acquisition info with Molly Pittman in front and content in videos with Ross or Suzzie or myself. We use Instagram to generate name recognition for those customer-facing employees as well as our products and services.

We are seeing that people are listening to the podcast episodes we promote, and subscribing to the show. We're seeing our downloads increase from Instagram source traffic, and our blogposts are gaining traction.

In our private community on Facebook we share informal pictures: "Here's what Deanne is doing around the office," or a video of Bryan skateboarding around our building. Nothing has indicated to us that marketers and small-business owners are shopping on Instagram, but they are looking for solutions on Instagram. We use the platform to add value to their research, and we are seeing a lot of people visiting our site after they've seen us on Instagram. It's growing our listener and reader base on our podcast and blog and leading to a growth in memberships and continuity products.

So instead of trying to send viewers directly into a funnel, you're doing value-only at first. Where do you go for inspiration?

Marder: Nordstrom does a terrific job at Instagram advertising, making me pause when I'm scrolling to look at everything in their screen. Their copy is really great, too. They paint a picture for you—"It's getting cooler out, fall is coming, are you prepared?" "You'll need the perfect dress when it's nice outside," " . . . the perfect sweater . . ." They're dressing their audience.

So what have been some of your most popular posts?

Marder: We promoted a podcast episode called "Everything I Learned About Paid Traffic, I Learned at a Kid's Party." We had a lot of people click and like the heck out of that episode. Now we're turning that into a regular piece of blog content that will work to retarget people through Facebook and Instagram. We pixel them and retarget to see if we can get them to opt in to an offer.

We also have success with lighter pieces. Ross wrote a post called "23 Weirdest Things Sold Around the Internet." People reacted really well to it because they saw us speaking to our audience in an unusual way without asking them to immediately buy anything. It was just quick content with a fun feature image, and they were more inclined to do what we wanted them to do.

Have you used tagging or hashtags or other Instagram strategies for page growth or getting engagements? What works for you?

Marder: Our social media manager is big on hashtags. We also have started including Google Trends in our strategy to keep our posts on-topic and current. It's like jacking the news to see how it can connect to digital marketing. So for example, maybe a trending company was considering selling something. We'll ask, "Are you a buyer?" and then hashtag it #honest #techcrunch #selling.

If you can join the conversation, search for the pain point you're trying to solve for your market and then continue digging to figure out which hashtags are working there and which will get you to the front page. And tag people when relevant. We're a big fan of tagging. Even if that person is not on Instagram, we can tag their Twitter handle and shoutout on Facebook and Twitter, "Hey, we featured you here."

All of these social networks are connected. The words you say on Instagram can easily reach people on Facebook or Twitter. Use hashtags that are relevant to your post and people who are searching for similar things, and tag the people you're speaking about or who would be interested. And don't just say, "Listen to this episode, Read this blog post." Tell them what they're going to get out of it. Make it benefit-heavy.

How can folks find out more about DigitalMarketer?

Marder: Go to www.DigitalMarketer.com or follow us @digitalmarketer.

FROM ONLINE TO OFFLINE WITH SHAUN BUCK

Did you see what you left there?!

If you aren't following up with Instagram followers once they are on your list, you are leaving a lot of money behind. The fortune is in the follow-up. And when most think of follow-up, they think of email. Just email.

Yes, email is important, but it should be just one tactic in your follow-up strategy. Employing different mediums of follow-up is vital. If you don't, you leave a lot of money on the table.

One of my go-to experts on this topic is Shaun Buck. Shaun is the CEO of NewsletterPro, a seven- (almost eight-) figure business. He started his company from scratch and has achieved that success with an offline product. (He also happens to be one of the nicest people I know. And he loves margaritas. I mean, what's not to love about that?)

I recently interviewed him about his philosophy on how to retain customers and the referrals they give you. Like me, Shaun believes the most important way to grow your business is to get customers and retain them.

From 2011 to 2014, Shaun grew his business by 2,975 percent. Along with a few more gray hairs for him, there were several key strategies in place. When I asked him how he achieved that, he told me there were two main secrets to his success:

1. Retain customers. (Shaun noted his average customer remains with him for approximately four years.)
2. Get each customer to bring a friend or two along.

He further explained that the conversion of new customers—whether referred from Instagram or another social media network, direct mail, or whatever source—is key. He used his own business as an example. From January to the end of April, his business's conversion figures were:

■ 35 percent of new customers were on their list for 0 to 30 days (these are the group most businesses pursue with passion).
■ 29 percent of new customers were on their list for 31 to 90 days (not ready to buy initially).
■ 7 percent were on their list for 91 to 365 days (they worked really hard to move this group up the sales funnel).
■ 29 percent were on their list for 365 days or more (holy biscuits and gravy!).

Most people, he said, give up way too early on their leads and think that if people don't buy right away it's not worth following up on them.

But following up is key.

People need to know who you are, what you do that can transform their lives, and that you are still in business. Or they won't buy from you. He further noted that most people (51 percent of sales) buy a product 90 days to 18 months after first obtaining the information about it. So if you implement a strategy to follow up, you will end up selling more and growing your business successfully.

There are two things that NewsletterPro focuses on:

1. Referrals—how can we get them to refer people to us (friends, family, or other businesses)?
2. Existing customers—how do we keep them for life?

Existing Customer Campaigns

They generally do this through contests or promotions for existing customers. For example, they ran a promotion that if existing customers referred one person who becomes a client (keeping it simple) they would receive a free trip to Las Vegas, including airfare, a couple of nights at a hotel, and a drive-your-favorite-sports-car experience.

When asked how he affords a campaign like that, Shaun advised that he simply asked himself how much he was willing to spend to get a new customer. Referrals don't cost as much to chase, and they tend to spend and refer other customers—making the investment in the referral campaign an even better option.

This path of action is obviously the opposite of what most people do (spend the least amount possible rather than preparing for the long term). So, so smart.

There is also an additional strategy in that if you are spending time with your existing customers, you are building a deeper relationship, creating opportunity to do more business together, or even finding a new partner. There are all kinds of potential that can come out of time spent together. By not being cheap, you will likely get dozens and dozens of referrals out of the campaign. A point to note is that the customers who get to go to Las Vegas (in this case) are the ones who have referred someone who has turned into a customer.

And any time in Las Vegas is a good time. (No, there won't be photos of that in *this* book!)

If you are wondering how to afford a campaign like the one NewsletterPro used (especially if cash flow is tight), don't forget that you can create your campaign now but not actually spend the money (i.e., gifting the prize) until the referrals become customers. So essentially those new customers will pay for your campaign. No laying out the cash ahead of the time.

Then how do you use a newsletter to promote a campaign like this? Shaun advised you do one of two things.

1. Congratulate everyone going to Las Vegas in the newsletter. Then make a point of saying to those who aren't going what they need to do to get invited. You teach your existing customers how to get referrals, and then call them to action by asking them to give you those referrals.

2. Include a free-standing insert in the newsletter. The insert again promotes the campaign, telling them what is happening and what to do to gain a ticket to Las Vegas.

Shaun further refers to a point Dan Kennedy makes that "direct marketing" (an actual physical paper newsletter) is the only reliable source he has as things change so rapidly. Shaun believes that in order to be successful you need to marry online and offline marketing. Business owners are normally in one camp or the other instead of finding a way to do both, resulting in huge growth. The reality is, newsletters are incredible. They do all of the following if not more:

- When you commit to publishing a newsletter, it establishes you as an expert.
- Although it's available to members, you can use it as a source of passive income (i.e., selling it to non-members).
- Use it before a prospect meeting (send a couple of issues)—establishing you as the expert.
- It hangs around longer than emails, which are easily deleted.
- It gives you the opportunity to include other things, like an insert highlighting a campaign.
- It shows you are willing to invest in your business and will be sticking around. Anyone can generate an online newsletter, but it takes time and money to create and print a physical newsletter.

Shaun makes the cover of their newsletter about them personally as a business and staff. People want to know about your life, business, etc. Pay attention to that portion in your newsletter whether it's a printed version or an online version.

Focus on Retention of Customers

You need to find out why people leave and fix it! One of the ways NewsletterPro prevents customers leaving is by establishing relationships. Find out what is happening in the lives of your customers. Little things—like sending a card and gift for a wedding, or sending flowers when someone passes away along with a sympathy card signed by the whole office—make a big difference.

Also don't forget to fix a problem when it is discovered. Only 4 percent of people will complain. Even if you lose a customer, you should still fix the problem so the next customer will not have to deal with it. If you focus on retention, your business will grow!

So go ahead and grab that print newsletter off the table you left behind yesterday. It's still there and just waiting for you to follow up.

#INSTAGRAMFORBUSINESS POSTABLES

■ *You* could be the next Apple. #InstagramforBusiness

■ You can create a tribe of loyal followers who maybe someday will get your logo tattooed on themselves, like the great brands of Nike or Harley-Davidson. #InstagramforBusiness

■ Before you begin to market and grow your platform to launch your product, program, or service via Instagram, develop your perfect prospect "avatar." #InstagramforBusiness

■ Your content needs to speak to your target market so clearly that to them it seems like you are a friend, not a business. #InstagramforBusinessk

■ No one wants to feel like they are the first to choose you to spend money with. Show them they aren't alone. #InstagramforBusiness

■ The most important thing when it comes to Instagram advertising is to track, measure, and scale once your data supports it. With that you can achieve incredible results. #InstagramforBusiness

■ If you fail to plan, you can plan to fail #InstagramforBusiness

Resource spotlight: Visit www.UGIGBook.com for an Instagram advertising template for maximum results.

Chapter 10

Instagram Stories and Instagram Live: Your 15-Plus Seconds of Fame

As Instagram is ever updating, so was this book as we were in final stages of going to print. Two updates were the introduction of Instagram Stories and Instagram Live. I twisted the arm of one of my in-house aficionados on Instagram Live, Samantha Melhorn to bring you the latest and greatest. Enjoy this guest chapter from Sam

They say you have eight seconds to grab your prospect's attention. It takes quite a bit of skill to generate a compelling message in such a short amount of time, but now marketers are called to face a further challenge. Instagram (and also Snapchat) is allowing people to create brief messages that disappear almost instantly. And users love it!

So, the next step beyond capturing attention is creating a message or visual that is memorable. Instagram's latest updates include the Stories and Live options. Both allow brands a unique way to interact with their fan base. *Stories* contain an interesting set of short video clips or images which will disappear after 24 hours, and the *Live* option notifies followers about videos that are being recorded in real time.

INSTAGRAM STORIES

Instagram Stories allows users to share moments of their day without permanently placing them on their profile, easing the fear of overposting.

There are three posting options: live, boomerang or normal. As these short videos or images are uploaded, they are grouped together in a mini slideshow using your profile picture as the cover photo. They can be found along the top of the Instagram app but disappear after just 24 hours.

Before Creating Your First Story

Adjust story settings: Click the week in the upper-right-hand corner of your profile page. Select "Story Settings." You can choose to allow replies from no one, everyone, or only people you follow (see Figure 10–1). You can also hide your story if there are people you do not wish to share it with in your audience.

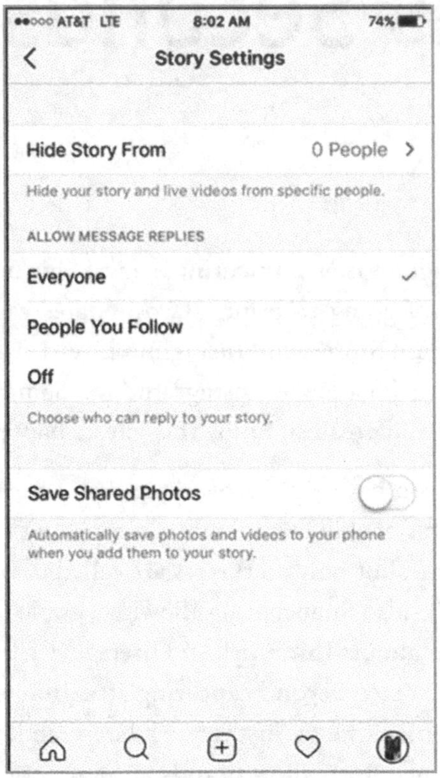

FIGURE 10–1. Story Settings Options.

Viewing Stories

The stories that appear along the top bar of your feed are organized left to right, from most recent to those already viewed. New stories will feature the colorful Instagram ring (see Figure 10–2 on page 199). When viewing, you cannot comment or like the story, but you have the option to send a direct message to the account owner.

FIGURE 10–2. Instagram Stories Appear at the Top of Your Feed.

Create Your First Story

Step 1. Tap the profile picture with the blue "+" from the top-left-hand corner of your feed (see Figure 10–3, page 200). Choose "Enable Camera Access" and/or "Enable Microphone Access."

Step 2. Select the appropriate post option:

Live. Recorded in real time and only available to those who engage while you're live. It disappears as soon as the broadcast finishes.

Normal. Images and videos disappear after 24 hours.

Boomerang. Small bursts of images played quickly forward and then backward.

Hands-free. Allows you to record without needing to hold your phone.

Step 3. Record or take photo!

Step 4. Edit options.

FIGURE 10–3. Select Your Post Option.

You can easily add filters, emojis, drawings, or text by using the tools illustrated below.

Change the filter. Instagram is known for its overlays and filters to dress up your photos. You can now add these to your stories too by sliding left or right over your image or video.

Add emojis, drawings, or text. Available on the top-right menu (see Figure 10-4, page 201).

Step 5. Save to post your story.

Save your video/photo to your device from the icon in the lower left, or select the arrow on the right for more options.

Send to select people. Your list of followers will appear, and you'll be able to choose specifically who you want to view your post.

Create a new group. Choose a group of people to allow access to your post.

That's it, you've just created your very first story.

FIGURE 10–4. Tools Inside the Stories Feature.

INSTAGRAM LIVE

This new feature engages users in a similar way to Periscope and Facebook Live. If your followers have Live Notifications turned on, they will receive an update when you are recording and be able to watch your video in real time. However, when the video is over, it doesn't stay on your profile or story. It disappears altogether, similar to Snapchat's six-second snippets.

To Create an Instagram Live

Step 1. Create a New Story.

Tap the profile picture with the blue "+" from the top-left-hand corner of your feed (see Figure 10–2, page 199). Choose "Enable Camera Access" and/or "Enable Microphone Access."

Step 2. Go Live!

Select the "Live" option. (Note: You cannot use flash in this mode.) When you are ready, tap "Start Live Video" to start recording. Instagram will notify your followers that you are doing a live broadcast so they can join in.

Step 3. Manage Live Broadcast.

As followers tune in, you will be able to see the number of viewers in the upper-left corner and their profile names at the bottom of the screen. Any viewer comments will also appear at the bottom, so you may respond or assess the engagement of your audience. You can disable the comment feature by tapping the three dots in the lower right and selecting "Turn Off Commenting."

Step 4. End the Broadcast.

When done, tap End in the upper right and select "End Live Video." This will prompt the analytics screen. Remember, your live video will not be saved to your Instagram Story and can't be viewed again.

Step 5. Review Live Analytics.

This screen tells you the total number of viewers who watched your broadcast. You can measure this number against your total follower count to determine what percentage of your fans engaged with your video.

A huge business benefit of using the Instagram Stories and Live features is that your account can reach followers who don't normally have Notifications turned on for your individual posts. They will automatically see your Instagram Story in the top bar of their feed.

As a business who wants to get the word out to your target market with as high of an ROI as possible, Instagram Live and Instagram Stories cannot be ignored. For now at least, these platforms allow you to reach your target market in droves . . . . for free. They have high interaction rates and are easy to use.

While you can still take advantage of these platforms, utilize them quickly for maximum results.

BUILDING AN INSTAGRAM EMPIRE WITH CODIE SANCHEZ

Codie Sanchez is an entrepreneur, international business expert, investor, Latina millennial, writer, and speaker looking to make us ask the question: *What if it was easy?* The message she shares across her social media accounts is that the struggle doesn't have to be real.

With more than 15,000 followers, your message is clearly taking Instagram by storm. What brought you to this point, and what drives you? What does your overall network and community look like right now? And what does your business look like?

Sanchez: I measure my network in a couple of different ways. Across all social networks, I have about 150,000 followers, including Instagram, Facebook, Twitter, and my email list. The second way I measure my network and my business is through the strategic relationships I build. I think it's important to not just focus on social networks because at the end of the day, you don't really know who's following you. Instead, I think about a strategic network in the way that now I have clients all over the world in my investment business. I get to consult with some of the biggest firms out there through my diversity and public speaking business.

Tell us about some of your different business enterprises and what they do.

Sanchez: My main business, or rather my biggest and most mature business, is the international investment firm, First Trust Portfolios. My team—from across Latin America, Chicago, New York, and Austin—sells investment products to institutions: pensions, sovereign wealth funds, those sorts of things. It's a business I built up over the last three years, after working in the industry for six years before that. Everyone on my team is female—that's pretty rare in the finance world. We've also built well over a billion-dollar business, which is amazing.

I recently exited a smaller startup called Threads Refined. That was an ecommerce fashion company. Now I'm building out what I guess you would call an online education and strategic consulting company at CodieSanchez.com. A core belief is that we need to have more diverse and conscious humans in positions of power if we want to create a more diverse and conscious world. I'm fascinated by the ability of social networks to build international brands for free with a click of a button. I don't think most big businesses understand the power of social media when used correctly. This is my experiment to see how I can utilize it.

How have you used the @CodieSanchez Instagram brand to build your tribe? Is it focused on Instagram, or does it cross platforms?

Sanchez: I'm really big on being able to control my own platform. I use Instagram to grow my email distribution list. Guess how many people use Myspace now? Does *anybody*? When Instagram stories came online, what happened to Snapchat? Usage dropped majorly, and so did the amount you got paid as an investor through Snapchat. So the only thing I know for certain is that change will come in every aspect of our lives and businesses. You have to apply that to social networks as well.

Instagram is a phenomenal platform and they've done the best job of any of them in protecting what is the beauty behind Instagram. It's not been allowed to become super salesy or cluttered and bot-driven, but eventually that's likely to change. This is why it's important to *own* your end clients. I'm not here to grow Instagram's platform, I'm here to grow *my* platform.

I use a Bitly link (which is essentially a URL shortener) in the Instagram bio, through a company of my friend Noah Kagan called SumoMe. Essentially it goes to a lead page to grab people's email address in return for a giveaway. Subscribers receive the giveaway by email auto-responder, and then the link takes them to my website.

When I started this business, I didn't have any emails because obviously my investment firm's clients were not in the same niche. Instagram has driven 30 to 40 percent of my current 50,000-subscriber list, followed by Facebook Live.

Wow. Growing a list that quickly doesn't just happen by luck. Tell us about the strategy behind your growth and how you've been able to see an ROI from your social media marketing.

Sanchez: I love the phrase "ROI." In business, "reach" is great, and "impressions" are great . . . but money is the only thing that talks. I committed to using Instagram for 365 days, posting daily, just over a year ago. Before that, I was a little bit snobby about social media. I would say, *"What are these people doing taking selfies all day? Go get a job."* About 60 days in to my commitment, I started to realize that one post a day isn't enough.

Any time I try something new in business, I try not to recreate the wheel entirely. I asked myself who was successful at social media? I looked at brands similar to mine like Marie Foleo and Tony Robbins. These are people I would aspire to have some similarity to, so I tried to mimic their techniques. I created a 15-step strategy based on what I saw, and those tactics have been in place for just about two months now. For me, it's not just about posting but about being strategic.

For someone who's just getting started, can you walk us through some of that plan?

Sanchez: First, I have a couple of Instagram dos and don'ts. Do make sure to use a good picture of yourself. And definitely use a link in your Instagram bio to direct viewers through AppSumo or Leadpages, which you can install on the back side of your website, so you can track leads and results.

Make sure to include a call to action in your bio—something kind of cute, but also offering value. Use emojis to draw attention to that offer, and be straight-forward about what you do and who you are. I get a little irked when I see people identify themselves as Chief Happiness Officer or Unicorn Chaser.

For posting, I have found that there are three things that matter in Instagram. First, make sure your content is valuable and insightful for people. Second, your content should look like your brand. I'm not a big believer in all the overbranded Instagram stuff. To me that feels corporate. You won't find my logo or super-curated, exact pictures on my account. It's a little edgier, like me. Finally, the most beneficial thing to growth through minimal output is reaching out to other humans who have a similar personality and getting into a relationship with them. If you're at the same user level, use share-for-share—have them post about you, and you about them. If you do that with authenticity, not just blasting people, you can get a couple hundred followers each time.

Did you just approach your personal network? How would you suggest someone start using share-for-share?

Sanchez: There are a couple of ways. If you don't have a lot of followers yet, you can pay for them. Pay for play! You can definitely DM [send a direct message] to some bigger accounts and pay for them to repost your stuff. Typically you will get followers based upon that.

I started out by looking at my friends' accounts who had a decent following and said, "Hey I'm trying to grow my account. Would you mind taking a picture and posting it, since we're out to dinner anyway?" I had them link my name in the post, so potential followers could see I was friends with influencers. Bear in mind, you always want to give more than you get. Whenever I asked for those shares, I would usually have posted something about them first. With social media they are a lot of selfish people who are always asking you to do things for them. Influencers get tired of that because it's a service they are typically compensated for.

The interaction should be mutually beneficial. See whose accounts are similar, with a similar amount of followers as you. Send them a DM like, "Hey, I'm trying to grow my following. Seems like you have similar followers/account/outlook. Maybe my followers would like to follow you, and yours follow me. Do you want to do a share-for-share?" You can link their name in the post comments and they can do the same, so hopefully you both grow. Just bear in mind, it's a skill and a job. It's not just going to happen overnight.

How do you use Instagram Live and Instagram Stories?

Sanchez: When I was at Summit at Sea, we had a little breakout with Gary Vaynerchuk. He tells it like he sees it. He says Facebook Live and Facebook Ads are the most underpriced way to market or advertise in the game right now. So if you have a business and you can sell something through links and use targeting to advertise to the right audience, you are going to be able to make the difference on what you've spent ad-wise and what you sell in a way you can't do in any other advertising mechanism.

So if you're a company or personal brand, you are crazy not to do some spending and research on Facebook Live and Facebook Ads. The same thing goes for Instagram except that Instagram doesn't have as in-depth reporting yet. Instagram stories are a great way for you to show your personality and that you're a real human—not like some of the accounts that are owned by people in other countries with essentially nothing behind them.

I like to do things like "Take Five," where I'll ask five questions to the person I'm with that day. My first question might be "Favorite Book?" That would be one Instagram story shot, and the next would be a video of the interviewee's answer. The next question might be "Best Quote?" That's a way to keep people engaged. You can also tag people in Instagram Stories now. Tagging bigger accounts, friends, and family and behind-the-scenes tagging creates a reciprocal effect.

How often do you use live video to communicate with your audience?

Sanchez: I should do more Instagram Live. Right now I do a lot of Facebook Live. I use it to give actual insight into helping people build lives and careers and relationships they love. On Instagram when I go live, it feels much more personal. I probably only do that once a week, but I use Instagram Stories daily. I don't profess to be the best at this, so if you're looking for accounts who've killed it in the Instagram game, check out fashion accounts like @happilygrey, who've been utilizing Instagram since the very beginning.

Any other tips?

Sanchez: Be true to yourself. Use Instagram in a way that is real and a little gritty. You don't have to tie it up in a bow all the time. I've never thought of Instagram as a popularity contest. At the end of the day no one cares how many Instagram followers you have. Make sure you focus on profits. Make sure you are true to yourself. Those things never go away. Once they are out there, they are out there.

Connect with Codie Sanchez for her products and educational programs: Instagram @codiesanchez, and at https://www.codiesanchez.com/.

BUILDING YOUR LUX TOOL BOX WITH INSTAGRAM APPS FOR SUCCESS

There are a bajillion (official count) apps you can use when it comes to Instagram marketing. I have discussed several throughout this book (I think I mention Word Swag almost every other page). But there are many more when it comes to photo editing, scheduling, and more. The following is a collection of some of the most popular.

Add Text to Images

- *Font Candy*. A variety of appealing typography designs can also be incorporated into your Instagram photos with Font Candy. Text can also be inverted into the background. Custom quote templates display your favorite sayings on your pics. Go to https://itunes.apple.com/ca/app/font-candy-creative-graphic/id661971496?mt=8Fused or http://easytigerapps.com/#fused.

- *Over*. Get creative with text design and placement with Over. With more than 200 fonts and a truckload of custom options and stock backgrounds, there's plenty of potential with this app. http://madewithover.com/

- *Quick*. Select your desired images, add the appropriate wording, and tinker with the font and size. After you get everything set up the way you want, post your image to Instagram. It's really that quick. www.overquick.com

- *SnapPen*. Add a touch of whimsy to your Instagram photos by scribbling all over them with SnapPen. The zoom feature allows for increased precision while adding markings to images with any of the five fluid pens. https://itunes.apple.com/ph/app/snappen/id723401906?mt=8

Galleries

- *Have2Have.It*. Take advantage of your clickable Instagram link by using this app to create a gallery of images followers can select to be directed to products or content. It also allows for easy tagging and conversion tracking. https://have2have.it/

- *Layout*. Remix up to nine images with an app that takes layouts to the next level. Select pics from your camera roll or take fresh pics with the Photo Booth feature. For the iPhone: https://itunes.apple.com/us/app/layout-from-instagram/id967351793?mt=8&ign-mpt=uo%3D4 or for Android devices: https://play.google.com/store/apps/details?id=com.instagram.layout.

- *PicCollage*. Seasonal stickers, backgrounds, and handy templates are some of the attractive features of this app. GIFs and stickers can be incorporated throughout your collections prior to posting. http://pic-collage.com/

- *Pic Stitch*. Present a collection of Instagram photos without the annoying pixelated look by using this free app. Choose from hundreds of layout options to create an attractive grid. Collages can be saved and posted as desired. Apple devices: https://itunes.apple.com/us/app/pic-stitch-1-photo-video-collage/id454768104?mt=8 or Android: https://play.google.com/store/apps/details?id=com.bigblueclip.picstitch&hl=en.

- *Pixlr*. A collage maker is combined with a top-quality photo editor on this app designed for mobile use. The hundreds of available editing options allow for plenty of attention to every detail of each photo you wish to post via Instagram. https://pixlr.com/

Image Quality

- *A Beautiful Mess.* Transform Instagram photos in seconds with custom filters. You'll also get access to hand-drawn doodles from Emma and Elsie, who created the popular lifestyle blog that inspired this app. www.abeautifulmessapp.com

- *A Color Story.* Add a splash of color and brightness to your Instagram photos with this easy-to-use app's hundred-plus filters. Forty movable effects, 20 free tools, and the ability to add curves and create custom filters make this app even more appealing. http://acolorstory.com/

- *Afterlight.* Russ, coral, and bay are among the 74 unique filters you'll have access to with this app. If you're posting landscape pics, you'll love the selection of 78 natural textures. Borders, including hashtags, can also be placed over your photos. http://afterlight.us/

- *BLACK.* Discover the power of black-and-white in the digital age. Described as an analog film emulator, this app lets you produce high-quality black-and-white photos with a cool retro look. A unique technical fix allows missing EXIF metadata to be corrected. https://itunes.apple.com/us/app/black-b-w-film-emulator/id939009354?mt=8

- *Camera Noir.* Mix things up with your Instagram displays by transforming some color images to shades of black and white. This black-and-white photo editor is high quality enough for professionals yet easy enough for everyone else. https://itunes.apple.com/us/app/camera-noir/id676866002?mt=8

- *Camera+.* The clarity filter is reason enough to download this app to jazz up your Instagram pics. The different shooting modes instantly improve the quality of your pics. The ability to separate exposure and focus is an equally appealing feature. https://itunes.apple.com/us/app/camera+/id329670577?mt=8

- *Enlight.* Forget cropping when you use Enlight to post your Instagram photos. Everything from contrast and color to exposure and curves can be adjusted with a few taps. Vintage filters and decals are just a few of the fun extras on this app. www.enlightapp.com

- *Facetune.* Say goodbye to dark circles, blemishes, and other imperfections with Facetune before posting photos on Instagram. You can even fix gray and thinning hair and readjust the focus by blurring out other people or background distractions in your pics. www.facetuneapp.com

- *Hipstamatic.* Produce retro-inspired images with an assortment of lens combinations available on this photography app. If you opt for Hipstamatic 300, effects can be changed after you've captured a photo. https://itunes.apple.com/us/app/hipstamatic-camera/id342115564?mt=8

- *InstaSize.* Quickly edit and post videos and photos with film-inspired filters. Use this app to add borders, stickers, and collage frames and take care of any necessary touch-ups. Available for both Apple and Android devices: www.instasize.com/.
- *Overgram.* Place one pic inside of another with an app that offers a wide range of free frames, screens, and assorted accessories. Filters can be applied to only the main image or all photos at once. https://play.google.com/store/apps/details?id=com.smagicteam.overgramcamera&hl=en
- *Perfect365.* Give your photos a one-tap makeover with this app. Imperfections, such as red eye and laugh lines, are easily edited out with a few taps. For Apple devices: https://itunes.apple.com/us/app/perfect365-custom-makeup-designs/id475976577?mt=8 or Android devices: https://play.google.com/store/apps/details?id=com.arcsoft.perfect365&hl=en.
- *Priime.* Add filters to your Instagram photos with this user-friendly app. Editing features allow for a multitude of fine-tuning and other adjustments necessary to create professional-looking images. https://priime.com/
- *SKRWT.* This app is especially useful if you're using shots of buildings and other structures within your Instagram photos. A responsive dial is used to separately adjust vertical and horizontal planes to correct distortion and perspective issues. http://skrwt.com/
- *Slow Shutter Cam.* Add shutter speed effects to Instagram images with the various capture modes available on this app. Tap the "Capture Settings" button on the lower toolbar to experiment with motion blur, light trail, low light, and other modes. http://www.cogitap.com/slowshutter/instructions.htm
- *Snapseed.* Achieve the same results you would get with professional photo editing software with Snapseed. Simply tap to make edits and retouch images. Photos can also be resized prior to posting or exporting. https://itunes.apple.com/ca/app/snapseed/id439438619?mt=8
- *Squaready.* If you're not satisfied with Instagram's layout and editing features, you'll love Squaready. It works especially well if you want to add some pizzazz to existing photos and display larger images. https://itunes.apple.com/us/app/squaready-smart-layouter-for/id440279995?mt=8
- *Superimpose.* Easily blend two separate photos into one pic with Superimpose. Masking tools allow you to remove a background from an image and add an entirely different one. The foreground can also be resized, rotated, and moved as you play around with placement before posting. www.superimposeapp.com
- *VSCO.* Share one image or an assortment of images all at once with VSCO. It's unique in that it's both a place to edit images and a platform itself where images and other content can be shared. https://vsco.co/store/app

Scheduling, Marketing, and Promotion

- *Hootsuite*. Instagram via Hootsuite allows you to promote photos on Instagram, comment on photos, engage with followers, and schedule posts. There's also the endless cross-promotional possibilities. https://hootsuite.com/

- *Iconosquare*. Download this app to keep track of the Instagram stats that matter most to you. In addition to tracking growth, you can also pinpoint days when followers aren't so active. https://pro.iconosquare.com/

- *Later*. Schedule and manage posts from your PC or mobile device with the app previously known as Latergramme. Easily view what's already been posted and see what you have scheduled. https://later.com/

- *Like2Buy*. A brand can be linked to its accompanying Instagram profile to allow browsers to shop by using this app. Photos can also be tagged and posts can be scheduled from the dashboard. https://www.curalate.com/product/like2buy/

- *Repost*. Effortlessly repost your photos and videos to your Instagram account with this app. It automatically gives credit to the source. http://repostapp.com/

- *ScheduGram*. Include ScheduGram among your set of scheduling apps to streamline your social management efforts. Images from the web can be easily cropped and enhanced with text before being stored for future posts. http://schedugr.am/

- *Shopseen*. Listings can be created for any store as inventories are instantly updated with this informative app. Instagram browsers can make purchases without being directed away from your page. www.shopseen.com/

- *Soldsie*. Sell content through your Instagram images with Soldsie. Your link will be used to present your content and essentially turn your Instagram page into a digital storefront. Traffic can also be generated from individual Instagram posts anywhere online. http://new.soldsie.com/how-it-works/

- *Sprout Social*. Grow your social media presence with this popular app by resizing images for Instagram to increase engagement. You also get access to useful analytics to track posts, hashtags, and engagement levels. www.sproutsocial.com

Video

- *Boomerang*. Create share-worthy mini-loop videos consisting of up to 20 photos. Your collection of photos can be continuously played backward and forward to put a new spin on photos that would otherwise have less of an impact individually. https://itunes.apple.com/us/app/boomerang-from-instagram/id1041596399?mt=8

- *Cinefy*. Produce instantly engaging videos for your Instagram page with this special effects and editing app for iPhone. Go full-on Hollywood with the selection of more than a hundred effects. www.cinefyapp.com

- *Clips Video Editor*. Described as "the simplest video editor in the world," this app is especially useful for preparing shorter clips for Instagram. Editing features make it easy to search larger videos for moments likely to attract attention. www.crunchbase.com/product/clips-video-editor#/entity

- *Flipagram*. Blend audio and movement with your Instagram photos. Allowing you to create musical stories, Flipagram lets you choose images and audio files from your library, set transition times between images, and superimpose text over your flipagrams. https://flipagram.com/

- *Hyperlapse*. The in-house stabilization feature on Instagram is enhanced with this app. You get professional quality time-lapse videos without the need to hire a production crew. https://hyperlapse.instagram.com/

- *Lapse It*. Use your mobile camera to capture images as time-lapse posts or stop-motion videos for your Instagram page. The award-winning app displays on-screen info as it captures and uploads directly to Instagram. www.lapseit.com.

- *Microsoft Hyperlapse Mobile*. Produce stable and smooth time-lapse videos or enhance videos already in your library. Features of this app include a choice of multiple speeds, resolution adjustments, and the option to stabilize without time-lapsing. https://play.google.com/store/apps/details?id=com.microsoft.hyperlapsemobile&hl=en

- *Vintagio*. Create vintage-quality videos with audio soundtracks and filters to produce videos mimicking silent films of yesteryear. The pro mode gives you the added option to add multiple videos, transitions, and photos. https://itunes.apple.com/us/app/vintagio/id335148458?mt=8

Video/GIF

- *DSCO*. Pronounced "disco," DSCO is a GIF-making app from VSCO. Capture and edit animated GIFs with an assortment of presets before uploading the results to your VSCO profile. After you've uploaded your GIFs, share the results via Instagram. https://vsco.co/dsco/collection/1

- *Giphy Cam*. Prepare your own GIFs for Instagram with Giphy Cam. It offers a nice selection of overlays and effects; and there's the emoji rendering, which is a fun feature all by itself. http://giphy.com/giphycam

- *Phhhoto*. Transform photos into instant moving pictures with this easy-to-use camera app. Visual creations can be transformed into attention-getting Instagram posts displayed as a continuous loop. https://phhhoto.com/

- *PicPlayPost*. Tell a story with your Instagram photos, GIFs, and videos by exploring the features available with this app. Different media forms can be easily blended to make your page more engaging. www.mixcord.co/partners/picplaypost.html

BECOMING INSTA-SOCIAL WITH ENTREPRENEUR

For more than 30 years, Entrepreneur Media has been setting the course for small business success. From startup to retirement, millions of entrepreneurs and small business owners trust the Entrepreneur Media family—Entrepreneur magazine, Entrepreneur.com, Entrepreneur Press, EntrepreneurEnEspanol.com, and industry partners—to point them in the right direction. The Entrepreneur Media family is regarded as a beacon within the small- to mid-size business community, providing outstanding content, fresh opportunities, and innovative ways to push publishing, small business, and entrepreneurship forward.

Entrepreneur Media is at the forefront of its social growth strategy, with now more than half a million @entrepreneur Instagram followers.

When did you join Instagram and what was the goal?

Entrepreneur: Our first post was of our January 2013 magazine cover featuring Sophia Amoruso. Starting an Instagram page was vital and necessary to increase our brand exposure. Like any business strategy, we started with a mission: to inform, inspire, and celebrate entrepreneurs. The platform allows us to take our print and online content and bring it into conversations that are trending.

Where do you go for inspiration?

Entrepreneur: True to our mission statement, we are always looking to accounts that celebrate people with inspirational and motivational content. Our favorite Instagram accounts are @HumansofNY which celebrates the human connection, and competitive accounts like @Wired which has great photography and visuals.

What were some of your most popular posts?

Entrepreneur: If we had to name just one form of entertainment that most Americans enjoy, it would likely be going to the movies. Add to that Kernel King's shared pain point of tasteless popcorn along with a colorful image, and we've buttered ourselves up for a good post (see Figure 10–5 on page 213).

Everyone knows that the number-one industry on Instagram is fashion, but what about the faces behind the clothes? Our interview with NYC-based designer Tanya Taylor led to one of our top-performing posts because of her alignment with the general Instagram user and the photographer's stunning photo (see Figure 10–6 on page 213).

Do you have any tips for businesses looking to grow their followers, or lessons you've learned along the way?

FIGURE 10–5. Bric "Kernel King" Simpson Designed a Lid for Movie Theater Popcorn to Allow Patrons to Evenly Distribute Butter and Other Seasonings Without Spills.

FIGURE 10–6. Tanya Taylor Is a Fashion Designer Who Successfully Bucks Tradition, Only Introducing Two Strong Collections per Year Instead of Four.

Entrepreneur: First, don't be afraid to partner with other accounts and share complementary content with each other's audiences. We've also learned that inspiration and positivity will get you further than "neutrality." People need to immediately know the reason why they're following you. Whatever it is, just make sure it's clear. For us at Entrepreneur, when you look at our page it's easy to see that we focus on success stories and provide tips and advice. In a platform like Instagram, your brand's mission needs to be translated visually.

Another lesson learned is that your Instagram account doesn't have to be your business name. It can be topical or a vertical related to your business that audiences can relate back to you. The goal should be to build a community.

Do you use any apps or tools for your Instagram account that you find especially helpful? If so, what are they?

Entrepreneur: We like using VSCO for editing photos and Iconosquare for statistics and community management. Iconosquare provides a great hashtag search that includes visual content.

How do you monetize on Instagram?

Entrepreneur: We recommend that you take advantage of using the link in the bio. That link should drive your audience to a solid landing page where you can convert them into buyers. Using photo posts is a great way to attract attention, and ensuring that the content you're providing is valuable and engaging can also lead to organic sales.

#INSTAGRAMFORBUSINESS POSTABLES

- Use the apps listed on pages 206 to 211 to get some amazing postables created from other chapters. #InstagramforBusiness

Resource spotlight: Visit www.UGIGbook.com to download a list of our favorite tools for marketing with results!

Chapter 11

The Final Word: Magical Results!

Maybe there's no magic button, but the results are magical! Ever see a testimonial like this?

> *It was so easy! I spent all day just surfing my feed while my follower count grew, as did my web traffic, email list, and sales. Plus, I got super skinny and my love life improved. And I never even had to get out of my pajamas. This is the best course, ever, and everyone should buy it!*

> —ANITA INTEGRADY

Many marketing "gurus" who are out there hawking books, goods, and services have magic potions for sale. "Take this and the results will be incredible." Their unscrupulous tactics are atrocious, but they are not the only ones to blame, of course.

Those buying the snake oil products and services are buying into a reality that even they know can't exist. They weren't forced to make those purchases, yet they make them, knowing the shortcut probably won't work.

There is no easy button, no magic potion, no manifestation you can do in order to get the results you are looking for. Real results will come from a successful strategy implemented and refined over time. Period.

There is great power in all of this, especially for the entrepreneur or small-business owner. Getting an ROI from Instagram doesn't require the advertising budget of a McDonald's or Pepsi. Making all of this work doesn't have to cost a lot. Sweat equity is the best equity you can invest in order to get an ROI from your Instagram marketing.

Or if you don't want to spend the time, hire a freelancer or firm that understands you and can get results. Real results. (As in, require them to open up their Ads Manager in front of you and show you the results.) Demand proof of success that is measurable, or do not give them your money. You worked too hard to earn each dollar you have to let someone else (or yourself) squander it away.

The most important thing to remember in all of this is, you have purpose and it needs to be shared with as many people as possible in order to serve them. You are not simply a business. You are a pain healer. When you match what you do with those who need it, you are solving their pain and making their life better.

Instagram marketing puts the tools in your hands to create the brand, message, audience, and business you are dreaming about. Stop dreaming and start doing.

You still reading? We're done—go out and fulfill your purpose!

Find a supportive friend who can cheer you on. Join a business networking group or mastermind. Come into our group, Marketing Insiders Elite (www.marketinginsiderselite. com). We would L.O.V.E. to have you.

Be with others who get it and will help keep you accountable to your fears. You owe it to your tribe. You owe it to the next person you were meant to help. You owe it to yourself.

#INSTAGRAMFORBUSINESS POSTABLES

■ There is no easy button, no magic potion, no manifestation you can do in order to get the results you are looking for. Real results will come from a successful strategy implemented and refined over time. Period. #Instagram-forBusiness

■ The most important thing to remember in all of this is, you have purpose and it needs to be shared with as many people as possible in order to serve them. #InstagramforBusiness

■ Nothing in life that is worth anything much is easy. #InstagramforBusiness

■ Be with others who get it and will help keep you accountable to your fears. #InstagramforBusiness

Resource spotlight: Visit www.UGIGbook.com for a "21-Day Instagram Sales Plan."

About the Author

Kim Walsh Phillips, @KWalshPhillips, is the world's number-one expert at empowering successful professionals to reach $1 million in annual revenue.

She is an award-winning speaker, author, podcaster, and busy CEO, leading three separate companies—Elite Digital Group, a direct-response social media agency; Elite Capital Advisers, a lead-generation firm for financial advisors; and Powerful Professionals, a community of high achievers closing in on the million dollar mark.

Kim has brought in more than a billion dollars online with her laser focus on increasing revenue through direct-response marketing. She is also the co-author of the best-selling book, *No B.S. Guide to Direct Response Social Media Marketing: The Ultimate No Holds Barred Guide to Producing Measurable, Monetizable Results with Social Media Marketing*, with Dan Kennedy.

She resides with her very tall husband, who is often asked to get things down from the ridiculously tall cabinets in their house, and their two glitter-and-all-things-pink-obsessed daughters, Bella and Katie, just outside of New York City.

Her secrets to success? Prayer, laughter, a great team, and coffee.

www.KimWalshPhillips.com (www.KimWalshPhillips.com)

Index